Praise for *America on the Brink*

"David Griffin's book forced me to confront the difficult truth that in many ways I remain an unrepentant American imperialist, if for no other reason than, as a dyed-in-the-wool Reagan Republican, I had never embraced the reality that American Imperialism was a "thing." But after reading his book, *America on the Brink,* I cannot hide from the fact that not only has my country become the modern-day equivalent of Ancient Rome, but that we have been thus my entire life. This awakening was David's final gift to me and the world, accomplished through a book that must be read by all who are struggling to define the role played by America in the world today. You can't solve a problem unless you first properly define it; David Griffin defines the scope and scale of the American problem. It is now incumbent upon us to find a solution."

SCOTT RITTER, former Chief Inspector for the UN in Iraq, author
Disarmament in the Time of Perestroika

"As a leading American public intellectual, the late Professor David Kay Griffin leaves us a legacy of forty well-researched books that brought him both disciples and antagonists. A distinguished professor of philosophy and theology, he broke new ground in the field of 'process studies' and post-modern philosophy in the wake of Alfred North Whitehead. This book is not theoretical philosophy, but an exercise in political common sense, raising pertinent questions for the survival of humanity and concretely applying philosophy to today's crises, including the existential struggle reflected in the Ukraine war. Unlike many of his peers, he never succumbed to mainstream narratives and groupthink. In 16 chapters Griffin exposes the dangers of American imperialism and denounces aggression and war crimes that have been committed in our name. The chapter 'Facing Up to the True Nature of the American Empire' is essential reading for every human rights activist, for every person who values truth and human dignity."

ALFRED DE ZAYAS, former UN Independent Expert on the Promotion
of Democracy and an Equitable International Order

Praise continued...

"At the end of World War II, the United States emerged as the world's richest and most powerful nation militarily. It has retained military superiority and the ability to shape financial structures and has used these to control much of the world's politics as well. It was also the most admired nation. It could have led the world by supporting the movements toward justice and local prosperity.

"David Griffin shows how, instead, it has used its military and financial power to prevent the sharing of the world's wealth with its people. This has led to loss of moral admiration. David knows that self-destructive aspects of our foreign policy go back much farther, but he begins his careful, objective, well-documented account with our replacement in Iran of the humanitarian and democratic Mossadegh by the corrupt and dictatorial shah. Again and again we have supported those who seek to increase the wealth of the great corporations against those who want to share the wealth with the people. That desire is attacked as Communist.

"This background helps us to understand that the crimes of our present enemies derive also from their interest in serving their people rather than the rich and their corporations. That our claims to lofty ideals are treated cynically in most of the world today, and that our goal of global dominance is crashing, should not surprise us.

"No one gives us a clearer picture of how we have engendered fear, suspicion, and hatred in much of the world, while still assuring ourselves about our virtue, than David Griffin. I strongly recommend this book for Americans who are able to learn the truth."

JOHN B. COBB., JR., Professor Emeritus of Theology,
Claremont School of Theology

AMERICA
on the
BRINK

HOW U.S. FOREIGN POLICY LED
TO THE WAR IN UKRAINE

DAVID RAY GRIFFIN

Clarity Press

ISBN: 978-1-949762-72-3
EBOOK ISBN: 978-1-949762-73-0

In-house editor: Daniel Athearn
Interior design: Becky Luening

Library of Congress Control Number: 2023933359

Clarity Press, Inc.
2625 Piedmont Rd. NE, Ste. 56
Atlanta, GA 30324, USA
https://www.claritypress.com

Table of Contents

David Ray Griffin, Indispensable Public Intellectual

Richard Falk

A Point of Departure

I found it sad that when David Ray Griffin died on November 25, 2022 so little public notice was taken to report on the death of one of the most important thinkers and public intellectuals of our time who illuminated our understanding of many crucial scholarly and public policy concerns. He did so in a consistently independent and progressive manner, making accurate use of relevant scholarship by others, whether ally or adversary. Late in life Griffin achieved fame for some (especially in Europe), shameful notoriety for others as the leading exponent of an alternative narrative of what really happened on 9/11 when the key symbolic sites of American wealth and power, the World Trade Center and the Pentagon, were attacked by terrorists in 2001, resulting in the death of 2996 persons.

The Price Paid for An Alternative Version of 9/11

The 20th anniversary of the attacks was recently observed with much understandable attention devoted to survival stories of individuals and coping strategies of the families of the victims. It was strange that despite all the media and governmental attention there was barely any notice of the intense controversy provoked by the events, not even a mention of the notable fact that earlier doubts about what actually happened on 9/11, as distinct from the official version, had disappeared from public view. Ignoring Griffin's death was further evidence that such silences were not accidental. Googling items under a name is one crude and fluctuating indicator of public importance in the digital age, and by this measure Griffin outscored the most prominent public intellectuals of our country and time by registering 25.2 million items as compared to 22.1 million for Samuel Huntington (on the right) and 17.9 million for Noam Chomsky (on the left).

To those who knew Griffin personally, whether or not persuaded by his dissenting views of 9/11, there was never a loss of respect for his rigorous scholarly standards or political independence and integrity. Throughout his life Griffin's work always exhibited the resolve of a probing thinker and fearless scholar who bravely followed the evidence wherever it led, however contrary to conventional wisdom the outcome of his research turned out to be. After the U.S. victory in the Cold War, and response to the 2001 attacks, Griffin's intellectual efforts became feverish, motivated by his worries that an America intoxicated by its power would imperil itself and the world, and even threaten the survival of the human species and life on the planet.

Griffin's friendship and exemplary role as a public intellectual was influential and inspirational for me and many others in several realms of thought long before his strong sense of duty drove him to devote most of the energy in his later life to an exposure of the realities of the 9/11 controversy as he interpreted them. Despite his 9/11 preoccupations Griffin took the time in this period to write a deeply researched alarmist book about the rising dangers of climate change, *Unprecedented: Can Civilization Survive the CO2 Crisis?* His earlier work along theological lines had focused on a philosophical and social rethinking of the nature of religion, with a full awareness of its economic, political, civiliza-tional, and ecological implications under conditions of modernity. It is impossible to summarize Griffin's wide-ranging interests, scholarly output, and leadership in organizing conferences and collective work among kindred scholars on the great questions haunting the future after the Cold War.

One feature common to almost all of his voluminous writing is unusual and stands out: Griffin's willingness to go beyond the bound-aries of what was deemed by conventional opinion to be "responsible thought" or "acceptable dissent" as relied upon by the self-censoring filters of the most influential media platforms. This helps explain what made Griffin's death a public happening that never happened. I have come to believe that it was not because his views aligned with the main currents of progressive thought in the United States and abroad. Something more sinister and distinct was at stake that is worth reflecting upon: that this unacknowledged blacklisting was a result of his public persona being linked so closely to views on 9/11 that governing elites wanted to discredit totally, enough so that they would be all but erased from public memory, with the desired effect of closing off debate, dialogue, and inquiry. Griffin kept writing, I believe, because he was scared of the broader consequences of what this closure meant for the future of the country and the world. Griffin believed a corrected and properly interpreted version of the 9/11 events might lead to a much needed reset in American foreign policy with respect to what he regarded as a suicidal geopolitical stance in the nuclear age.

The Unspoken Vendetta against Trespassers of the 'No-Go' Zones of Public Policy

Like Noam Chomsky, or Jean-Paul Sartre before him, Griffin had distinguished himself by way of breakthrough scholarship long prior to venturing onto the precarious terrain of controversial politics. Yet Chomsky, eminent as a linguist before he ventured into public space with devastating critiques of the U.S. role in the world, will be recognized and even celebrated whether dead or alive as a progressive public intellectual almost everywhere in the world, raising the elusive question as to what are these elusive differences among such notable public intellectuals.

In my view there are certain "no-go" zones that Chomsky and Sartre more or less respected, not from prudence, but due to their beliefs and interests. In contrast, Griffin continuously breached such limits during his long productive scholarly life.

For several decades before 9/11 Griffin had continuously challenged conventional ideas and beliefs as an author and academic activist. For instance, his early philosophical and theological works took seriously the truth claims of parapsychology and reports confirming life after death. Such beliefs were anathema to those who accepted the tenets of modern science that subscribed to mechanistic and materialist views of causation as providing thought with the only authoritative criteria of the real. Griffin's creativity as theologian centered on stripping religion of supernaturalism, while enlarging our understanding of religion as consistent with more expansive views of scientifically verified reality.

Griffin proceeded by affirming the continuous relevance in the modern world of a stress on experientially validated philosophical assessments. In this vein he was following in the traditions set by the philosophical work of Alfred North Whitehead and Charles Hartshorne, and his lifelong theological partner, John Cobb, with whom he founded "process theology" associated with the Claremont Graduate School of Theology. If Griffin had stopped here, his contributions would be appreciated by devoted followers in a few relatively esoteric academic circles, and there would be little reason to be puzzled as to why his unconventional work and life did not receive the wider public recognition it deserved. Actually, an imaginative obit writer might have been impressed by Griffin's work and depicted his life as centering on a maverick's challenge to the dogmas of truth, currently strictly adhered to by the scientific community and conditioning the most influential currents of religious thought.

Griffin's later work on 9/11 set off a different set of alarms that produced a "conspiracy of silence" with respect to his overall record of scholarly excellence, certainly of great enough weight to have earned Griffin sufficient eminence to make his death a public event worthy of notice and commentary. The controversies surrounding the true nature of the assassinations of the Kennedy Brothers, Martin Luther King, Jr., and Malcolm X give some indication of the high costs paid by those that venture into such no-go zones.

Griffin's Public Persona Erased in the U.S. for Being a No-Go Trespasser

After much puzzlement, I have come to explain this neglect of such an outstanding scholar as almost solely an indirect consequence of Griffin daring to challenge the official version of the 9/11 attacks of 2001 on the World Trade Center and Pentagon. Not only did he mount this challenge by publishing a book provocatively entitled *The New Pearl Harbor: Disturbing Questions About the Bush Administration and 9/11* (2004), but he followed this carefully crafted critique with an incredible additional eleven books that refuted every facet of the official version of these events, and gained a worldwide following for what had become a crusade to bring about a reliably objective inquiry rather than a thinly rationalized whitewashing of official culpability. Griffin deeply believed and hoped that disclosures made possible by the research and their documented presentation would lead in due course to positive results.

What may have been even more inflammatory than the accusation that the government and the media had orchestrated a massive coverup of 9/11 were Griffin's views of the motivations and consequences involved. Undoubtedly most incriminating from the perspective of Washington and the threats posed by Griffin to its matrix of ideological control was his well-evidenced belief that this denial of 9/11 truth was tied to an underlying foreign policy agenda that had fueled past war-making and imperial interventions and were deemed integral to implementing the post-Cold War neoconservative resolve to fill permanently the geopolitical vacuum created by the Soviet implosion. By doing so, the U.S. was seeking to exert control over the whole world on behalf of neoliberal variants of world capitalism operating under the security blanket of American militarism, consisting of a gigantic global network of foreign bases, widespread covert coercive maneuvers throughout the world, and a series of regime-changing interventions. The latter often masked as "democracy promotion" and "state-building" as in Afghanistan in 2002, Iraq after 2003, and several other countries.

Griffin found his audiences around the world through well attended lectures, foreign media outlets, and most of all through his defiant books on why it was vital to get the true story of 9/11 as widely disseminated as possible. He fully earned his international celebrity by linking the exposure of the 9/11 events to the before and after stories of American foreign policy in a series of outstanding books, *Bush and Cheney: How They Ruined the United States and the World* (2015); *The American Trajectory: Divine or Demonic* (2018). Both of these books connect the grandiosity of the past national claims of Manifest Destiny and "American Exceptionalism" to the neoconservative determination to make the entire world subject to U.S. hegemony.

Griffin's steadfastness, passion, and talents were most dramatically saved for his dying days in a hospice where he lay heavily medicalized because of pain but determined to make one last attempt to alert the America he loved about the disastrous future that was being scripted in a geopolitically bellicose and inflammatory manner.

What follows is Griffin's final testament: *America on the Brink: How U.S. Foreign Policy Led to the War in Ukraine* (2023).

This book is indispensable reading for all who want to understand why the current behavior of the United States is hell bent in pursuit of a geopolitical path that is dooming the prospects of the human species for a peaceful, humane, and ecologically stable future. Hopefully, it will also in time produce a most deserved recognition of David Griffin as one of the greatest public intellectuals of our time.

Editor's Note

This book was in process, though largely completed, when David Ray Griffin became unable to proceed with it due to the progression of his illness. Even so, he continued proposing further changes and corrections while in palliative care, relying on the assistance of his wife, Ann Jaqua, to transmit his communications. I did not live in the same city, but insofar as I had assisted with many of his books previously and am familiar with his writings, David proposed that I compose any further text that might be needed to complete it. David wanted the book to keep abreast of events in Ukraine as far forward in time as possible, and he remained involved up to the time that he could no longer communicate. While Diana Collier, Editorial Director of Clarity Press, had discussed the book with David at some length and had a major role in shaping it into its final structure, my role was primarily that of completing the writing, including a few updates in the Ukraine chapter concerning events after his passing on November 25, 2022.

America on the Brink supplements the historical analysis of U.S. foreign policy begun in David's earlier book, *The American Trajectory: Divine or Demonic?* An important spur for the new project was the war between Ukraine and Russia that began in February 2022. He strongly felt the need to fill in the historical background to this conflict about which the American public was and remains largely uninformed or misinformed.

Chapter 1 recounts the historical thinking on the idea of America as an imperial power: the claims that have been made either that America is not imperialist at all, or that it represents a new kind of empire serving noble ends and/or is only reluctantly or "accidentally" imperialist. David concludes that the U.S. pursues a malign imperialism, and he makes this case by relating how one politically conservative scholar, Andrew Bacevich, came to recognize and criticize the imperialist nature of American foreign policy.

The next thirteen chapters provide a series of historical illustrations of the imperialist orientation of American foreign policy, briefly recounting post-World War II U.S. interventions in a range of countries and the consequences for the peoples of these lands, leading fatefully to the war in Ukraine, the topic of the penultimate chapter. The core of the book, this chapter details American responsibility for creating the conditions that led to the Russian invasion, for ignoring genuine opportunities for avoidance and settlement, and indeed for stoking the fires through ongoing provision of military and financial support.

A concluding chapter provides a summary evaluation of American interventionist foreign policy and lays out the possibility of a more auspicious and ethical approach to engagement with the world that recognizes contemporary realities. A moral basis for foreign policy is proposed drawing on principles shared by the world's great religions.

—*Daniel Athearn*

The Making of an Anti-Imperialist

The idea of an "American empire," along with the related idea of "American imperialism," has had an interesting history. In the nineteenth century, the idea was openly discussed, even celebrated. The reigning assumption was that the emerging American empire, unlike all previous empires, would be a benign, even a benevolent, empire. It would be an "empire of liberty," bringing freedom wherever it spread. By the twentieth century, however, the term "imperialism" had acquired such negative connotations that politicians and even respectable intellectuals ceased speaking of American imperialism, except to deny the existence of any such thing. In 1983, for example, President Ronald Reagan declared: "We're not in the business of imperialism, aggression or conquest.... We threaten no one."[1]

The negative connotations of the word "imperialism," moreover, spread to the word "empire," so that at the very time the United States was creating the most extensive empire the world had ever known, the mainstream narrative denied that there *was* an American empire.

The main rationale for denying the existence of an American empire was the equation of "empire" with the kind of *colonial* empire Great Britain had. Making that equation and then overlooking the awkward fact that America did have a few formal colonies enabled American leaders to deny that they ruled over an ever-growing empire. This ploy ignored the fact that American business and political leaders had made

---

1   Ronald Reagan, "Remarks at the Annual Washington Conference of the American Legion," February 22, 1983; quoted in Andrew J. Bacevich, *The New American Militarism: How Americans Are Seduced by War* (Oxford: Oxford University Press, 2005), 185.

a conscious decision to create a different kind of empire: a *neo-colonial* empire, sometimes called an *informal* empire. As Ludwell Denny said in 1930: "We shall not make Britain's mistake. Too wise to try to govern the world, we shall merely own it."[2] By "merely" owning countries, without having formal colonial offices, America could sustain the myth, at least among its own people, that it was not an imperial power.

Although politicians and most intellectuals regarded as respectable supported this myth, a few intellectuals were able to remain respectable while admitting the existence of an American empire by stipulating that America's empire differed from all previous empires in two respects. First, America had acquired its empire accidentally. As Ernest May's 1961 study, *Imperial Democracy: The Emergence of America as a Great Power* put it: "Some nations achieve greatness," said May, but "the United States had greatness thrust upon it."[3]

The second obligatory statement was that the American empire, unlike all previous empires, is *benign*. A classic statement of this view can be found in a 1967 book by Ronald Steel entitled *Pax Americana*. Writing as the criticism of the Vietnam War was heating up, Steel acknowledged that "by any conventional standards for judging such things," America is "an imperial power," having an empire "the scope of which the world has never seen."[4] However, Steel argued, "America has been engaged in a kind of welfare imperialism, empire building for noble ends rather than for such base motives as profit and influence"— the chief noble end being "permitting other nations to enjoy the benefits of freedom, democracy, and self-determination."[5] When America intervenes, Steel said, it does so with "the most noble motives and with the most generous impulses."[6]

---

2   Ludwell Denny, *America Conquers Britain* (193), cited in Titus Alexander, *Unraveling Global Apartheid: An Overview of World Politics* (Cambridge: Polity, 1996), 148.

3   Ernest R. May, *Imperial Democracy: The Emergence of America as a Great Power* (New York: Harcourt, Brace, & World, 1961), 270; quoted in Andrew J. Bacevich, *American Empire: The Realities and Consequences of U.S. Diplomacy* (Cambridge: Harvard University Press, 2002), 7.

4   Ronald Steel, *Pax Americana* (New York: Viking Press, 1967), 15, 14.

5   Steel, *Pax Americana*, 16–17, 18.

6   Steel, vii. When I first encountered these statements, I assumed that they were made with tongue in cheek. But Steel clearly meant them. In the meantime, however, he has developed a very different attitude towards the American empire, as evident in

The most effective way to show the falsity of these views—that American has no empire or that, if it does, its empire is an accidental, benign empire—would be to rehearse the story of U.S. imperialism.

But this would be a very long story. It would need to begin with the displacement of the Native Americans, which involved the extermination of about 10,000,000 of them.[7] It would need to include the institution of slavery, which, besides all the other evils, probably involved the deaths of another 10,000,000 human beings.[8] This story would need to explain why in 1829 the South American hero Simon Bolivar said: "It seems to be the destiny of the United States to impoverish [the rest of] America." This story would need to deal with the theft of what is now the American Southwest from Mexico.[9] It would need to deal with the increasing number of invasions after the American Civil War in countries such as Guatemala, El Salvador, Chile, Brazil, and Venezuela.[10] It would need to deal with so-called Spanish-American Wars of 1898–1902, during which America took control of Cuba, Puerto Rico, the Philippines, Hawaii, and Guam.[11] It would need to explain why the war to deny independence to the Filipinos led to the formation of the Anti-Imperialist League, with one of its members, William James, saying: "God damn the U.S. for its vile conduct in the Philippine Isles."[12] This story of American imperialism would also need to tell of America's

---

Steel's *Temptations of a Superpower* (Cambridge: Harvard University Press, 1995).

7   See David E. Stannard, *American Holocaust: The Conquest of the New World* (New York: Oxford University Press, 1992), 267–68; Francis Jennings, *The Founders of America: From the Earliest Migration to the Present* (New York: Norton, 1993), 395.

8   See Stannard, *American Holocaust*, 317. I reached the estimate of 10,000,000 by extrapolating from Stannard's figures for all of the Americas.

9   See Richard W. Van Alstyne, *The Rising America Empire* (1960; New York: Norton, 1974).

10 See Walter LaFeber, *Inevitable Revolutions: The United States in Central America*, 2nd ed. (New York: Norton, 1993).

11 Philip S. Foner, *The Spanish-Cuban-American War and the Birth of American Imperialism*, 2 vols. (New York: Monthly Review, 1972); Stuart Creighton Miller *"Benevolent Assimilation": The American Conquest of the Philippines, 1899–1903* (New Haven: Yale University Press, 1982).

12 On many of the leading members of the League, see Robert Beisner, *Twelve Against Empire: The Anti-Imperialists, 1898–1902* (New York: McGraw-Hill, 1968). For the writings of one of its prominent members, see Jim Zwick, ed., *Mark Twain's Weapons of Satire: Anti-Imperialist Writings on the Philippine-American War* (Syracuse: Syracuse University Press, 1992).

interventions further abroad—in Japan in 1854, China in 1900, Russia in 1918, and Hungary in 1919.[13] Back in this hemisphere, this story would need to address America's theft of Panama from Colombia in 1903, then its repeated interventions in the Dominican Republic, Haiti, Nicaragua, Costa Rica, Guatemala, and El Salvador, with lengthy occupations of some of those countries.[14] It would need to explain its imperial aims in World War II, which led it to install right-wing postwar governments in Greece, France, Italy, Japan, Korea, and the Philippines, even though this meant turning against the Resistance movements, which had fought alongside the Allies against the Fascist powers.[15] This story would then need to explain, against deeply entrenched mythology, how the Cold War was far more the result of the imperial ambitions of the United States than those of the Soviet Union.[16] It would also need to tell of the great number of countries in which the United States overthrew constitutional governments, such as Iran (1953), Guatemala (1954), Brazil (1961–1964), the Dominican Republic (1965), Greece (1965 and 1967), Indonesia (1965–66), and Chile (1973), as well as its later interventions in Nicaragua and El Salvador.[17] This story of U.S. imperialism would

---

13   See Lloyd C. Gardner, Walter F. LaFeber, and Thomas J. McCormick, *Creation of the American Empire* (Chicago: Rand McNally, 1973), and Walter LaFeber, Richard Polenberg, and Nancy Woloch, *The American Century: A History of the United States*, 5th ed. (Boston: McGraw-Hill, 1998).

14   See Walter LaFeber, *Inevitable Revolutions* and also *The Panama Canal: The Crisis in Historical Perspective* (New York: Oxford University Press, 1978).

15   See Laurence Shoup and William Minter, *Imperial Brain Trust: The Council on Foreign Relations and United States Foreign Policy* (New York: Monthly Review Press, 1977); David F. Schmitz, *Thank God They're On Our Side: The United States and Right-Wing Dictatorships, 1921–1965* (Chapel Hill: University of North Carolina Press, 1999); Gabriel Kolko, *The Politics of War: The World and United States Foreign Policy 1943–1945* (New York: Pantheon, 1968, 1990); and *Confronting the Third World: United States Foreign Policy 1945–1980* (New York: Pantheon, 1988).

16   See Kolko, *The Politics of War*; Walter LaFeber, *America, Russia, and the Cold War: 1945–1990*, 6th ed. (McGraw Hill, 1990); Melvin Leffler, *A Preponderance of Power* (Stanford: Stanford University Press, 1992); and Carolyn Eisenberg, *Drawing the Line: The American Decision to Divide Germany, 1944–1949* (Cambridge: Cambridge University Press, 1996).

17   See Schmitz, *Thank God They're On Our Side*; William Blum, *Killing Hope: U.S. Military and CIA Interventions Since World War II* (Monroe, Maine: Common Courage, 1995); Noam Chomsky, *Year 501: The Conquest Continues* (Boston: South End, 1993); Jonathan Kwitny, *Endless Enemies: The Making of an Unfriendly*

need to describe America's 30-year effort to prevent the unification and independence of Vietnam, a process that included merciless bombings of Laos and Cambodia.[18] It would then need to describe the policies that have led to such hatred of America in the Arab and Muslim worlds.[19] This story would need, furthermore, to tell of other levers ensuring U.S. domination, such as the economic policies behind these interventions and America's posture with regard to nuclear weapons.[20]

So, although telling this story in detail would be the most effective way to argue that America's empire is neither accidental nor benign, this obviously would take up at least several chapters. However, there is a quicker way to make this case, thanks to the publication in 2002 of a book by the respected historian Andrew Bacevich entitled *American Empire*.[21] Bacevich is a conservative. But he is an *honest* conservative, who tells the truth about the American empire, pointing out that it is neither accidental nor benign.

World (New York: Penguin Books, 1986); Piero Gleijeses, *Shattered Hope: The Guatemalan Revolution and the United States, 1944–1954* (Princeton: Princeton University Press, 1991); Peter Kornbluh, *Nicaragua: The Price of Intervention: Reagan's Wars against the Sandinistas* (Washington, D.C.: Institute for Policy Studies, 1987); and LaFeber, *Inevitable Revolutions*.

18 See George McT. Kahin, *Intervention: How America Became Involved in Vietnam* (New York: Anchor, 1987), and Marilyn B. Young, *The Vietnam Wars: 1945–1990* (New York: HarperPerennial, 1991).

19 See Noam Chomsky, *Fateful Triangle: The United States, Israel, and the Palestinians*, updated ed., Foreword by Edward Said (Cambridge: South End, 1999); Charles D., Smith, *Palestine and the Arab-Israeli Conflict: A History with Documents*, 4th ed. (Boston: Bedford/St. Martin's, 2001); Phyllis Bennis, *Before and After: US Foreign Policy and the September 11th Crisis* (New York: Olive Branch, 2003); Richard Labevière, *Dollars for Terror: The United States and Islam* (New York: Algora, 2000); Eqbal Ahmad, *Terrorism: Theirs and Ours* (New York: Seven Stories, 2001); John K., Cooley, *Unholy Wars: Afghanistan, America and International Terrorism*, 2nd ed. (London: Pluto, 2000); Dilip Hiro, *Iraq: In the Eye of the Storm* (New York: Nation Books, 2002).

20 See Robert J. Lifton and Richard Falk, *The Political and Psychological Case Against Nuclearism* (New York: Basis Books, 1982); Francis A. Boyle, *The Criminality of Nuclear Deterrence: Could the U.S. War on Terrorism Go Nuclear?* (Atlanta: Clarity Press, 2002); and Helen Caldicott, *The New Nuclear Danger: George W. Bush's Military-Industrial Complex* (New York Press, 2002).

21 Andrew J. Bacevich, *American Empire: The Realities and Consequences of U.S. Diplomacy* (Cambridge: Harvard University Press, 2002).

There have, of course, been previous intellectuals who have told these truths, but they have been left-leaning thinkers, such as Charles Beard, Noam Chomsky, Richard Falk, Walter LaFeber, William Appleton Williams, and Howard Zinn.[22] Their account of the American empire could be and has been easily dismissed by mainline thinkers as distorted by a left-wing agenda.

Bacevich, however, has no such leftist agenda. We can assume, therefore, that insofar as his account contradicts the standard denial of the existence of an American empire along with the standard portrayal of this empire as accidental and benign, it is not distorted by ideological bias.

The Reality of the American Empire

As Bacevich points out, it is still considered impolitic for those in office to admit to the existence of an American empire. In his West Point speech in June of 2002, President Bush said: "We don't seek an empire." Likewise, when Secretary of Defense Donald Rumsfeld was asked by an Al-Jazeera correspondent in 2003 if the Bush administration was bent on "empire-building," Rumsfeld replied: "We don't seek empires. We're not imperialistic. We never have been. I can't imagine why you'd even

---

22   See Richard W. Van Alstyne, *The Rising America Empire* (1960; New York: Norton, 1974); Noam Chomsky, *American Power and the New Mandarins* (1967; New York: Vintage Books, 1969); and *Rogue States: The Rule of Force in World Affairs* (Cambridge: South End Press, 2000); Richard Falk, "Imperialism in Crisis," an introduction to Mansour Farhang, *U.S. Imperialism: From the Spanish-American War to the Iranian Revolution* (Boston: South End Press, 1981); Lloyd C. Gardner, Walter F. LaFeber, and Thomas J. McCormick, *Creation of the American Empire* (1973); Walter LaFeber, *The New Empire: An Interpretation of American Expansion 1860–1898* (1963; Ithaca: Cornell University Press, 1998); Harry Magdoff, *The Age of Imperialism: The Economics of U.S. Foreign Policy* (New York: Monthly Review, 1966, 1969); Thomas J. McCormick, *China Market: America's Quest for Informal Empire, 1893–1901* (Chicago: Quadrangle Books, 1967); Michael Parenti, *Against Empire* (San Francisco: City Lights, 1995); Laurence Shoup and William Minter, *Imperial Brain Trust: The Council on Foreign Relations and United States Foreign Policy* (New York: Monthly Review Press, 1977); William Appleton Williams, *The Tragedy of American Diplomacy* (1959; New York: Norton, 1988) and *Empire as a Way of Life: An Essay on the Causes and Character of America's Present Predicament* (Oxford: Oxford University Press, 1980); and Howard Zinn, *A People's History of the United States* (New York: Harper, 1980, 1990).

ask the question."[23] But many imperialists who are outside the government no longer feel the need to deny the obvious.

For example, in 2000, Richard Haass, soon to become the director of policy planning in Colin Powell's State Department, gave an address titled "Imperial America," in which he called on Americans to "re-conceive their global role from one of a traditional nation-state to an imperial power."[24] In January of 2001, neocon Robert Kagan criticized "Clinton and his advisers" for "having the stomach only to be halfway imperialists."[25]

Only after the attacks of September 11, 2001, did the language of empire become really prominent. Early in 2002, columnist Charles Krauthammer wrote: "People are coming out of the closet on the word 'empire.'" Believing this a good thing, Krauthammer said that Americans need to face up to the responsibilities entailed by the fact that they are now "undisputed masters of the world."[26]

Bacevich himself provided the ultimate example of this new willingness of conservatives to admit the obvious. Against those who still tried to pretend that America is not the head of a worldwide empire, Bacevich wrote:

> Holding sway in not one but several regions of pivotal geopolitical importance, disdaining the legitimacy of political economic principles other than its own, declaring the existing order to be sacrosanct, asserting unquestioned military

---

23 Remarks by the President at 2002 Graduation Exercise of the United States Military Academy, June 1, 2002. http://www.whitehouse.gov/news/releases/2002/06/20020601-3.html; Department of Defense press conference, April 23, 2003, quoted in Rahul Mahajan, *Full Spectrum Dominance: U.S. Power in Iraq and Beyond* (New York: Seven Stories Press, 2003), 9.

24 Quoted in Bacevich, *American Empire*, 219. Haass, to be sure, paid deference to the long-standing distaste for "imperialism" by adding: "An imperial foreign policy is not to be confused with imperialism." But he probably realized that this is a distinction without a difference.

25 Robert Kagan, "The Clinton Legacy Abroad," *Weekly Standard*, January 15, 2001; quoted in Bacevich, *The New American Militarism*, 85.

26 Krauthammer's statements, originally published in Emily Eakin, "All Roads Lead To D.C.," *The New York Times*, Week In Review, March 31, 2002, are quoted in Jonathan Freedland, "Is America the New Rome?", *The Guardian*, September 18, 2002, G2: 2–5.

supremacy with a globally deployed force configured not for self-defense but for coercion: these are the actions of a nation engaged in the governance of empire.[27]

Some of these imperialists were quite frank in their advocacy of the unilateral use of American power. In an essay in the *Atlantic Monthly* in 2003, Robert Kaplan publicly argued that America should use its power unilaterally to "manage an unruly world," leaving behind "the so-called international community" and especially the United Nations, whose Security Council "represents an antiquated power arrangement unreflective of the latest wave of U.S. military modernization."[28] Richard Perle said that the Bush administration had already brought about this change. In a commentary entitled "Thank God for the Death of the UN," Perle said: "Its abject failure gave us only anarchy. The world needs order." That order was to be provided, of course, by the USA.[29]

Why the American Empire Is Not Accidental

This new openness by its supporters concerning the reality of the American empire is generally coupled, however, with the view that Bacevich calls the "The Myth of the Reluctant Superpower," according to which "greatness was not sought; it just happened."[30] Using as an example Ernest May's previously quoted statement that the United States, without seeking it, "had greatness thrust upon it."[31] Bacevich provided a more complete characterization of this myth, writing that:

In this view, American policy is a response to external factors. The United States does not act in accordance with some predetermined logic; it reacts to circumstances. . . . [T]he United

---

27 Bacevich, *American Empire*, 243–44.
28 Robert Kaplan, "Supremacy by Stealth: Ten Rules for Managing the World," *The Atlantic Monthly*, July/August, 2003.
29 Richard Perle, "Thank God for the Death of the UN," *The Guardian*, March 21, 2003.
30 Bacevich, *American Empire*, 7.
31 Ernest R. May, *Imperial Democracy: The Emergence of America as a Great Power* (New York: Harcourt, Brace, and World, 1961), 270; quoted in Bacevich, *American Empire*, 7.

States—unlike other nations—achieved pre-eminence not by consciously seeking it but simply as an unintended consequence of actions taken either in self-defense or on behalf of others.[32]

Bacevich himself, he admitted, had previously accepted this myth. He had assumed that American foreign policy was actually guided by its stated objectives, which were "quite limited—to protect our homeland, to preserve our values, to defend our closest allies."[33] On the basis of these assumptions, he believed that the American participation in the Cold War was a purely defensive effort to contain Soviet expansionism, that the Soviet Union wanted to establish a worldwide empire while the United States did not. He assumed, accordingly, that after winning the Cold War, the United States would greatly reduce its military budget, its weapons programs, and its overseas deployments. But instead, he wrote,

in the decade following the fall of the Berlin Wall, . . . [t]he United States employed military power not merely in response to a crisis. . . . It did so to . . . anticipate, intimidate, preempt . . . and control. And it did so routinely and continuously. In the age of globalization, the Department of Defense completed its transformation into a Department of Power Projection.[34]

More generally, he reported, the objectives of U.S. foreign policy "aimed at nothing short of a full-scale transformation of the international order."[35] Realizing that he had been operating with faulty assumptions, Bacevich began his rethinking of what American foreign policy was all about by delving into the works of two leftist critics of U.S. policy, Charles Beard and William Appleton Williams. According to Beard, America intervened abroad not selflessly to help others but to advance its own commercial empire.[36] Besides coming to accept this view, Bacevich also came to agree with the basic point of Williams's view about the American

---

32   Bacevich, *American Empire,* 7.
33   Bacevich, viii.
34   Bacevich, 127.
35   Bacevich, viii.
36   Bacevich, 14–17.

empire—that, far from just having grown "like Topsy," it "emerged out of a particular worldview and reflected a coherent strategy."[37] The scope of this "grand strategy," which "has not changed in a century," added Bacevich, "is nothing short of stupendous."[38]

So, America did not acquire its worldwide empire accidentally, but by means of a consciously formulated strategy, which was executed about equally by Republican and Democratic administrations for well over a century.

Why the American Empire Is Not Benign

The idea that America acquired its empire accidentally is usually a subordinate point, made to support a claim more crucial to the defense of America's imperial role—namely, that it is benign.

I earlier quoted Ronald Steel's 1967 statement of this view. But, as I intimated earlier, this idea extends back to the founding of the nation and even before. In *The Rising American Empire*, Richard Van Alstyne reports that "before the middle of the eighteenth century, the concept of an empire that would take in the whole continent was fully formed."[39] From the outset, moreover, the idea of the American empire as an "empire of liberty," hence an "empire of right," was repeatedly articulated. For example, a poem by David Humphreys, a protégé of George Washington, included these lines:

> Our constitutions form'd on freedom's base,
> Which all the blessings of all lands embrace;
> Embrace humanity's extended cause,
> A world of our empire, for a world of our laws.[40]

America's cause, in other words, is identical with humanity's cause, which is freedom. This claim, which has since then been repeated countless times, was reiterated in President Bush's address to the nation

---

37   Bacevich, 30. This quotation is Bacevich's summary of the position of Williams.
38   Bacevich, ix, 6.
39   Richard Van Alstyne, *The Rising American Empire*, vii.
40   Anders Stephanson, *Manifest Destiny: American Expansion and the Empire of Right* (New York: Hill and Wang, 1995), 19.

on September 7, 2003. Defending his administration's policy in Iraq, he closed his address by saying: "We are serving in freedom's cause, a cause that is the cause of all mankind." Given this identity, the spread of the American empire would be a blessing for all.

This idea was most characteristically expressed in the phrase "manifest destiny," which was coined in 1845.[41] Although originally the phrase referred only to the mission of the United States "to overspread the continent," an editor named Debow wrote in 1850:

> We have a destiny to perform, a "manifest destiny" over all Mexico, over South America, over the West Indies and Canada.... The gates of the Chinese empire must be thrown down.... The eagle of the republic shall poise itself over the field of Waterloo...and a successor of Washington ascend the chair of universal empire![42]

Debow and others who thought in these terms assumed that other nations should not take offense, because America's universal empire would be a "democratic empire." Although America would, like previous great nations, exercise imperialism, it would be a "New Imperialism," one "destined to carry world-wide the principles of Anglo-Saxon peace and justice, liberty and law."[43]

As I mentioned earlier, in the 20th century, as the negative connotations that accrued to the word "imperialism" tainted the word "empire," this kind of talk became infrequent. Although the old notion of America as a benign empire was still occasionally articulated, as illustrated by Steel's *Pax Americana*, most defenders of American policy simply denied, at least by omission, that America had an empire of any sort.

After the crumbling of the Soviet Union, however, the idea of America as a benign imperial power began to be stated more frequently. In a widely cited 1990 essay, "The Unipolar Moment," Charles Krauthammer said that although people usually "recoil[] at the thought of a single dominant power for fear of what it will do with its power...[,] America is the exception to this rule," because "the world generally

41   Stephanson, *Manifest Destiny*, xi.
42   Van Alstyne, *The Rising American Empire*, 159.
43   Stephanson, 90.

sees it as benign," as a power that "acts not just out of self-interest but a sense of right."[44] In 1998, Robert Kagan published an essay entitled "The Benevolent Empire."[45] In 2001, Krauthammer wrote: "[W]e are not just any hegemon. We run a uniquely benign imperium. This is not mere self-congratulation; it is a fact manifest in the way others welcome our power."[46] In 2002, Dinesh D'Souza, after saying that "America has become an empire," added that happily it is "the most magnanimous imperial power ever."[47] In 2003, Krauthammer again asserted that America's claim to being a benign power is not mere "self-congratulation," this time saying that the truth of this claim is verified by America's "track record."[48] Also in 2003, Michael Ignatieff wrote:

> America's empire is not like empires of times past, built on ... conquest.... [It] is a new invention ..., an empire lite, a global hegemony whose grace notes are free markets, human rights and democracy.... It is the imperialism of ... good intentions.[49]

Having written his essay to defend military intervention in Iraq, Ignatieff said that America's good intentions include the aim to replace dictatorships with democracies. In 2005, Krauthammer said that "the strengthening and spread of democracy" is "[t]he great project of the Bush administration."[50] The day before, in the inaugural address for his second term, President Bush himself said that "the policy of the United

---

44 Charles Krauthammer, "The Unipolar Moment," in *Foreign Affairs* 70/1 (1990–91): 295–306, at 304–5.]

45 Robert Kagan, "The Benevolent Empire," *Foreign Policy*, Summer 1998: 24–35.

46 Charles Krauthammer, "The Bush Doctrine: ABM, Kyoto, and the New American Unilateralism, *Weekly Standard*, June 4, 2001.

47 Dinesh D'Souza, "In Praise of an American Empire," *Christian Science Monitor*, April 26, 2002.

48 Charles Krauthammer, "The Unipolar Era," in Andrew J. Bacevich, ed., *The Imperial Tense: Prospects and Problems of American Empire* (Chicago: Ivan R. Dee, 2003), 47–65, at 59. This track record, he says, proves that "the United States is not an imperial power with a desire to rule other countries." (This essay was originally published in the Winter 2003 issue of *The National Interest*.)

49 Michael Ignatieff, "The American Empire: The Burden," *New York Times Magazine*, January 5, 2003: 23–27, 50–54, at 24, 52.

50 Krauthammer, "Tomorrow's Threat," *Washington Post*, January 21, 2005.

States [is] to seek and support the growth of democratic movements and institutions in every nation and culture."[51]

Bacevich agreed with these men that it is good to be forthright about the existence of the American empire. But he rejected their attempt to justify this empire by claiming that America's intentions are benign. He dismissed, for example, the conceit that "the United States [has] fought [in wars] for altruistic purposes, seeking to end war itself and to make the world safe for democracy."[52] He ridiculed the claim "that the promotion of peace, democracy, and human rights and the punishment of evil-doers—not the pursuit of self-interest—[has] defined the essence of American diplomacy." And he rejected the claim that "[t]o the extent that interests [have] figured at all, . . . American interests and American ideals [have been] congruent."[53]

Bacevich spoke instead of "the unflagging self-interest and large ambitions underlying all U.S. policy" and of the aim of the U.S. military "to achieve something approaching omnipotence: 'Full Spectrum Dominance.'"[54] He mocked the claim that while such power wielded by others would be threatening, "it is by definition benign" in America's hands because the leader of the free world "does not exploit or dominate but acts on behalf of purposes that look beyond mere self-interest."[55] Bacevich knew that time and time again the U.S. government had intervened to dominate and exploit other countries. Finally, whereas members of the benign empire school claimed that America intervened in countries such as Iraq in order to promote peace and democracy, Bacevich pointed out that in previous countries in which America has intervened, "democracy [did not] flower as a result." America intervened instead "to sustain American primacy."[56]

The view of Andrew Bacevich the conservative seems not far from those of Noam Chomsky the radical, who summed up the effect of U.S. interventions in the title of one of his books, *Deterring Democracy*.[57]

---

51 "Inaugural Address by George W. Bush," *The New York Times*, January 20, 2005. http://www.nytimes.com/2005/01/20/politics/20BUSH-TEXT.html
52 Bacevich, *American Empire*, 7.
53 Bacevich, 46.
54 Bacevich, 4, 133.
55 Bacevich, 52.
56 Bacevich, 115, 196.
57 Noam Chomsky, *Deterring Democracy*, 2nd ed. (New York: Hill and Wang, 1992).

After the world witnessed the Bush administration's response to 9/11, comparisons of America with Rome became commonplace. In 2002, an article appeared in a London newspaper asking, "Is America the New Rome?" Saying that "the word of the hour is empire," the author said that "suddenly America is bearing its name."[58] In that same year, Krauthammer wrote that America is "no mere international citizen" but "the dominant power in the world, more dominant than any since Rome."[59]

Bacevich also answered this question in the affirmative. Pointing out that Charles Beard had argued in 1939 that "America is not to be Rome,"[60] Bacevich added that in the 1990s "most citizens still comforted themselves with the belief that as the sole superpower the United States was *nothing* like Rome." However, Bacevich noted: "The reality that Beard feared has come to pass: like it or not, America today *is* Rome."[61]

As Bacevich's comments made clear, this idea includes the point that America is no more benign than Rome. Although Rome's rulers spoke of *Pax Romana*, with one of its emperors assuming the title "Pacifier of the World,"[62] this pacification was achieved by means of its overwhelming military might, which the Romans used ruthlessly. As a Caledonian chieftain at the time put it, the Romans "rob, butcher, plunder, and call it 'empire'; and where they make desolation, they call it 'peace.'"[63]

The Romans used their overwhelming power not merely to conquer but also to terrorize and thereby intimidate their conquered subjects to keep them in line. When the Roman legions were sent on expeditions, accordingly, their main mission was usually "to punish, to avenge, and

58   Jonathan Freedland, "Is America the New Rome?" *The Guardian*, Sept. 18, 2002.
59   Charles Krauthammer, "The Bush Doctrine," *Time*, March 5, 2001, quoted in Chalmers Johnson, *The Sorrows of Empire: Militarism, Secrecy, and the End of the Republic* (New York: Henry Holt [Metropolitan Books], 2004), 68.
60   Bacevich, *American Empire*, 242 (quoting Charles Beard, *Giddy Minds and Foreign Quarrels* [1939], 87).
61   Bacevich, *American Empire*, 244.
62   Richard A. Horsley, *Jesus and Empire: The Kingdom of God and the New World Disorder* (Minneapolis: Fortress, 2003), 197.
63   Tacitus, *Agricola* 14.1; quoted in Horsley, *Jesus and Empire*, 31.

to terrify—that is, to reassert a certain state of mind in the enemy"—a state of "awe and terror."[64]

America's Move Toward Complete Global Dominance

Since the United States became the only superpower, its leaders expressed rather openly their intention to use their power in a similar way. In 1992, Colin Powell, then head of the Joint Chiefs of Staff, told members of Congress that America requires sufficient power to "deter any challenger from ever dreaming of challenging us on the world stage." Powell even said: "I want to be the bully on the block," implanting in the mind of potential opponents the realization that "there is no future in trying to challenge the armed forces of the United States."[65] It is rather sobering to read these comments in light of the fact that Powell was later, in comparison with others in the Bush-Cheney administration, considered a dove.

Also in 1992, in any case, similar ideas were expressed in the draft of the Pentagon's "Defense Planning Guidance" (DPG) document, authored by Paul Wolfowitz, who would become George W. Bush's assistant secretary of defense, and Lewis "Scooter" Libby, who would become Vice-President Cheney's chief of staff. This document stated: "Our first objective is to prevent the re-emergence of a new rival. . . . [W]e must maintain the mechanisms for deterring potential competitors from even aspiring to a regional or global role." This document, Bacevich said, "was in effect a blueprint for permanent American global hegemony."[66]

Bacevich, considering Wolfowitz to be the document's primary author, refers to it as "Wolfowitz's Indiscretion" because, instead of using the standard language of American statecraft, promising to use American power "to assure the survival and success of liberty," this document was too candid, "openly suggest[ing] that calculations of power and self-interest rather than altruism and high ideals provided the

---

64 Susan P. Mattern, *Rome and the Enemy: Imperial Strategy in the Principate* (Berkeley: University of California Press, 1999), 117, 172.
65 Colin Powell, testimony to the U.S. Congress, 1992.
66 Bacevich, *American Empire*, 44.

proper basis for framing strategy."[67] When the document was leaked and portions of it printed in the press, the resulting furor, in which Wolfowitz was "roundly denounced," led the Pentagon to withdraw and rewrite the document.

However, Bacevich pointed out, its basic ideas would reappear in later documents, including *The National Security Strategy of the United States of America*, published in September 2002. This document, known as *NSS 2002*, said: "We must build and maintain our defenses beyond challenge" so that we can "dissuade future military competition." With statements such as "our best defense is a good offense,"[68] moreover, this document introduced the doctrine of *preventive* warfare, which involves attacking other countries before they pose an immediate threat.

In stating these and related policies, *NSS 2002* was adopting many of the recommendations of a document entitled *Rebuilding America's Defenses*, which was published in 2000 by the Project for the New American Century (PNAC). Many of its founders went on to become central figures in the Bush II administration, including Cheney, Libby, Wolfowitz, Richard Armitage, John Bolton, Richard Perle, Donald Rumsfeld, James Woolsey, and Zalmay Khalilzad. Especially noteworthy is the fact that Libby and Wolfowitz, who had co-authored the draft of the 1992 Defense Planning Guidance document, were directly involved in the production of this 2000 document.[69]

Rebuilding America's Defenses emphasized the importance of getting greatly increased funding for the technological "revolution in military affairs," at the center of which was the U.S. Space Command.

The U.S. Space Command

The purpose of the Space Command, which is essentially a new branch of the military, is spelled out quite explicitly in a document published in February of 1997 called "Vision for 2020," at the head of which is this mission statement: "U.S. Space Command—dominating the space

---

67   Bacevich, *American Empire*, 44–45.
68   *The National Security Strategy of the United States of America*, September 2002 (available at www.whitehouse.gov/nsc/nss.html), 29–30, 6.
69   *Rebuilding America's Defenses: Strategy, Forces and Resources for a New Century*, (Project for the New American Century, September 2000). https://www.newamericancentury.org

dimension of military operations to protect U.S. interests and invest-ment."[70] This 1997 document engaged in no sentimental propaganda about the need for the United States to dominate space for the sake of promoting democracy or otherwise serving humanity. It instead said: "The globalization of the world economy . . . will continue with a wid-ening between 'haves' and 'have-nots.'" In other words, although the official line is that U.S.-led economic globalization will make everyone better off, the Pentagon knew that as America's plutocratic domination of the world economy increases, the poor will get still poorer while the rich get still richer. This will make the "have-nots" hate America all the more, so we need to be able to keep them in line.[71] We can do this through "Full Spectrum Dominance," which means being dominant not only on land, on the sea, and in the air, as we are today, but having control of space as well.

The only part of this three-part program that received much public discussion was the so-called Missile Defense Shield. A second part, which involved surveillance technology that can zero in on any part of the planet with such precision that every enemy of U.S. forces can be identified, was already well on the way to being realized.[72] The third part involved putting actual weapons in space, including laser cannons, which have the offensive potential, as one writer put it, to "make a cruise

---

70 General Howell M. Estes III, USAF, United States Space Command, *Vision for 2020*, February 1997. http://www.fas.org/spp/military/docops/usspac/visbook.pdf This document begins by saying: "During the rise of sea commerce, nations built navies to protect and enhance their commercial interests. During the westward expansion of the continental United States, military outposts and the cavalry emerged to protect our wagon trains, settlements, and railroads. The emergence of space power follows both of these models. Over the past several decades, space power has primarily supported land, sea, and air operations. . . . During the early portion of the 21st century, space power will also evolve into a separate and equal medium of warfare. The medium of space is the fourth medium of warfare—along with land, sea, and air. Space power . . . will be increasingly leveraged to close the ever-widening gap between diminishing resources and increasing military commitments. . . . The emerging synergy of space superiority with land, sea, and air superiority, will lead to Full Spectrum Dominance."

71 This is, of course, not a divergence from prior policy. See, for example, the quotation from George Kennan in Chapter 9.

72 The developments achieved already by 1998 are described in George Friedman and Meredith Friedman, *The Future of War: Power, Technology and American World Dominance in the 21st Century* (New York: St. Martin's, 1998).

missile look like a firecracker."[73] With laser weapons on our satellites, the United States would be able, as the document says, "to deny others the use of space," thereby giving America total and permanent dominance.

Although the U.S. military's intention to weaponize space was previously known only by a few people, it was revealed by Tim Weiner in a *New York Times* front-page story in May 2005.[74] Pointing out that the Air Force was seeking a presidential directive to field "offensive and defensive space weapons," Weiner quoted the head of the Space Command, General Lance Lord, as saying that the goal is "space superiority," defined as "freedom to attack as well as freedom from attack."

In light of Bacevich's previously quoted observation that the U.S. military was seeking "to achieve something approaching omnipotence," we can point out that the name of one of the Space Command's programs, "Rods from God," does suggest that it seeks the kind of destructive omnipotence attributed to God by traditional theists—destructive power that is intended to be used to dominate other nations. Weiner referred to a strategy called Global Strike, which, according to Lord, will involve the "incredible capability" to destroy things "anywhere in the world. . . in 45 minutes."

The aggressive purpose of the U.S. Space Command's program was announced in the logo of one of its divisions: "In Your Face from Outer space."[75] Such aggressive, offensive aims were also stated frankly elsewhere. In a 2003 book entitled *Full Spectrum Dominance*, Rahul Mahajan pointed out that *Rebuilding America's Defenses* made the following "remarkable admission":

> In the post-Cold-War era, America and its allies . . . have become the primary objects of deterrence and it is states like Iraq, Iran and North Korea who most wish to develop deterrent capabilities. Projecting conventional military forces . . . will be far more complex and constrained when the American

---

73   Jack Hitt, "The Next Battlefield May Be in Outer Space."

74   Tim Weiner, "Air Force Seeks Bush's Approval for Space Weapons Programs," *The New York Times*, May 18, 2005. http://www.nytimes.com/2005/05/18/business/18space.html?th&emc=th

75   Hitt, "The Next Battlefield May Be in Outer Space." For a brief overview of this project, see Karl Grossman's *Weapons in Space*.

homeland . . . is subject to attack by otherwise weak rogue regimes capable of cobbling together a minuscule ballistic missile force. Building an effective . . . system of missile defenses
is a prerequisite for maintaining American preeminence.[76]

In other words, although the name "missile defense shield" suggests that
the system's purpose is deter attacks from other nations, its real purpose
is to *prevent other nations from deterring America.* The idea is that if
a nation that wishes not to become part of the American empire has a
modest number of nuclear missiles, we could eliminate most of them
with a first strike. Then if the few surviving ones were launched at the
United States, the missile defense shield would be able to intercept them
(even though it would probably not be good enough to protect us from
a large-scale attack). On this basis, we could take over countries such
as North Korea, even if they have some nuclear weapons. Advocates of
the system have been remarkably willing to admit that the purpose of
this "defense" system is offensive. The Bush administration's national
security advisor, Condoleezza Rice, for example, said that the purpose
of the missile defense system would be to protect America's "freedom of
action." Lawrence F. Kaplan, the editor of *World Affairs,* was even more
candid, saying: "Missile defense isn't really meant to protect America.
It's a tool for global domination."[77]

Full spectrum dominance, which the weaponization of space will
provide, is for the sake of completing what Richard Falk has labeled "the
global domination project," which he characterized as "an unprecedented exhibition of geopolitical greed at its worst."[78] A similar judgment
would have been made by Adam Smith, who criticized the "vile and

---

76   Rahul Mahajan, *Full Spectrum Dominance: U.S. Power in Iraq and Beyond* (New
      York: Seven Stories Press, 2003), 53–54, quoting *Rebuilding America's Defenses,*
      54.

77   Condoleezza Rice, "Remarks on Foreign Policy Issues," November 16, 2000;
      Lawrence Kaplan, *New Republic* 224 (March 12, 2001), cover text; both quoted in
      Bacevich, *American Empire,* 223.

78   See "Resisting the Global Domination Project: An Interview with Prof. Richard
      Falk," *Frontline,* 20/8 (April 12–25, 2003), and Falk's *The Great Terror War* (New
      York: Olive Branch Press, 2002), xxvii.

selfish maxim of all for ourselves and nothing for other people," which
has been followed by "the masters of mankind in every age."[79]

The New American Militarism

In his 2003 book, *The Sorrows of Empire*, which was subtitled *Militarism,
Secrecy, and the End of the Republic*, Chalmers Johnson said that the
United States is "something other than what it professed to be"—that
in reality it is "a military juggernaut intent on world domination."[80]
At the end of *American Empire*, published in 2002, Andrew Bacevich
suggested that the topic of "civil-military relations" was a dangerously
neglected topic.[81] He then developed this theme in a 2005 book entitled
The New American Militarism, in which he says that America has become a "military Leviathan."[82]

In using the adjective "new," Bacevich made a twofold point. On
the one hand, militarism did not suddenly develop under the Bush-
Cheney administration. It had been a bipartisan project, which had been
developing for some time, especially since the end of the Vietnam War.
On the other hand, Bush and his advisors "have certainly taken up the
mantle of this militarism with a verve."[83] At the heart of this enthusiasm
is what Bacevich calls a marriage of "military metaphysics," meaning
"a tendency to see international problems as military problems," with
utopian expectations as to what can be achieved by military means.[84]

Besides having greater enthusiasm for military adventures, the
Bush-Cheney administration added two new dimensions: "the Bush
doctrine of preventive war," which Bacevich calls "the clearest articulation of the new American militarism,"[85] and the closely related idea
that it is perfectly acceptable to use military force to bring about "regime
change" in other countries.

---

79   See Robert Brank Fulton, *Adam Smith Speaks to Our Times* (Boston: Christopher
     House, 1963), 388–89.
80   Chalmers Johnson, *The Sorrows of Empire*, 33, 4.
81   Bacevich, *American Empire*, 298.
82   Andrew J. Bacevich, *The New American Militarism*, 54.
83   Bacevich, *The New American Militarism*, 4–6.
84   Bacevich, *The New American Militarism*, 2, 3, 7.
85   Bacevich, *The New American Militarism*, 147.

While referring to the idea of preventive war as a "Bush doctrine," Bacevich knows that neither this idea nor that of regime change originated in the mind of George W. Bush. These doctrines were instead products of the neoconservative movement, which "laid the intellectual foundation of the new American militarism."[86]

A central part of laying this foundation was the concerted effort to get Americans to accept and even take pride in the fact that their country is an imperial power. The statements by Krauthammer and others quoted earlier followed on a suggestion made some years earlier by Irving Kristol, one of the founders of the neoconservative movement. In 1986, with the end of the Cold War on the horizon, Kristol said that the United States needed to move toward a foreign policy of "global unilateralism." He said that it would be difficult to get most fellow Americans to accept this policy, however, because "we are an imperial power with no imperial self-definition."[87] One of the central goals of neocons—as members of the movement are often called—was to instill this new self-definition.

The foundation for the doctrine of preventive war in particular was especially laid by what Bacevich called "second-generation neoconservative thinking,"[88] in which leading roles were played by several thinkers quoted earlier, including Robert Kagan, Lawrence Kaplan, Charles Krauthammer, William Kristol, and Richard Perle. For these neocons, the United States should, in Kagan's 1996 words, "use [its military strength] actively to maintain a world order which both supports and rests upon American hegemony."[89]

From this neocon perspective, Bacevich said, the purpose of the Department of Defense is not primarily to defend and to deter but "to transform the international order by transforming its constituent parts." The United States had not been able to use war for this purpose earlier because "the proximate threat posed by the Soviet Union had obliged

86   Bacevich, *The New American Militarism*, 72. For the efforts of the neoconservatives with regard to the doctrines of regime change and preventive war, see pp. 85–86, 90.

87   Bacevich, 80, quoting Gary Dorrien, *The Neoconservative Mind: Politics, Culture, and the War of Ideology* (Philadelphia: Temple University Press, 1993), 117, who quoted Kristol's statement from the *Wall Street Journal*, March 3, 1986.

88   Bacevich, 83.

89   Bacevich, quoting Robert Kagan, "American Power—A Guide for the Perplexed," *Commentary* 101 (April 1996).

the United States to exercise a certain self-restraint," but once this threat was gone, "the need for self-restraint fell away."[90]

In Bacevich's eyes, as this statement showed, these thinkers had never favored U.S. self-restraint on the basis of international law and morality. They had merely tolerated it as long as prudence demanded it. But once the bipolar world became unipolar, with only one superpower, they believed that America should use its power, without self-restraint, to achieve its interests.

Bacevich pointed out, moreover, that the present policy of the Department of Defense is in line with the advice of the neocons: Its primary mission now is "global power projection," with "defense per se figur[ing] as little more than an afterthought."[91]

The conclusion that the end of the Cold War led U.S. leaders to use military forces primarily for power projection is, Bacevich pointed out, supported by relative numbers. "During the entire Cold War era, from 1945 through 1988, large-scale U.S. military actions abroad totaled a scant six," but from the fall of the Berlin wall in 1989 to the attack on Iraq in 2003, there were nine such actions. We went, in other words, from 6 in 48 years to 9 in 14 years! Speaking as a military man himself, Bacevich observed that "the tempo of U.S. military interventionism had become nothing short of frenetic."[92]

To be capable of using its strength in this proactive, transformative way, the U.S. military needed massive funding. The need for ever higher levels of military spending, accordingly, is a central—perhaps *the* central—theme of the neocons.

And yet the neocons, who came largely to guide policy in Washington, want us to spend still more of our tax dollars on the military. If recent history is any guide, moreover, they will get their way. It is time for people of peaceable faith to realize that our country is not in the hands of other people of peaceable faith. It is in the hands of people of greed, served by fanatics animated by militaristic imperialism.

The following chapters illustrate how American imperialism has affected a number of countries in recent decades. These accounts greatly enlarge upon this theme as presented in an earlier work, *The American*

---

90   Bacevich, *The New American Militarism*, 85.
91   Bacevich, 17.
92   Bacevich, 19.

Trajectory: Divine or Demonic? Two additional post-war episodes that illustrate militaristic and amoral foreign policy in general were adequately covered in the earlier book: the terrorist bombings across Europe arranged by NATO and the CIA and blamed on Communists in order to influence politics in those countries in service to perceived Cold War imperatives,[93] and the use of atomic bombs on Japan, which still is falsely believed by much of the public to have been necessary to bring about a surrender but is likely to have been motivated by geostrategic considerations.[94]

---

93 David Ray Griffin, *The American Trajectory: Divine or Demonic?*, Clarity Press, 2018, 310–322.
94 Griffin, *The American Trajectory*, 153–166

2

Creating Hatred in Iran

BP is one of the world's largest oil-and-gas companies. In 2010, it became notorious for being responsible for the *Deepwater Horizon* oil spill, the largest-ever accidental release of oil in marine waters. This release resulted in severe environmental and economic consequences, for which BP was heavily fined. But BP, previously known as British Petroleum, was earlier responsible for an event with even more disastrous consequences.

In the 1940s, British Petroleum was known as the Anglo-Iranian Oil Company, though it was entirely owned by Great Britain. It was exploiting Iran terribly and keeping it in poverty, because it was giving Iran only 16 percent of the profits, even though the going rate was 50 percent.[1] After Britain refused to negotiate, the Iranians nationalized the company in 1951. This move was led in the parliament by Mohammad Mossadegh, who had been elected prime minister. Defending Iran's decision to the UN Security Council, Mossadegh said:

> My countrymen lack the bare necessities of existence. Their standard of living is probably one of the lowest in the world. Our greatest natural asset is oil. This should be the source of work and food for the population of Iran.... [T]he revenue from it should go to improve our conditions of life. As now organized, however, the petroleum industry has contributed practically nothing to the well-being of the people.... The

---

1   Stephen Kinzer, *All the Shah's Men: An American Coup and the Roots of Middle East Terror* (John Wiley), 2003), 50, 89; Stephen Kinzer, *Overthrow: America's Century of Regime Change from Hawaii to Iraq* (Henry Holt, 2006), 117.

oil resources of Iran, like its rivers and mountains, are the property of the people of Iran. They alone have the authority to decide what shall be done with it, by whom and how.[2]

Mossadegh's statement was made in response to the British spokesman, who had said that the oil beneath Iran's soil was "clearly the property of the Anglo-Iranian Company."[3] This attitude was expressed by the British Chancellor of the Exchequer, who said that Mossadegh's attitude failed to recognize the fact that "our own economic viability was at stake, which was much more important than Persia's."[4]

The UN Security Council rejected the British claim. In response the UK organized, with American support, an economic blockade, which plunged the already impoverished country into destitution. Although Mossadegh had offered Britain compensation based on assessed value and precedent, and even offered the British a discounted price for oil, British leaders in late 1952 approached the CIA about organizing a coup. They suspected that President Truman would not support such a plan, but they believed that the incoming Eisenhower administration would be amenable. They were right.

The Eisenhower administration had many reasons to desire regime change. Iran's nationalization of a foreign oil company, if allowed to stand, might inspire similar seizures elsewhere.[5] Also, if there were a friendly government in Tehran, Iran could be used for surveillance of the Soviet Union and for protecting U.S. interests in the Gulf region.[6] Furthermore, Eisenhower's secretary of state, John Foster Dulles, and his brother, Allen Dulles, the new director of the CIA, had both previously worked for the law firm representing Standard Oil of New Jersey, which would certainly get a big share of a coup to take over the oil company.[7] In addition, the Dulles brothers were strongly anti-Communist.[8]

---

2   Stephen Kinzer, *All the Shah's Men,* 123–24.

3   Kinzer, 121.

4   Kinzer, 129.

5   Walter LaFeber et al., *The American Century: A History of the United States Since 1941,* 5th ed. (Boston: McGraw-Hill, 1998), 385.

6   William Blum, *Killing Hope: US Military and CIA Interventions Since World War II,* 70.

7   Blum, *Killing Hope,* 71.

8   Audrey R. Kahin and George McT. Kahin, *Subversion as Foreign Policy: The Secret*

The Eisenhower administration swept into office by charging the Democrats with having lost both China and Korea to the Communists. A British intelligence agent then sold the Dulles brothers on the coup by telling them that Mossadegh was a Communist who would lead Iran to Communism. This claim was totally false: Mossadegh was a convinced democrat, who did not allow Communists in his government.[9] Unsurprisingly, the Dulles brothers nonetheless argued that America needed to overthrow Mossadegh to prevent Iran from going Communist.

To organize the coup, the Dulles brothers chose Kermit Roosevelt, a grandson of President Theodore Roosevelt. The idea that the CIA would orchestrate such a coup was opposed by several members of the CIA, especially Roger Goiran, who was the chief of the CIA station in Tehran. Goiran warned that if such a coup was carried out, Iranians would forever view the United States as a supporter of "Anglo-French imperialism." But Allen Dulles fired Goiran and ordered the coup to go ahead.[10]

Notably, Roosevelt planned the coup along with a former Nazi collaborator, General Zahedi, and the young shah of Iran. Roosevelt convinced the shah to join the coup by telling him that, if Mossadegh were left in power, he would lead to a Communist Iran;[11] for the shah, though, the prospect of attaining personal power was very probably a factor as well.

Roosevelt's coup plan, dubbed Operation Ajax, had many lines of attack.

- First, a campaign in the streets, the mosques, and the press would undermine Mossadegh's popularity, as he would be portrayed as corrupt, pro-Communist, and anti-Islam.

- Second, thugs would be paid to launch staged attacks on religious leaders, making them appear to be ordered by Mossadegh.

Eisenhower and Dulles Debacle in Indonesia (Seattle: University of Washington Press, 1995), 4; Stephen Kinzer, *Overthrow: America's Century of Regime Change from Hawaii to Iraq* (Henry Holt, 2006), 4, 114, 117.

9   Kinzer, *Overthrow,* 121.
10   Kinzer, *All the Shah's Men,* 164.
11   Kinzer, *All the Shah's Men,* 10.

- Third, General Zahedi would bribe military officers to be ready to help with the coup.

- Fourth, members of the parliament would also be bribed.

- Fifth, on "coup day," thousands of paid demonstrators were paid to stage a massive anti-government rally, and the bribed members of parliament would arrange a vote to demand Mossadegh's resignation.

- Sixth, army units under Zahedi's control would arrest Mossadegh and take charge of command posts, police and radio stations, and the national bank.

- Seventh, General Zahedi would accept the shah's nomination to be the prime minister.[12]

Although the U.S.-backed ouster of Mossadegh was bitterly denounced by the people of Iran, the young shah gave thanks to Allah and the CIA—as presumably did Standard Oil, which started receiving 40 percent of Iran's oil profits. In spite of having earlier pointed out that Mossadegh had "acquired a reputation as an honest patriot"[13] the *New York Times* now declared that his ouster would be a good learning experience:

> Underdeveloped countries with rich resources now have an object lesson in the heavy cost that must be paid by one of their number which goes berserk with fanatical nationalism.[14]

"Fanatical nationalism" was, of course, the idea that a country's resources should benefit its own people, rather than the corporations of America and its allies. This object lesson provides an example of the way in which the U.S. government has, like Rome and other empires, used terror in one place to intimidate elsewhere.

The after-effects of this object lesson were even more deadly. Although Allen Dulles declared that Iran had been saved from a

---

12 Kinzer, *All the Shah's Men*, 10, 163.
13 Blum, *Killing Hope*, 70.
14 Noam Chomsky, *Deterring Democracy*, 2nd ed. (New York: Hill and Wang, 1992), 50 (quoting the *New York Times*, August 6, 1954).

"Communist-dominated regime,"[15] democratic freedom was not to be the result. The coup gave Mohammad Reza Shah the opportunity to become a dictator, as the CIA gave him over $1 billion a year, with which he bought weaponry and crushed dissent by whatever means necessary. The shah's regime instituted, in the words of Amnesty International, "a history of torture which is beyond belief."[16] This torture was the work of the shah's secret police, SAVAK, which was trained by Norman Schwarzkopf, Sr. (the father of the man who was to lead U.S. forces in the first Bush administration's attack on Iraq, discussed later).[17]

For saddling the Iranian people with this regime and stealing their one source of wealth, America earned their long-term hatred, which was manifested later when the shah was replaced in 1979 by the rabidly anti-American government headed by Ayatollah Khomeini, which allowed students to take over the American embassy in Tehran and hold its diplomats hostage. One of the militant students explained later that the hostage-taking was a delayed reaction to Operation Ajax.[18]

Prior to Operation Ajax, Iranians had admired America, liking it much better than both Britain and the Soviet Union.[19] But America's Operation Ajax, followed by its apparent intent to bring the despised shah back, followed by Iran's holding of American hostages, led to a state of long-term hatred between these two countries.

Interestingly, Eisenhower had asked why it was not possible "to get some of the people in these down-trodden countries to like us instead of hating us."[20] He answered his own question when he OK'd the plan of the Dulles brothers to overthrow Iran's beloved leader, Mohammad Mossadegh.

This episode, pointed out Kinzer, had another effect:

Operation Ajax taught tyrants and aspiring tyrants there that the world's most powerful governments were willing to

---

15   LaFeber, *The American Age*, 518.
16   Blum, *Killing Hope*, 72.
17   William Rivers Pitt, *War On Iraq* (New York: Context Books, 2002), 17.
18   Pitt, *War On Iraq*, 17; Kinzer, *Overthrow*, 202.
19   Kinzer, *All the Shah's Men*, 85–86.
20   Kinzer, 158.

tolerate limitless oppression as long as oppressive regimes were friendly to the West and Western oil companies.[21]

A final observation: Kermit Roosevelt warned the CIA that its success in Iran should not be taken as evidence that it could overthrow governments at will. "The Dulles Brothers, however, took it to mean exactly that," observed Kinzer. "They were already plotting to strike against the left-leaning regime in Guatemala."[22]

---

21 Kinzer, 204.
22 Kinzer, 202.

3

Deterring Democracy in Guatemala

Insofar as America has acknowledged that it is imperialistic, it has portrayed its imperialism as benign because, although it pursues its own self-interests, it does so by promoting the growth of democratic governments around the world. This self-evaluation is true, however, only if "democratic governments" are, by definition, governments that support American interests. Given the more standard definition, which speaks of governments that are freely elected (without outside influence), reflect the interests of the majority, and protect human rights, American influence has generally been used for—to use the title of one of Noam Chomsky's books—"deterring democracy."[1]

This fact has nowhere been more clearly illustrated than in Guatemala, where the Eisenhower administration in 1954 overthrew what author Piero Gleijeses called "the first truly democratic government in Guatemala's history" and "the best government it has ever had." The United States thereby returned Guatemala, for the remainder of the

---

1   This section is based primarily upon the two definitive accounts: Piero Gleijeses, *Shattered Hope: The Guatemalan Revolution and the United States, 1944–1954* (Princeton: Princeton University Press, 1991), and Nick Cullather, *Secret History: The CIA's Classified Account of Its Operations in Guatemala 1952–1954* (Stanford: Stanford University Press, 1999), which draws on both Gleijeses's book and CIA files, which were originally intended only for internal CIA use. Their accounts differ significantly from older accounts, especially with regard to the communism of Jacobo Arbenz, the importance of the United Fruit Company, and the cause for the success of the US operation. There is a newer book: Mario Overall and Dan Hagedorn, *PBSuccess: The CIA's Covert Operation to Overthrow Guatemalan President Jacobo Arbenz June–July 1954* (Helion and Company). But its new material deals only with the use of air power by the CIA and the Guatemalan Air Force.

century and beyond, to the condition that has led it to be called "the land of eternal tyranny."[2]

In doing so, the Eisenhower administration also destroyed the man most responsible for the ten years of democracy that Guatemala enjoyed from 1945 to 1954, Jacobo Arbenz. Strangely, the Guatemalan side of this story revolves around four men whose name began with "Ar": Arévalo, Arana, Armas, and Arbenz himself. The decisive factor, however, would be a fifth "Ar": the Army.

Once the center of Mayan civilization but having none of the resources that interested Spain, Guatemala had become a neglected, impoverished country during the three centuries of Spanish rule. At the end of the 19th century, however, the rising demand for coffee provided a source of riches. The indigenous peoples, accordingly, were further dispossessed of their land and forced to provide inexpensive labor for the large landholders.[3] Then the market for coffee collapsed during the global financial crisis of 1929, providing further cause for unrest among the native population. In response, Guatemala's wealthy class, wanting a "strong leader" to thwart any challenge to their interests, selected Jorge Ubico, who modeled himself on Napoleon, Franco, and Mussolini. Living up to his "reputation for efficiency and cruelty" during his 13-year dictatorship, he legalized the murder of natives by landowners, crushed labor unions, and had spies and secret police everywhere, creating a society of fear.[4]

Although hated by the masses, Ubico was appreciated by the Guatemalan upper class—and also by the U.S. government and corporations, to which he was deferential. He was especially generous to the biggest U.S. enterprise, the United Fruit Company (UFCO), to which he gave free land and a free hand.[5] Although Washington's support had been unstinting, FDR's administration finally, in response to a student-led uprising, encouraged Ubico to resign, confident that he would be replaced by another deferential leader.[6] And this is what would have happened, had it not been for a young army captain, Jacobo Arbenz.

---

2   Gleijeses, *Shattered Hope*, 3.
3   Gleijeses, 10; Nick Cullather, *Secret History*, 9.
4   Gleijeses, 9–19.
5   Gleijeses, 19–21; Cullather, *Secret History*, 10.
6   Gleijeses, 22–23.

Having no money to attend university, Arbenz had won a scholarship to the military academy, where he had excelled, first as a student and then as an officer. But he was an unusual officer, one "whose concern for the future of his country was intense," one who told his future wife, "I would like to be a reformer."[7] The occasion for embarking on this course was provided by General Federico Ponce, who, after Ubico's resignation, brought his troops to the Guatemalan Congress, thereby "persuading" it to make him president.

Furious, Arbenz resigned from the army in protest and then led a victorious battle against Ponce's forces. Although the other soldier most responsible for the victory, Francisco Arana, wanted to set up a military government, Arbenz insisted that they prepare for free elections and thereby civilian rule. The elections, Arbenz told his wife, "will be completely free. Therefore, Arévalo will win [and] we will have written a brilliant and patriotic page in our history."[8]

He was referring to Juan José Arévalo, who became president after "the revolution of 1944," which had begun with the student-led revolt against Ubico. Given Arévalo's Ph.D. in education and his emphasis on spiritual matters—he called himself, in opposition to the materialist concerns of the Marxists, a "spiritual socialist"—he seemed safe enough to the upper classes and U.S. businesses.

And he *was*, being firmly committed to capitalism. He did, to be sure, introduce some significant reforms, allowing workers the right to unionize and permitting the passage of a Labor Code. Believing in political freedom, he even tolerated communists, although he did not legalize their party. But he did not touch the biggest issue, the fact that 2 percent of the landowners owned 72 percent of the land, while most of the rest were crowded onto parcels too small to feed a family.[9] He also did not change the country's extremely regressive tax code, which, among other things, allowed U.S. corporations to pay little.[10]

In spite of the moderate nature of Arévalo's reforms, however, the upper classes and American corporations—which were outraged by any deviation from the conditions they had enjoyed under Ubico—protested,

---

7   Gleijeses, *Shattered Hope*, 135–35.
8   Gleijeses, 53, 140; Cullather, *Secret History*, 11.
9   Gleijeses, 36–37.
10   Gleijeses, 41–47, 91, 117, 377.

with UFCO (the United Fruit Company) complaining to Washington that it was being "persecuted" and that Arévalo was a communist.[11] Although the Truman administration spent much time debating whether Arévalo was, in fact, a communist, it decided that there was no basis to take action.[12]

But Arana, now the chief of the armed forces, precipitated a crisis. Having been encouraged by the landed elite to stage a coup, he gave Arévalo an ultimatum: either be deposed or else replace his ministers with those chosen by Arana. Instead of accepting the ultimatum, Arévalo simply had Arana dismissed, then ordered Arbenz, who was the minister of defense, to have him arrested. When Arana resisted arrest, he was killed by Arbenz's men in a shootout.[13] Upon hearing of Arana's death, his supporters revolted but were defeated by the loyalist forces, skillfully led by Arbenz.[14]

With his prestige reinforced—he had saved democracy again— Arbenz won a landslide victory in the next presidential elections, in spite of being opposed by the landed elite.[15] The only other challenge was an inept coup attempted by one of Arana's former officers, Castillo Armas, who was captured but later escaped from prison, thereby becoming available to become an American tool.[16]

In any case, Arbenz, taking office in March of 1951, quickly articulated the moral vision behind the reforms he envisaged:

> I grant great importance to economic policy, but only as a means to achieve our social goals. All the riches of Guatemala are not as important as the life, the freedom, the dignity, the health and the happiness of the most humble of its people. How wrong we would be if—mistaking the means for the

---

11 Gleijeses, 94, 96, 99–100, 103, 105.

12 Gleijeses, 119–21.

13 Although there were rumors that Arbenz simply had Arana murdered, this was, Gleijeses showed, most improbable. The rumors persisted partly because Arévalo, rather than telling the truth about Arana's betrayal, claimed that he was killed by right-wing reactionaries. Although Arbenz had advised Arévalo simply to tell the truth, he remained silent (Gleijeses, 67–71).

14 Gleijeses, 54–56, 59, 62–71.

15 Gleijeses, 73, 83; Cullather, *Secret History*, 11.

16 Gleijeses, 81–83.

end—we were to set financial stability and economic growth
as the supreme goals of our policy, sacrificing to them the well
being of our masses.... Our task is to work together in order
to produce more wealth.... But we must distribute these riches
so that those who have less—and they are the immense majority—benefit more, while those who have more—and they are
so few—also benefit, but to a lesser extent. How could it be
otherwise, given the poverty, the poor health, and the lack of
education of our people.[17]

Although this statement was unsettling to the landed elite and
U.S. companies, it was generally dismissed as mere rhetoric, especially
because nothing changed during the next year. Arbenz, however, was
working quietly but intensely with his advisers on an integrated plan to
carry out his redistributive vision, at the center of which was agrarian
reform.[18]

Presented to a stunned Congress in April of 1952, Decree 900 was
approved in June, with implementation beginning in January of 1953—
the month the Eisenhower administration came to power.[19] Although
it was a moderate program, expropriating only uncultivated land from
larger estates, it was extremely successful, being implemented with little
violence, resulting in an immediate increase in production (rather than
a temporary decrease, as in most such programs), and helping a large
percent of Guatemala's people.[20] As Piero Gleijeses pointed out, Arbenz
had "accomplished a unique feat: the first true agrarian reform of Central
America.... For the first time since the Spanish conquest, the government returned land to the Indians."[21] The landed elite, UFCO, and the
U.S. government, however, had different perspectives.

Although UFCO was duly paid for expropriated land, it claimed
that the amount was far too little. The problem resulted from the fact that
Decree 900 stipulated that the amount paid for expropriated land would
reflect the value that had been declared by the owners for tax purposes.

17   Gleijeses, *Shattered Hope*, 150.
18   Gleijeses, 144–45.
19   Gleijeses, 145, 150–51, 231.
20   Gleijeses, 152, 155–60, 163.
21   Gleijeses, 135, 160.

UFCO had been declaring that the land was worth only $1 million, but it now claimed that the expropriated land was really worth $19 million. Although UFCO thereby admitted that it had been grossly undervaluing its land to keep its taxes down, the U.S. State Department endorsed its claim of unjust treatment.[22]

The Eisenhower administration, having had the CIA overthrow the government of Iran in 1953, decided to have a repeat performance in Guatemala. Contrary to most previous accounts, however, the fact that the Eisenhower administration was closely connected with UFCO was probably not a primary reason for this decision. Far more important was the very fact that the agrarian reform *was successful*. It was a classic case of "the threat of a good example." As a letter to the assistant secretary of state for inter-American affairs put it:

> Guatemala has become an increasing threat to the stability of Honduras and El Salvador. Its agrarian reform is a powerful propaganda weapon; its broad social program of aiding the workers and peasants in a victorious struggle against the upper classes and large foreign enterprises has a strong appeal to the populations of Central American neighbors where similar conditions prevail.

American leaders did not, of course, advance this reason in their public discussions. The *expressed* concern was that Arbenz's government constituted a "Soviet beachhead" in Central America.[23] This, however, was not true.

It *is* true, contrary to some accounts, that Arbenz had become a communist and had communist friends, who served as his "kitchen cabinet," helping him formulate the plan for agrarian reform. But Arbenz had become a convinced communist through reading Marx, finding that the Marxian analysis illuminated the situation of Guatemala, and also through the fact that the communist intellectuals in Guatemala were hardworking, dedicated, incorruptible people who were, like Arbenz,

---

22 Gleijeses, 151, 164.
23 Gleijeses, 257, 262, 298.

genuinely concerned to help their country, especially the poor.[24] There
was no connection to the Soviet Union whatsoever; the two countries
did not even have diplomatic relations.[25]

Even if there had been, this would have provided no justification
for the United States to overthrow a duly elected government.[26] After all,
the U.S. government was busy establishing "beachheads" all around the
Soviet Union. The claim that it had a right to do this while the Soviets had
no right to assist governments in the Western Hemisphere was just one
more example of American double standards. But this argument need
not even be made in this case, because there was no Soviet connection.

Given Washington's mindset, however, the mere fact that Arbenz
was a Marxist, combined with the fact that he was in the process of
carrying out successful and popular land reform—thereby establishing
a precedent that people in neighboring countries might want to dupli-
cate—was sufficient for Washington to set in motion a plan to get rid of
Arbenz.[27]

Although much has been made in some accounts of razzle-dazzle
orchestrated by the CIA, the coup was successful simply because the
United States bribed, persuaded, and intimidated the Guatemalan army.
Hence, when Castillo Armas led a little band of soldiers across the border from Honduras, he was victorious not because of CIA tricks, as some
accounts have claimed, but only because the Guatemalan army had decided not to fight. They had been told that Armas' army was simply a
proxy for the Americans, so that if it was defeated, the U.S. military

---

24 Gleijeses, *Shattered Hope*, 78–79, 140–41, 143–46, 182, 190, 192, 216, 233–34;
    Cullather, *Secret History*, 142.
25 Cullather, 107–8.
26 When David Atlee Phillips, then a recent CIA recruit, was tapped for the assignment,
    he reportedly said: "But Arbenz became President in a free election. What right do
    we have to help someone topple his government and throw him out of office?"
    This story was told by Phillips himself in *The Night Watch: Twenty-five Years of
    Peculiar Service* (New York: Athenaeum, 1977), 34–35.
27 This was actually the Eisenhower administration's second attempt to overthrow
    Arbenz. After the first attempt, Arbenz discovered and published evidence
    of American involvement. The US State Department called the accusations
    "ridiculous and untrue," adding: "It is the policy of the United States not to interfere
    in the internal affairs of other nations" (Blum, *Killing Hope*, 78). What it meant, of
    course, is that it is the policy of the United States to lie whenever it gets caught.

would invade the country in full force.[1] This intimidation worked. Arbenz was forced from office due to this threat from the United States. Secretary John Foster Dulles, of course, gave the American people a different interpretation, saying that the "people of Guatemala have now been heard from."[2]

The puppet subsequently installed by U.S. officials scuttled land reform, outlawed labor unions, killed labor organizers, and banned political parties and opposition newspapers.[3] Longer term, the U.S. overthrow of Guatemala's fledgling democracy resulted in decades of state terror, much of it carried out by death squads. "Over the next three decades," wrote Walter LaFeber, "Guatemala's military rulers racked up the worst human rights record in the Western Hemisphere."[4]

The U.S. intervention also resulted in widespread poverty, with some 20,000 people, mainly children, dying of hunger each year, and many other children avoiding this fate only through prostitution.[5] According to a 2014 report: "Guatemala suffers from a level of inequality and widespread poverty that is extreme even within Latin America. According to the World Bank's Guatemala Poverty Assessment, many developing countries are poor, multi-ethnic, and overwhelmingly rural. Yet Guatemala stands out for the magnitude of these characteristics."[6]

The "land of eternal tyranny" had, beginning in 1944, experienced ten years of hope. But American foreign policy was committed, as suggested by the title of a book by William Blum, to *Killing Hope*. Accordingly, the hope of the Guatemalans became, as the title of the book by Piero Gleijeses put it, a *Shattered Hope*. In Eisenhower's memoirs, nevertheless, the overthrow of Arbenz was listed as one of his proudest accomplishments.[7]

---

1   Gleijeses, *Shattered Hope*, 246–47, 254, 256, 305, 313, 335, 338–39, 341, 365, 375, 380; Cullather, *Secret History*, 60, 64, 68, 82, 84–85, 89.
2   Schmitz, *Thank God*, 196.
3   Blum, *Killing Hope*, 82.
4   Walter LaFeber, "Illusions of an American Century," in Andrew J. Bacevich, ed., "The Short American Century," 158–86, at 168.
5   Chomsky, *Year 501*, 174–76.
6   "Telling Common Hope's Story 2014."
7   Gleijeses, *Shattered Hope*, 235, citing Dwight D. Eisenhower, *Mandate for Change, 1953–1956* (Garden City: Doubleday, 1963), 421–27, 573–75.

4

Pushing Neighboring Cuba
Toward Communism

Known as the July 26 Movement because its first major attack occurred on July 26, 1953, Fidel Castro's campaign to overthrow Batista's U.S.-supported regime had gained substantial backing by 1958. By January 1, 1959, the July 26 Movement took control. Had Eisenhower and Dulles considered this movement even remotely communist, they would have eliminated it long before this. And their assessment was correct. Castro was a middle-class lawyer; he was not strongly anti-American; he desired foreign investment and U.S. aid; and his Movement had no relation, except one of mutual hostility, with Cuba's Communist Party. Shortly after coming to power, he even suggested at an Organization of American States (OAS) meeting that the USA provide a $30 billion, ten-year package to Latin America to overcome social conditions that could bring communists to power.[1]

Castro did, however, speak critically of the 60 years of American control, of the resulting impoverishment of the Cuban masses, and of the military presence at Guantánamo, and he declared that Cuba would henceforth be neutral in the Cold War.[2]

This neutralist nationalism was crucial, because if it were emulated by other countries, the status of the United States as the de facto ruler of the noncommunist world would be threatened. "A defection by any significant number of Latin American countries to the ranks of neutralism," a NSC paper had declared in February, "would seriously

---

1   Gabriel Kolko, *Confronting the Third World: United States Foreign Policy 1945–1980* (New York: Pantheon, 1988), 141.
2   Blum, *Killing Hope*, 192.

impair the ability of the United States to exercise effective leadership of the Free World."[3] Compared with a communist government, in fact, a neutralist nationalistic government was far more dangerous, because it would probably be more influential. It would also be more difficult to overthrow without facing severe criticism.[4]

Washington's ire was increased when Castro introduced a land reform law. Although it was rather mild, it did affect U.S. business interests. Washington took retaliatory action in October of 1959, not only blocking a sale of jet fighters from Britain but also beginning a series of bombing and strafing attacks on Cuba.[5] This twofold action, leading Castro to conclude that Washington would soon try to overthrow his government, led him to turn to Moscow to purchase arms.[6]

Castro was right about U.S. intentions. Allen Dulles, director of the CIA, had begun planning for an invasion, and by March of 1960 Eisenhower had approved Dulles's covert plan to "bring about the replacement of the Castro regime with one more devoted to the true interests of the Cuban people and more acceptable to the U.S."—but, of course, "in such a manner as to avoid any appearance of U.S. intervention."[7] The CIA began training Cuban exiles, composed largely of former supporters of Batista, and even hired a mobster to assassinate Castro.[8]

Washington's hostility increased further when Castro nationalized the sugar industry and then the American oil companies—after they had refused to refine Soviet oil.[9] Cuba was driven into even greater dependence on the Soviets by Washington's imposition of an embargo. Given the fact that America had, during the previous 60 years, structured Cuba's economy to be almost totally dependent on its own, this embargo was devastating.

---

3   Schmitz, *Thank God*, 227.
4   Kolko, *Confronting the Third World*, 142.
5   Kolko, 141; Schmitz, *Thank God*, 219; Blum, *Killing Hope*, 186.
6   Kolko, 141–42.
7   Schmitz, *Thank God*, 220, citing "A Program of Covert Action against the Castro Regime," March 17, 1960.
8   Blum, *Killing Hope*, 192; Warren Hinckle and William Turner, *Deadly Secrets: The CIA-Mafia War Against Castro and the Assassination of J.F.K.* (New York: Thunder's Mouth, 1992), xv–xvi, 24–25.
9   Kolko, 142–43.

When John Fitzgerald Kennedy (JFK) became president in 1961, he inherited the CIA's invasion plan. Holding a similar view of the problem posed by Castro, he approved the invasion in April, which would become known as the Bay of Pigs debacle. Although the Kennedy men hoped to repeat the 1954 overthrow of Arbenz in Guatemala, Castro's military, unlike Arbenz's, remained loyal to him.[10] The invasion was a complete failure; furthermore, it forced Castro to become even more dependent on the Soviet Union. That same month, Castro for the first time proclaimed the Cuban revolution to be socialist. A few months later, an alliance between Castroism and the Communist Party was formed, and that December Castro announced his acceptance of Marxism-Leninism.[11]

From then on, the U.S. war against Castro—which involved not only a continuation of the economic embargo but also a continuing series of attacks aimed at further destroying the Cuban economy—could be justified as an attempt to rid the hemisphere of a Communist dictatorship. Most Americans, nevertheless, had little knowledge of this war, which was called the "dirtiest, most secret war in American history."[12] And to this day few Americans know that Castro was deliberately pushed into association with the Soviet Union and the Communist Party by the United States itself.

In any case, Cuba's dependence upon the Soviet Union and its fear of another American invasion, combined with Washington's hostility to Cuba, communism, and the Soviet Union, would lead to the missile crisis of 1962. From the Cuban point of view, the missiles provided by the USSR were necessary to deter another U.S. invasion. From the point of view of the Soviet leaders, the missiles in Cuba were parallel to the American missiles in Turkey and Western Europe pointed at the USSR. In the words of Premier Nikita Khrushchev,

> the United States had no moral or legal quarrel with us. We hadn't given the Cubans anything more than the Americans were giving to their allies. We had the same rights. . . . Our

---

10   Walter LaFeber, *Inevitable Revolutions: The United States in Central America* (New York: Norton, 1984), 149.

11   Kolko, *Confronting the Third World*, 144.

12   Hinckle and Turner, *Deadly Secrets*, xi.

conduct in the international arena was governed by the same rules and limits.

Khrushchev failed to realize, however, that America's purported moral superiority gave it special rights. As *Time* magazine explained, anyone who accepted Khrushchev's argument was suffering from "intellectual and moral confusion":

> The purpose of the U.S. bases [in Turkey] was not to blackmail Russia but to strengthen the defense system of NATO, which had been created as a safeguard against Russian aggression.... [Also] there is an enormous moral difference between U.S. and Russian objectives.... The U.S. bases, such as those in Turkey, have helped keep the peace since World War II, while the Russian bases in Cuba threatened to upset the peace. The Russian bases were intended to further conquest and domination, while U.S. bases were erected to preserve freedom. The difference should have been obvious to all.[13]

As with many statements justifying America's double standards, it is hard to tell whether this one was written with tongue in cheek.

In any case, the advantage provided to the U.S. by Castro's embrace of Marxist-Leninism was great, given the true nature of the "Cuban threat." This threat, JFK was told by a team he had appointed to evaluate Latin America, is "the spread of the Castro idea of taking matters into one's own hands." This idea has great appeal, they reported, because "the distribution of land and other forms of national wealth greatly favors the propertied classes." That by itself was not a problem, of course, but only the fact that "the poor and underprivileged, stimulated by the example of the Cuban revolution, are now demanding opportunities for a decent living."[14]

Given Washington's concept of "national security," according to which it is threatened unless the whole world, and especially the whole Western Hemisphere, follows U.S. leadership, Cuba was a threat to U.S.

---

13   Blum, *Killing Hope*, 185, quoting *Time,* November 2, 1962.
14   Chomsky, *Rogue States*, 2, citing "American Republics," vol. XII of *Foreign Relations of the United States* (US Dept. of State, 1961–63), 13–14, 33.

national security. As a U.S. diplomat to Mexico pointed out, however, "If we publicly declare that Cuba is a threat to our security, forty million Mexicans will die laughing."[15]

But now American leaders did not have to make this ludicrous claim. Having forced Castro into embracing Marxism and the USSR, U.S. leaders could portray themselves as nobly standing up for human rights, while conveniently ignoring the fact that in terms of social and economic rights—such as the rights to food, health care and education— Cuba, in spite of the embargo, far excelled all the Latin American countries in the American camp.[16] This fact was, of course, precisely what made the Cuban threat—the threat of a good example—so dangerous.[17] As the CIA told the White House in 1964:

> Cuba's experiment with almost total state socialism is being watched closely by other nations in the hemisphere, and any appearance of success there could have an extensive impact on the statist trend elsewhere in the area.[18]

Given the American government's task of helping U.S. business, successive administrations would make every attempt, from tightening the embargo to sporadic military strikes on economic targets, to make sure the Cuban economy would not thrive.

15　Chomsky, *Year 501*, 146, quoting Ruth Leacock, *Requiem for Revolution* (Kent State University Press, 1990), 33.

16　In 1980, the World Health Organization reported that "Cuba has the best health statistics in Latin America." In 1992, a report in Australia said that "despite the economic difficulties, the average Cuban is still better fed, housed, educated, and provided for medically than other Latin Americans." Both reports are quoted in Chomsky, *Year 501*, 151–52.

17　Washington's concern for the human rights of the Cuban people has been so great that in 1997 it continued its embargo on medicine to Cuba because supplying it would be "detrimental to US foreign policy interests" (Chomsky, *Rogue States*, 148).

18　LaFeber, *Inevitable Revolutions*, 157.

[5]

Brazil: Centerpiece of the Alliance for Progress

JFK's Alliance for Progress, which was created in response to Castro's victory in Cuba, declared that it would discontinue support for "dictatorships or regimes based on plutocracies," because that policy had "lent plausibility to the Communist charge that America's only interest was to enlarge her investment opportunities and markets, and to the Marxian charge that American capitalism equated to imperialism."[1] Intending "peaceful revolutions," JFK's basic idea was that economic aid could be used to create a growing middle class and a democratic alternative to both right-wing dictatorships and left-wing revolutions.[2]

Brazil was to be the centerpiece of the Alliance.[3] Brazil's economy had long been dominated by America's. Gerald Haines, the senior historian of the CIA, frankly said that Washington had guided "Brazilian industrial development for the benefit of private U.S. corporations," developing "a neocolonial relationship, with Brazil furnishing the raw materials for American industry and the United States supplying Brazil with manufactured goods." Any industrial development in Brazil had to be "complementary to U.S. industry. . . . Brazilian development was all right as long as it did not interfere with American profits and dominance."[4] As a result, Brazil had become one of the most economically divided societies in the world, with an enormous gap between the rich and the poor.

---

1 Schmitz, *Thank God*, 238–39.
2 LaFeber, *Inevitable Revolutions*, 149.
3 Schmitz, *Thank God*, 269.
4 Chomsky, *Year 501*: 159, quoting *Gerald Haines, The Americanization of Brazil*.

In 1961, João Goulart, the vice-president, was elevated to the presidency when the former president was forced out of office by the Kennedy Administration, which was angered by his refusal to support the U.S. embargo against Cuba.[5] Goulart, a Roman Catholic, a millionaire landowner, and a critic of Castro, was not even close to being a communist. But he, like his predecessor, did favor moderate economic nationalism and social reform, which led him to raise the minimum wage, to initiate some mild agrarian changes, and to restrict the profits of U.S. businesses. Also, favoring democracy and neutralism, he opposed sanctions against Cuba and extended democratic rights to communists, even appointing some of them to government posts. Being suspicious of U.S. machinations, furthermore, he promoted nationalist over pro-American officers in the military.[6]

In the minds of these U.S.-trained officers as well as the Brazilian plutocrats and Washington officials, these actions raised the possibility that Goulart was planning to establish a communist dictatorship—which, even if a mere possibility, had to be eliminated.[7]

The Kennedy Administration, besides starting to discuss a coup with Brazilian officers, began increasing the percentage of Alliance funds going for military aid. The CIA spent millions of dollars supporting anti-Goulart candidates and an anti-Goulart propaganda campaign, spreading stories about outrages he was allegedly planning.[8]

A few months after Kennedy's assassination, the administration of Lyndon Baines Johnson (LBJ) gave the military planners the green light for the coup, which became known as the March 31 Revolution. Although Secretary of State Dean Rusk would later swear to Congress

---

5   Schmitz, *Thank God*, 269; Blum, *Killing Hope*, 156.
6   Blum, *Killing Hope*, 164–66; Chomsky, *Year 501*, 162; Schmitz, *Thank God*, 269.
7   The language used by US officials reflects the fact that there was no evidence that Goulart was a communist. The charges were that "we *may be* witnessing the early stages of an attempted slow-motion coup"; there is a "*danger* that he will become a captive of the left"; there is "a *good chance* that the course of Brazilian politics will continue moving toward leftist solutions"; there are "*fears* of Goulart's intentions to maneuver a Left-wing takeover"; Goulart "*may be able* to neutralize [the] military …bulwark against a Leftist takeover"; "a communist takeover is *conceivable*"; and, most frightening, present tendencies "*could* lead ultimately to …an extreme leftist regime with a strongly anti-US character" (Schmitz, *Thank God*, 270–73; emphases added).
8   Blum, *Killing Hope*, 166; Schmitz, *Thank God*, 271–72.

that the United States had nothing to do with it, Washington sent oil, money, and arms.[9] After the coup's success, the American ambassador called it "the single most important victory for freedom in the hemisphere in recent years," the meaning of which was clarified by the CIA's statement that the change "will create a greatly improved climate for private investment."[10]

Freedom in the layperson's sense, however, was not facilitated. The March 31 Revolution, which was said to be necessary to prevent a *possible* left-wing dictatorship, ushered in an *actual* right-wing military dictatorship that, besides lasting for two decades, was especially brutal. The people were subjected to "disappearances," death squads, extreme torture, and gang rapes of women in front of their husbands and children—all underwritten by Uncle Sam. The income of this already extremely inegalitarian country was redistributed upward.

By the 1980s, in spite of having the world's eighth largest economy, fueled by billions of dollars in U.S. aid and investment, Brazil ranked among the worst countries of the world in terms of health, education, and general welfare. Over two-thirds of the population were malnourished, hundreds of thousands of children were dying of starvation each year, and millions of children were surviving only by becoming slaves or prostitutes—at least until murdered for the price their organs would bring.

Washington never withdrew support for this regime, which survived until Brazil's economy, having followed the IMF's neoliberal, wealth-producing policies, collapsed.[11] The fact that America supported this regime while persecuting Cuba's, with its successful promotion of health care and education in spite of a crippling embargo, by itself showed that America was not fit to run the world.

---

9   Blum, *Killing Hope*, 167–69.
10   Schmitz, *Thank God*, 276, 275.
11   Blum, *Killing Hope*, 170–71; Chomsky, *Deterring Democracy*, 227–28; *Year 501*, 165–69, 177.

[6]

Dominican Republic: The Johnson Doctrine and the Credibility Gap

Although the brutal dictatorship of Rafael Trujillo in the Dominican Republic had received unwavering U.S. support for almost three decades, Batista's fall to Castro's forces in Cuba in 1959 gave U.S. policymakers several reasons to begin plans for Trujillo's removal: the realization that right-wing dictators might be fostering revolution rather than checking it; the criticism by Latin American governments that America, while always opposing leftist governments no matter how good, supports right-wing governments no matter how bad; and Eisenhower's realization that, because these countries believed "that the Trujillo situation is more serious than the Castro situation," they will not "reach a proper level of indignation in dealing with Castro" until Trujillo is eliminated.[1]

While Eisenhower hesitated, for fear that the elimination of Trujillo would open the door for a left-leaning government, the new Kennedy administration, ready to show that it would oppose right-wing dictatorships, apparently gave the green light, and in May of 1961 Trujillo was assassinated by a conservative group.[2] Then, after almost two years of new right-wing governments backed by the USA, Juan Bosch was elected president with a large majority in the first free election in the country's history.

This is what JFK's administration said it supported, and Bosch was the kind of moderate reformer it hoped to promote in the hemisphere. But in September of 1963——only seven months after his election——Bosch

---

1   Blum, *Killing Hope*, 175; Schmitz, *Thank God*, 231.
2   Blum, *Killing Hope*, 176.

was removed in a U.S.-sanctioned coup. The reforms themselves—land reform, higher wages, and some modest nationalization of businesses—upset the upper class, the military, and U.S. companies.[3] What most bothered Washington, however, was that Bosch, a believer in democracy, maintained that communists should not be persecuted unless they broke the law. Observing all this, the CIA said that, because of insufficient evidence, "the possibility that he was secretly pro-communist or a party member could not be ruled out."[4]

Given the U.S. principle that, with regard to communism, one is guilty until proven innocent, the Dominican Republic's seven months of democracy was terminated by a military coup. "Democracy," explained *Newsweek*, "was being saved from communism by getting rid of democracy."[5]

In April of 1965, however, a group of "constitutionalists" instigated a rebellion to return Bosch to power. LBJ had just intensified U.S. involvement in Vietnam to prevent its "going communist" on his watch and evidently saw the Dominican Republic in the same light. "If the Castro-types take over the Dominican Republic," a close advisor told him, "it will be the worst domestic political disaster any Administration could suffer."[6] Within days, 23,000 marines were in the country, preventing the military government from being overthrown by the citizens trying to restore constitutional rule.

This intervention violated not only the Charter of the United Nations but also the Charter of the Organization of American States (OAS), which prohibits intervention "directly or indirectly, for any reason whatever, in the internal or external affairs of any other state." That, however, was an irrelevancy to LBJ, who, expressing himself with his usual delicacy, said that the OAS "couldn't pour piss out of a boot if the instructions were written on the heel."[7]

Attempting, nonetheless, to justify the intervention, LBJ offered three of the standard excuses: American lives at risk, rebel atrocities,

---

3   Blum, 179; Schmitz, *Thank God*, 260.
4   Schmitz, *Thank God*, 258.
5   Blum, 180.
6   Schmitz, 284.
7   LaFeber, *Inevitable Revolutions*, 158, quoting Philip Geyelin, *Lyndon B. Johnson and the World* (1966), 254.

and communist domination of the rebel movement—telling a national audience that "the establishment of another communist government in the Western Hemisphere" could not be permitted.[8] The administration then launched a massive propaganda campaign to convince the world of the truth of its claims. American reporters in the Dominican Republic, however, refuted all of them. The claim of communist domination, which was most emphasized, was undermined by the twofold fact that no communists could be found and that the Communist Party in the Dominican Republic, the CIA reported, had been "unaware of the coup attempt."[9]

After hearings conducted later that year, Senator William Fulbright, chairman of the Senate Foreign Relations Committee, concluded that the administration had used the communist threat and danger to American lives only as a pretext to prevent Bosch's government from returning to power. Another Senate critic, Frank Church, said that U.S. leaders "downgrade freedom by equating it with the absence of communism" and "upgrade a host of dictatorial regimes by dignifying them with membership in what we like to call the 'Free World.'"[10] The *New York Times* asked why American soldiers should be sent to kill Dominicans who were "fighting and dying for social justice and constitutionalism."[11]

One legacy of this intervention, due to the number of the government lies that were exposed, was the entry of the expression "credibility gap" into American popular language.[12] While that legacy reflected the perspective of much of the public, Washington, reflecting another perspective, launched an attack on the concept of non-intervention, calling it obsolete. LBJ said that "with enemies of freedom talking about 'Wars of national liberation,' the old distinction between 'Civil War' and 'International War' has already lost much of its meaning." LBJ's statement revealed perhaps more than he intended: From the perspective of a government that sees itself as the rightful government of the whole world, there *is* no distinction between civil and international wars.

---

8   LaFeber, *Inevitable Revolutions*, 157.
9   Schmitz, *Thank God*, 284–85; Blum, *Killing Hope*, 182–183.
10   Schmitz, *Thank God*, 284–85; Blum, *Killing Hope*, 182–183.
11   Young, *The Vietnam Wars*, 152.
12   Blum, *Killing Hope*, 183, citing David Wise, *The Politics of Lying* (1973), 32.

In any case, the House of Representatives, evidently sharing this perspective, passed a resolution (315 to 52) justifying the unilateral use of force on foreign territory by any nation that considers itself threatened by "international communism, directly or indirectly." Although the House Resolution referred to "any nation," it meant, of course, only America and its junior partners. The essence of this "Johnson Doctrine," commented Richard Barnet, is "a virtually unlimited claim of legitimacy for armed intervention in civil strife."[13]

For the people of the Dominican Republic, the legacy was predictable. In the election of 1966, the people, having been massively propagandized and told in effect that the military occupation would not end unless they voted for the U.S.-backed candidate instead of Bosch, did so. As a result, in William Blum's summary statement:

> The rich became richer and the poor had . . . hungry babies; democracy remained an alien concept; the police and military regularly kidnapped, tortured and murdered opponents of the government and terrorized union organizers. . . . The pot was sweetened for foreign investors. . . . And the men who ran the United States . . . were satisfied.[14]

The United States did not limit its regime-change interventions only to the Western Hemisphere, of course. We will turn next to an illustration in Asia, then one in Europe.

---

13 Blum, *Killing Hope*, 183, citing Richard Barnet, *Intervention and Revolution* (1972), 178–79.
14 Blum, 184.

[7]

Indonesia: Paving the Way to Hell

Indonesia, the world's largest Islamic country, had long been a colony of the Netherlands. At the end of World War II, during which Indonesia had fallen under Japanese control, America initially supported the attempt by the Netherlands to regain control of Indonesia, just as it had supported France's effort to regain control of Vietnam. Eventually, however, America pressured the Netherlands to withdraw, partly because it had refused to obey a Security Council order. (The French effort in Vietnam was able to continue, by contrast, because France had veto power, so there were no Security Council resolutions against it.) The battle for Indonesia's independence was led by Sukarno, who was then elected president.

However, America found him insufficiently obedient to its wishes. Sukarno was not a communist, he did not allow any members of the Communist Party (the PKI) into his cabinet, and he even ruthlessly suppressed Soviet-oriented communists. But he did not persecute *nationalistic* communists, who had sided with him against the Soviet-oriented communists.[1]

The Eisenhower administration became obsessed with the possibility that, because of Sukarno's tolerance of the PKI, this organization might become strong enough "to take power through legal . . . means" (even though it was the smallest of Indonesia's four major parties). Washington hence decided on a covert policy, in the words of Secretary

---

1   Kahin and Kahin, *Subversion as Foreign Policy,* 32, 40, 42–43, 50–51; Chomsky, *Powers and Prospects: Reflections on Human Nature and the Social Order* (Boston: South End, 1996), 190. It was only with the publication of the book by the Kahins in 1995 that the information about America's 1965 intervention was made public. It had been kept secret for 30 years and is evidently still unknown to most Americans.

of State John Foster Dulles, "to bring about a new government on Java" (which is Indonesia's dominant island, where most of the people live).[2] The plan was to exploit the dissatisfaction of the outer islands with the central government in Java (in Jakarta), thereby turning their movement for a federal system into a full-blown civil war.

This war, which occurred in 1957, was supported by massive military assistance and generous funding, courtesy of American taxpayers, who were not informed that their money was being used to foment war against a democratically elected government. The idea was to establish a pro-American government on the island of Sumatra, which has Indonesia's oil, then use it as a base for taking over the whole country.[3] However, in spite of the massive American support given to the rebels, Java's forces held them off, partly because they foiled an American plan for a false flag operation. (The plan was to burn the U.S.-owned oil fields on Sumatra, then blame it on the Javanese, to provide, in the words of a U.S. soldier, "a pretext to send in marines.")[4]

One result of this imperialist adventure, which fulfilled Sukarno's prediction that American support for the rebels would be the "way to hell," was the loss of some 40,000 Indonesian lives.[5] But that was merely a foretaste of the hell to come.

Fearing that Indonesia's parliamentary system would allow the PKI to win the 1959 elections, Washington bribed the army to postpone the elections and then to eliminate the parliamentary system altogether.[6] Later, in 1965, the U.S. Ambassador to Indonesia, in view of the fact that the PKI had become stronger, told President Johnson that "an unsuccessful coup attempt by the PKI might be the most effective development to start a reversal of political trends."[7]

Within months there was such an attempt, fabricated by the CIA and the Pentagon in collusion with army strongman General Suharto, who blamed the coup on the PKI. Suharto then used this "failed coup

---

2   Kahin and Kahin, *Subversion as Foreign Policy*, 91, 92, 93, 126, 161.
3   Kahin and Kahin, 10, 15, 74, 84, 87–88.
4   Kahin and Kahin, 149–51; cf. 124.
5   Kahin and Kahin, 86, 99, 102, 119–20, 128, 132, 134, 136, 138, 140, 150–51, 158, 161, 186, 216.
6   Kahin and Kahin, 193–94, 208.
7   Kahin and Kahin, 225.

attempt" as a pretext to begin a general slaughter, for which the Johnson administration provided arms and "shooting lists."[8]

The resulting holocaust resulted in the deaths of one to two million people; the CIA itself compared it to the Nazi and Soviet mass murders.[9] Many of the victims were simply peasants, school teachers, and union organizers accused of being communist sympathizers. In addition, hundreds of thousands of people were put in jail or concentration camps, many for the rest of their lives.[10]

The long-term consequences were also devastating. Indonesia would not enjoy free elections or representative government for the rest of the century.[11] Landlessness increased, wages fell, and Indonesia became the poorest nation in Southeast Asia, with much of the population living in stark poverty with insufficient food.

America's 1965 intervention in Indonesia did, however, serve a few interests. Suharto, being careful not to upset the United States, ruled the country dictatorially until 1999 and became "a fabulously wealthy man." And Indonesia, having been saved, like Iran, from the nationalists, became a "paradise for investors."[12]

The CIA was extremely proud of the 1965 intervention, regarding it as a model for future operations.[13]

---

8 On arms, see Noam Chomsky, *Year 501*, 126, and Gabriel Kolko, *Confronting the Third World: United States Foreign Policy 1945–1980* (New York: Pantheon, 1988), 181. On shooting lists, see Kathy Kadane, *San Francisco Examiner*, May 20, 1990. For additional evidence of U.S. responsibility, see Kahin and Kahin, *Subversion as Foreign Policy*, 123, 225, and Blum, *Killing Hope*, 195–97.

9 Kahin and Kahin, *Subversion as Foreign Policy*, 227–28; Noam Chomsky and Edward S. Herman, *The Washington Connection and Third World Fascism* (Montreal: Black Rose, 1979), 207.

10 Kahin and Kahin, 227–28; Noam Chomsky, *Rogue States: The Rule of Force in World Affairs* (Cambridge: South End Press, 2000), 6, 144; Chomsky and Herman, *The Washington Connection*, 208–9, 228; John Stockwell, *The Praetorian Guard: The U.S. Role in the New World Order* (Boston: South End, 1991), 72.

11 Kahin and Kahin, 194; 217; Chomsky and Herman, *The Washington Connection*, 209–10.

12 Kolko, *Confronting the Third World*, 185; Chomsky and Herman, *The Washington Connection*, 209–10.

13 Ralph W. McGehee, *Deadly Deceits: My 25 Years in the CIA* (New York: Sheridan Square Publications, 1983), 57–58; Stockwell, *The Praetorian Guard*, 72–73.

[8]

Whacking a Flea, Screwing Greece's Constitution

The U.S. devotion to fostering democracy in the land of its birth illustrated in the 1940s was manifested again in the 1960s, by which time Greece had become a central base of American power, with dozens of U.S. military installations and a vast intelligence network closely intertwined with the CIA. In 1964, George Papandreou became prime minister. Having been installed by the British and having led the oligarchy's war against the left in the 1940s, he should have been fully acceptable to U.S. officials.

But Papandreou had moved toward neutralism and was also resisting Washington's solution to its dispute with Cyprus, having had his ambassador explain to LBJ that it would be unacceptable to Greece's parliament and in violation of its constitution. "Then listen to me, Mr. Ambassador," LBJ reportedly replied,

> fuck your Parliament and your Constitution. America is an elephant. Cyprus is a flea. If these two fleas continue itching the elephant, they may just get whacked by the elephant's trunk. . . . We pay a lot of good American dollars to the Greeks. . . . If your Prime Minister gives me talk about Democracy, Parliament and Constitutions, he, his Parliament and his Constitution may not last very long.[1]

---

1   David McGowan, *Understanding the F-Word: American Fascism and the Politics of Illusion* (iUniverse, 2001), 161.

They did not. In 1965, the CIA helped King Constantine bribe enough members of Papandreou's party to topple his government.[2]

Part of Washington's reason for wanting Papandreou removed involved his son, Andreas Papandreou, who was a member of his father's cabinet. In this role, he had learned that the KYP—the Greek equivalent of the CIA—had become a shadow government, with powers beyond the control of the formal government, and that the KYP was closely linked to the CIA, so that the United States could virtually control Greek policy.[3] Although young Papandreou was unsuccessful in most of his attempts to reform and regulate the KYP, he was able to transfer the KYP agent who served as the liaison with the CIA, George Papadopoulos.

In any case, after having been removed in 1965, George and Andreas Papandreou were about to be returned to power by the voters in 1967. Two days before the election, however, a military junta, led by Papadopoulos, staged a coup. Claiming that the action was necessary to prevent a Communist takeover, Papadopoulos made himself prime minister. The Johnson administration, knowing months before that such a coup was being planned, let it occur. The CIA was, in fact, surely involved in the planning. Papadopoulos, who had been on the CIA payroll for 15 years, was widely considered "the first CIA agent to become Premier of a European country."[4]

In any case, by removing both the elder and the younger Papandreou, the American elephant had eliminated two irritating fleas with one whack.

As its reward for being the locus of this historic event, Greece experienced a seven-year nightmare, with thousands subjected to extreme forms of torture, some for merely criticizing the government. American leaders, however, defended Greece's military junta, which one U.S. general called "the best damn Government since Pericles." The Papadopoulos regime appreciated this support, with one notorious torturer regularly telling his victims: "You can't fight us, we are Americans."[5]

---

2   Blum, *Killing Hope,* 216.
3   Blum, 217.
4   Blum, 218.
5   Blum, 215, 220.

[9]

The Invasion of Panama

In 1989, the Soviet Union collapsed. For U.S. imperialists, this development created both an opportunity and a problem. The opportunity was obvious: It meant that the goal to make the American empire universal would no longer be obstructed by another nation of comparable strength. "In the two decades that followed the end of the Cold War," reported Walter LaFeber, "the United States carried out more military interventions than it had during the previous forty-five years of waging that war."[1]

The problem was that the disappearance of the Soviet Union meant that "the communist menace" could no longer provide an enemy of global scope to serve as an excuse for American interventions around the world. Moreover, to most Americans, including many in Congress, massive military spending no longer seemed necessary. There was much talk of a "peace dividend," meaning that tax dollars previously used for military spending could be devoted to matters such as health, education, and the environment. This was a serious threat. As Stephen Shalom pointed out in *Imperial Alibis*, a new rationale for continued high levels of military spending was needed.[2] This chapter provides one example of how Washington behaved under the new situation.

---

1   Walter LaFeber, "Illusions of an American Century," in Andrew J. Bacevich, ed., *The Short American Century* (Harvard University Press, 2012), 158–86, at 182.

2   See Stephen Rosskamm Shalom, *Imperial Alibis: Rationalizing U. S. Intervention after the Cold War* (Boston: South End, 1993). The need for this rationale also provided the theme of Noam Chomsky's introduction to his *Deterring Democracy* (see the next note).

The collapse of the Soviet Empire was symbolized by the fall of the Berlin Wall on November 9, 1989. Just a little over a month later, on December 20, 1989, the administration of George H. W. Bush invaded Panama in what was called, with or without a straight face, "Operation Just Cause." This operation was meant to provide at least part of the answer to the question of how the United States could continue overturning governments.

The attack on Panama was massive. Washington originally claimed that only 200 Panamanian civilians were killed, then raised the figure to around 500.[3]

But the Central American Human Rights Commission said, as did Catholic and Episcopal Churches, that an estimate of 3,000 would be conservative. The title of the Commission's report was "Panama: More than an Invasion, . . . a Massacre."[4] Eyewitnesses reported that U.S. helicopters fired at strictly civilian buildings, that U.S. troops shot at ambulances and bayoneted wounded people to death, and that U.S. tanks ran over dead bodies and even a bus, killing all its passengers.

Especially singled out for attack was the El Chorillo neighborhood. At 1:00 AM, while its residents were sleeping, it was attacked by tanks, helicopters, rockets, and flame-throwers. People burned to death in the incinerated buildings or leaped from their windows. People running through the streets in panic were cut down in crossfire and crushed by tanks.[5] This "bloodbath," said a spokesperson for El Chorillo's refugees, killed over 2000 people and created 15,000 refugees.[6]

What was the reason for this massive attack on this tiny, helpless country? What was the "just cause"? One of the reasons given, "to protect American lives," was based on an incident on the night of December 16–17. Four U.S. marines, after approaching a sensitive Panamanian roadblock, were fired at, with one being killed, another wounded. The Pentagon claimed that the soldiers were unarmed and had simply gotten

---

3   Noam Chomsky, *Deterring Democracy*, 2nd ed. (New York: Hill and Wang, 1992), 164; William Blum, *Killing Hope: U.S. Military and C.I.A. Interventions Since World War II* (Common Courage, 2008), 305.

4   Chomsky, *Deterring Democracy*, 164–65 (quoting *Brecha*, CODEHUCA, "Report of Joint CODEHUCDA-CONADEHUPA Delegation," January–February 1990, San José).

5   Blum, *Killing Hope*, 305.

6   Chomsky, *Deterring Democracy*, 165.

lost. The *Los Angeles Times*, however, revealed that the marines were armed and had provoked the response with obscenities and disobedience to an order to get out of their car.[7] The conclusion that this incident was merely a pretext for the invasion is reinforced by evidence showing that the war had been planned for some time in advance.[8]

That evidence is supported, furthermore, by the fact that the White House, with the aid of the compliant U.S. media, had orchestrated a campaign to demonize Panama's ruler, General Manuel Noriega, months before.[9] This media campaign provided reasons that were later used to justify the invasion—that Noriega had stolen the 1989 election and that he was involved in the drug racket. However, the U.S. Government had long known about Noriega's involvement with drugs and had supported him when he stole the election in 1984.[10]

Still another sign that the invasion occurred for reasons other than the publicly provided ones was that, although in October of 1989 the Panamanian Defense Forces had Noriega in custody and offered to turn him over to the United States, the Bush Administration declined the offer.[11] Furthermore, a European diplomat reported that shortly after the invasion began, he telephoned the U.S. military to tell them that Noriega was in the flat of his mistress's grandmother, but he was told that the military "had other priorities."[12]

As for the real reasons for the invasion, one factor was that the exposure of Noriega's drug dealing, combined with his failure to hew the U.S. line on Nicaragua, made him no longer a useful client. This

---

7   Blum, *Killing Hope*, 310 (citing the *Los Angeles Times*, December 22, 1990).

8   For one thing, when General Max Thurman was appointed the new Commander-in-Chief of the Southern Command, he was reportedly told by Admiral William Crowe, Chairman of the Joint Chiefs of Staff, that Bush would be calling for large-scale military action in Panama in the near future; see Blum, *Killing Hope*, 311 (citing Kevin Buckley, *Panama: The Whole Story* [1991], 193, who in turn cited the *Washington Post National Weekly Edition*, January 22–28, 1990).

9   The success of the campaign was illustrated by ABC's Ted Koppel, who said: "Manuel Noriega belongs to that special fraternity of international villains, men like Qaddafi, Idi Amin, and the Ayatollah Khomeini, whom Americans just love to hate," so that "strong public support for a reprisal was all but guaranteed" (ABC TV, quoted in *The Progressive*, February 1990, and in Chomsky, *Deterring Democracy*, 145).

10 Chomsky, *Deterring Democracy*, 153, 180; Blum, *Killing Hope*, 306–9.

11 Blum, *Killing Hope*, 309.

12 Blum, 310.

fact was especially crucial at this time because the administration of the Panama Canal was scheduled to pass back into Panamanian hands on January 1, 1990. The invasion put the government back into the hands of the white-skinned pro-American elite, which had been displaced in 1968.[13] The Bush administration's original plan, in fact, had been to establish a U.S. military government, but it later decided to install a local man, Guillermo Endara, as president. Of course, said a Pentagon study, Endara's government was "merely a facade."[14] It was a facade to hide the fact that Washington established direct control over ministries and institutions through which it could, in the words of a Mexican journal, "permanently control all the actions and decisions of the government."

With the establishment of this parallel government, the journal continued, "things have returned to the way they were before 1968."[15] What had happened in 1968 was a coup, led by General Torrijos, which had displaced the rule of the white elite, who constitute about 8 percent of the population. Although Torrijos and his successor, Noriega, were dictators, they were populist dictators, and their two decades of rule brought remarkable changes. In Chomsky's words:

> Black, Mestizo, and Indigenous Panamanians gained their first share of power, and economic and land reforms were undertaken. . . . [I]nfant mortality declined from 40 percent to less than 20 percent and life expectancy increased by nine years.... Indigenous communities were granted autonomy and protection for their traditional lands, to an extent unmatched in the hemisphere.[16]

Obviously, such a condition could not be allowed to stand indefinitely. The reversion to the pre-1968 state of things was confirmed by a report in the *Miami Herald* the following June (1990), which said:

> Six months after the U.S. invasion, Panama is showing signs of growing prosperity—at least for the largely white-skinned

---

13   Chomsky, *Deterring Democracy*, 159–60.
14   Blum, *Killing Hope*, 313 (citing *The Nation*, October 3, 1994: 346).
15   Chomsky, 169 (quoting *Excelsior*, February 28, 1990).
16   Chomsky, 168 (quoting *Excelsior*).

business class that has regained its influence. . . . The upper class and the middle classes are doing great. . . . But the poor are in bad shape. . . . The Catholic Church has begun to denounce what it sees as a lack of government concern for the poor.[17]

The massive attack on El Chorillo was part of this project to aid Panama's elite class. The owners of this neighborhood had wanted "to transform this prime piece of real estate into a posher district," but Noriega had stood in the way, allowing the poor to live there rent-free. U.S. forces removed this obstacle "by bombing the neighborhood into rubble and then leveling the charred ruins with bulldozers."[18] This violent gentrification of El Chorillo was simply part of the economic purpose of the invasion, as suggested by the fact that Bush afterwards announced that $1 billion in aid would be given to rebuild Panama—at least $600 million of which would enrich American banks and corporations.[19]

Still another motive was suggested by a human rights commission report that "the U.S. Army used highly sophisticated weapons—some for the first time in combat—against unarmed civilian populations."[20] Among these weapons were F-117A stealth fighters, which were used to bomb facilities that had no fighter planes or even any radar. An aviation journal, explaining the likely rationale, said:

> By demonstrating the F-117A's capability to operate in low-intensity conflicts, . . . the operation can be used by the Air Force to justify the huge investment made in stealth technology [to] an increasingly skeptical Congress.[21]

The same conclusion was reached by a retired military officer. Saying "100 Special Forces guys" would have sufficed to capture Noriega, he

---

17   Andres Oppenheimer, *Miami Herald*, June 20, 1990.
18   Chomsky, 169. The first of the two quotations is from an article by Pamela Constable in the *Boston Globe*, July 11, 1990.
19   Chomsky, 163.
20   Chomsky, 166.
21   Chomsky, 166 (quoting *Aviation Week and Space Technology*, January 1, 1990).

suggested that "this big operation was a Pentagon attempt to impress Congress just when they're starting to cut back on the military."[22]

When President Bush was asked by a reporter, "Was it really worth it to send people to their death for this? To get Noriega?", Bush replied that "every human life is precious, and yet I have to answer yes, it has been worth it."[23] The U.S. House of Representatives, showing no interest in the question of how many Panamanian civilians were killed, passed a resolution 389-26 commending the president for his handling of the invasion and expressing sadness over the loss of 23 American lives.[24] Some human lives are obviously more precious than others.

In light of the interests served by the U.S. invasion of Panama, the government's justification for it was especially revealing. Article 51 of the UN Charter restricts the use of force by any nation to self-defense, and then only until there is time for the Security Council to act. But the American Ambassador to the UN informed it, on the day of the invasion, that this article "provides for the use of armed force . . . to defend our interests."[25] With this interpretation, the United States was saying that it had the right to invade any country not simply for "self-defense," as virtually everyone else understood it, but also for the sake of defending any interest whatsoever.

The fact that U.S. leaders now felt free to announce this new doctrine was suggested by the fact that on the day after the invasion, General Colin Powell, the new Chairman of the Joint Chiefs of Staff, said: "We have to put a shingle outside our door saying, 'Superpower lives here.'"[26]

The people of Latin America, however, did not need this shingle. An article in *El Tiempo*, calling Operation Just Cause an "imperialist invasion of Panama," said: "We live in a climate of aggression and dis-respect . . . [in] absolute submission . . . to the service of an implacable superpower." An editorial, denouncing "international totalitarianism in the guise of democracy," said that Bush "declared plainly to Latin America that for the North American government, there is no law—only

---

22   Chomsky, *Deterring Democracy*, 166.
23   Blum, *Killing Hope*, 305.
24   Chomsky, 157.
25   *Associated Press*, December 20, 1989.
26   *Washington Post*, December 21, 1989: 36.

its will—when imposing its designs on the hemisphere."[27] As the rest of the world would soon come to see, however, this policy was not to be limited to the Western Hemisphere.

That same day—January 5, 1990—a story in the *Boston Globe* said that former assistant secretary of state Elliott Abrams, who was convicted in the Iran-Contra Scandal, expressed pleasure over the invasion of Panama. Now that developments in Moscow have lessened the prospect for a small operation to escalate into a superpower conflict, Abrams said, "[George H.W.] Bush probably is going to be increasingly willing to use force."[28] That prediction would come true a year later.

---

27 *El Tiempo*, January 5, 1990.
28 Quoted in an article by Stephen Kurkjian and Adam Pertman, *Boston Globe*, January 5, 1990.

[10]

The 1991 Attack on Iraq

Although Saddam Hussein's invasion of Kuwait was as illegal as was the U.S. invasion of Panama, he had understandable reasons for it. Kuwait was exceeding its OPEC quota of oil production by 40 percent, thereby driving down the price of oil. This violation was costing Iraq billions of dollars and thereby preventing its economic recovery—a recovery necessary for it to pay back the $90 billion it had borrowed for its war with Iran. Kuwait was also reportedly using slant drilling under the border to steal oil from Iraq's oil fields. At the same time, while other creditors were being patient, Kuwait was demanding immediate payment of the billions that Iraq had borrowed from it, hoping to use this as leverage to force a favorable settlement of its long-term border dispute with Iraq.[1]

Saddam explained all this to the U.S. ambassador, April Glaspie, at a meeting he had requested on July 25, 1990, after his troops were already massed on the Iraq-Kuwait border, ready to attack. He had good reason to expect American support, since his Baath Party had come to power through a CIA-engineered coup; Washington had allowed him to slaughter Kurds with impunity; and it had supported him during his long war with Iran, even turning a blind eye to his use of poison gas against Kurds and Iranians. Saddam knew, moreover, that the United States had no respect for the United Nations or international law generally. Saddam could well have assumed that he and the Americans had what could be called a "barbarians' agreement."

Besides all this, Ambassador Glaspie told him (the conversation was, unbeknownst to her, being tape recorded): "We have no opinion on

---

1   Dilip Hiro, *Iraq: In the Eye of the Storm* (New York: Thunder's Mouth Press/Nation Books, 2002), 33–34; Chomsky, *Deterring Democracy*, 195–96.

the Arab-Arab conflicts, like your border disagreement with Kuwait," adding that "[Secretary of State] James Baker has directed our official spokesmen to emphasize this instruction."[2] On August 1, Saddam sent his forces into Kuwait, evidently having understood Glaspie's statement as a green light to invade the tiny country to his south—as George H.W. Bush had recently done to a tiny country to *his* south.[3]

The Bush Administration, however, immediately expressed outrage at this violation of international law.[4] The UN General Assembly, ironically, had just condemned Bush's invasion of Panama as a "flagrant violation of international law and of [Panama's] independence, sovereignty, and territorial integrity." But there was no Security Council resolution against the United States because the U.S. representative, of course, vetoed all attempts to pass one.[5] Then the United States, with no apparent sense of shame, used carrot-and-stick tactics to get the Security Council to pass resolutions condemning Iraq, demanding its withdrawal from Kuwait, and authorizing the use of "all necessary means" to compel it to withdraw if it had not done so by January 15, 1991.[6]

The Bush administration was ready to provide those means. Claiming that Saddam was ready to invade Saudi Arabia next, Bush within days sent troops there in what was called Operation Desert Shield. The Bush administration then assembled a coalition of forces that began its attack in January of 1991.

The attack, dubbed Operation Desert Storm, dropped over 100,000 tons of explosives, the equivalent of about 6 Hiroshima atomic bombs,[7] on Iraq, targeting "civilian infrastructure, including power, sewage,

---

2   Quoted in Nafeez Mosaddeq Ahmed, *Behind the War on Terror: Western Secret Strategy and the Struggle for Iraq* (Clairview Books, 2003), 75, from the *New York Times*, September 23, 1990, and July 17, 1991.

3   Hiro, *Iraq*, 34; Noam Chomsky, *Rogue States: The Rule of Force in World Affairs* (South End Press, 2000), 21–22; Ahmed, *Beyond the War on Terror*, 75.

4   Chomsky, *Deterring Democracy*, 185.

5   Chomsky, *Rogue States*, 22; *Deterring Democracy*, 187.

6   This, of course, is only one of hundreds of cases in which, in parallel situations, one violation of international law is condemned by the UN while the another is not, due to the veto power held by the leading imperialist states, which they exercise on their own behalf and on behalf of their client states. The fact that these states have permanent veto power means that the enforcement of international law is not even close to impartial.

7   Hiro, *Iraq*, 37–39.

and water systems"—targets, points out Noam Chomsky, "having little relation to driving Iraq from Kuwait" but "designed for long-term U.S. political ends."[8]

Late in February, Iraq announced that, having accepted a peace plan offered by Moscow, it was withdrawing from Kuwait immediately and unconditionally. As it was retreating in surrender, U.S. planes attacked the head and tail of the long convoy, thereby immobilizing it. U.S. forces then began slaughtering the Iraqi troops in what American soldiers called a "turkey shoot" (thereby using a term U.S. troops had used in the Philippines a century earlier). Evidently 25 to 30 thousand Iraqis were killed during this 40-hour slaughter.[9]

Estimates of how many Iraqis were killed in Operation Desert Storm range from 60,000 to well over 100,000.[10] Some 30,000 of these deaths occurred after America had encouraged a popular uprising against Saddam's regime. When the Shias responded, fearing the emergence of an Islamic government in alliance with Iran, American forces then gave Saddam a free hand to slaughter the Shias.[11]

Evidence that Saddam Fell into an American Trap

Two months after the attack began, Claude Cheysson, who had formerly been France's foreign minister, said: "The Americans were determined to go to war" and Saddam "walked into a trap."[12] This opinion had already been expressed a month and a half before the attack by the Iraqi ambassador to the United States, who said that Ambassador Glaspie's avowal of U.S. neutrality on the dispute between Iraq and Kuwait was "part and parcel of the setup."[13] Most Americans would, of course, be suspicious of claims made by Iraqi and even French spokespersons. But there is considerable evidence that they were right.

---

8   Chomsky, *Deterring Democracy*, 410.
9   Chomsky, 410; Hiro, *Iraq*, 38–39.
10 Hiro, 39.
11 Hiro, 40–43.
12 "Setting the American Trap for Hussein," *International Herald Tribune*, March 11, 1991.
13 *Los Angeles Times*, November 1, 1990, quoted in Blum, *Killing Hope, 323.*

This evidence includes: (a) U.S. motives for a war with Iraq; (b) Kuwait's behavior; (c) U.S. behavior; and (d) physical and testimonial evidence of collusion between U.S. and Kuwaiti leaders.

U.S. Motives for War with Iraq

There were several reasons why the U.S. government, including the Pentagon, might have wanted a war with Iraq at that time.

First, the attack on Panama had not been sufficient to end the calls for huge cutbacks in military spending, now that the Cold War was over. President Bush was railing against those who would "naïvely cut the muscle out of our defense posture," but news reports said that "the administration and Congress are expecting the most acrimonious hard-fought defense budget battle in recent history" and that "tensions have escalated" between Congress and the Pentagon."[14] Shortly after Iraq's invasion of Kuwait, Bush argued that, in the words of the *Washington Post*, it "underscores the need to go slowly in restructuring U.S. defense forces."[15] After U.S. troops were deployed to Saudi Arabia, Lawrence Korb, former assistant secretary of defense, said this deployment "seems driven ... by upcoming budget battles on Capitol Hill."[16] If he was right, the plan worked. "Operation Desert Shield," reported the *Los Angeles Times* in October, "forged a major change in the political climate of the negotiations, forcing lawmakers who had been advocating deep cuts on the defensive." As a result, the budget agreement reached in October would preserve much of the funding that had been spent "each year to prepare for a major Soviet onslaught on Western Europe."[17]

A second possible motive was provided by the fact that Bush's popularity was declining. Although his approval rating in January, following his invasion of Panama, had been at 80 percent, by July it had dropped to 60 percent. Again, if this was a motive, it worked. After the bombing began, his approval rating rose to 82 percent, his highest ever.[18]

---

14 *Washington Post*, January 13, February 12, and June 16, 1990; quoted in Blum, *Killing Hope*, 320.
15 *Washington Post*, August 3, 1990.
16 *Washington Post*, November 25, 1990.
17 *Los Angeles Times*, October 18, 1990.
18 *The Gallup Poll: Public Opinion 1991* (Wilmington, Delaware, 1992).

Although these first two motives could have been satisfied by wars in any one of many places, there were also motives related to Iraq in particular. One of these was the fact that the United States was being edged out of its dominating position in the Gulf. It had fallen to fourth place among arms suppliers and many Gulf States, including Saudi Arabia, were refusing to allow a permanent U.S. military presence. This problem was also solved by the Gulf War: the United States sold some $60 billion worth of arms in the ensuing decade and its military presence in the Gulf increased dramatically. [19]

A fourth possible motive reflected the fact that although the United States had supported Saddam during his war with Iran and had even shielded him from any consequences after his use of poison gas, he was becoming increasingly less subservient. Besides supporting the Palestinian cause, he was becoming a new spokesman for Arab nationalism, warning of the danger that "the Arab Gulf region will be ruled by American will," with the result that the distribution and price of oil would be dictated on the basis of American interests alone.[20] The U.S. attack on Iraq, followed by the brutal sanctions, showed not only Saddam but the leaders of other countries in the region the danger of challenging U.S. hegemony in the region, even verbally.

Finally, as Saddam's statement illustrated, U.S. hegemony in the region was so important because of the region's oil. As the notorious draft of the Pentagon's Defense Planning Guidance document of 1992 stated in a paragraph mentioning Iraq's invasion of Kuwait, "our overall objective is to remain the predominant outside power in the region and preserve U.S. and Western access to the region's oil."[21]

---

19 Ahmed, *Beyond the War on Terror*, 67–68, 86, citing Robert Dreyfuss, "The Thirty-Year Itch," *Mother Jones*, March/April 2003.

20 Quoted in Ralph Schoenman, *Iraq and Kuwait: A History Suppressed* (Santa Barbara: Veritas Press, 1992), 11–12.

21 This document, authored primarily by Paul Wolfowitz and Lewis Libby, was leaked to the *New York Times*, where it was discussed in Patrick Tyler, "US Strategy Plan Calls for Ensuring No Rivals Develop," *The New York Times*, March 8, 1992. For the resulting furor because of the document's openly imperialistic language, see Andrew J. Bacevich, *American Empire: The Realities and Consequences of U.S. Diplomacy* (Cambridge: Harvard University Press, 2002), 43–46.

Kuwait's Behavior

That the Bush administration had wanted Iraq to invade Kuwait, thereby providing an excuse for the United States to go to war, is also suggested by Kuwait's behavior leading up to the invasion.

In the first place, Kuwait had taken several actions certain to anger Saddam. It had been extracting oil from that portion of the Rumaila oilfields that Iraq, in the border dispute, claimed as its own. It had also been using slant-drill technology (supplied by the United States) to steal oil from the part of Rumaila that is indisputably Iraq's. Then, as soon as the Iran-Iraq ended in August of 1988, Kuwait drastically increased its oil production, thereby violating OPEC agreements and causing crude oil prices to plummet from $21 to $11 a barrel, thereby costing Iraq $14 billion a year. To make things worse, in mid-1989, Kuwait greatly increased production again, costing Iraq still more billions. By 1990, this economic warfare had so decimated Iraq that, although Saddam had expected his economy to recover quickly after the war so that he could repay his loans, it was in worse condition than at the war's end. At the same time, Kuwait was demanding immediate repayment of the $30 billion it had loaned Iraq.[22]

In addition to behaving in this clearly unreasonable way, Kuwait's leaders rebuffed every attempt by Saddam to enter into negotiations— and did so in a way that one senior U.S. official called "nasty" and "arrogant."[23] When these leaders did respond to Saddam's financial demands, which involved many billions of dollars, they offered "an insulting half-million dollars."[24]

As suggested by several observers—including Jordan's King Hussein and a political science professor at Kuwait University—this behavior by tiny little Kuwait was clearly irrational unless it had been encouraged by a very powerful ally.[25]

---

22 Ahmed, *Beyond the War on Terror*, 69–70.

23 Knut Royce, "A Trail of Distortion against Iraq," *Newsday*, January 21, 1991, quoted in Ahmed, *Beyond the War on Terror,* 69.

24 Blum, *Killing Hope*, 323.

25 *San Francisco Chronicle*, March 13, 1991; Milton Viorst, "A Reporter at Large: After the Liberation," *The New Yorker,* September 30, 1991; both cited in Ahmed, *Beyond the War on Terror*, 70, 72.

U.S. Behavior

The idea that the United States might have encouraged Kuwait's provocative behavior before the invasion by Iraq is suggested not only by the
existence of U.S. motives to attack Iraq, discussed above, but also by
U.S. behavior, both before and after Iraq's invasion of Kuwait.

Before the invasion, the U.S. military had worked out plans for an
attack on Iraq. In the Pentagon's planning in 1990 for possible wars,
"the Soviet threat" had been replaced by "the Iraqi threat." War games
involved responses to an Iraqi invasion of Kuwait and with bombing
targets in Iraq.[26] The overall planning for the war against Iraq was under the direction of General Norman Schwarzkopf, who would later
be put in charge of the war itself. "After the war," reports professor of
international law Francis Boyle, "Schwarzkopf referred to 18 months
of planning for the campaign"[27]—which would mean that planning had
begun over a year before Iraq's invasion of Kuwait. Part of this planning
involved secretly expanding a network of military-intelligence bases in
Saudi Arabia.[28] The planning also involved sending "massive quantities
of United States weapons, equipment, and supplies" to these bases in
January 1990—eight months before Iraq's invasion of Kuwait.[29]

The Bush administration's behavior after Iraq's invasion of Kuwait
provided additional evidence that it was bent on war. In the first place,
the Bush administration, in order to justify Operation Desert Shield,
falsely claimed that top-secret satellite photographs taken in the middle
of September (1990) showed that over a quarter million Iraqi troops
and 1500 tanks were in southern Kuwait, ready to invade Kuwait. Jean
Heller of the *St. Petersburg Times* (of Florida), after obtaining photos
from Soviet commercial satellites for the same period and having them
examined by experts, exposed the lie in a story headlined "Photos Don't

---

26 Major James Blackwell, *Thunder in the Desert: The Strategy and Tactics of the
    Persian Gulf* War (New York: Bantam Books, 1991), 85–86; Los *Angeles Times*,
    August 5, 1990; *Washington Post*, June 23, 1991; all cited in Blum, *Killing Hope*,
    324.

27 Francis A. Boyle, "US War Crimes During the Gulf War," *New Dawn Magazine*,
    No. 15 (September–October 1992).

28 Gen. Carl E. Vuono, U.S. Army Chief of Staff, "A Strategic Force for the 1990s
    and Beyond," *US Army* (January 1990), 1–17, cited in Ahmed, *Beyond the War on
    Terror*, 65.

29 Boyle, "US War Crimes."

Show Buildup."[30] Although this story was published on January 6, 1991, mainstream news outlets failed to pick it up and the U.S.-led attack went ahead as scheduled ten days later. "To this day," reported a story in the *Christian Science Monitor* in 2002, "the Pentagon's photographs of the [alleged] Iraqi troop build-up remain classified."[31]

Besides lying about the deployment of Iraqi troops in Kuwait, the Bush administration colluded with Kuwait to manufacture a lie about their behavior. This lie—that Iraqi troops had ripped premature babies from incubators in Al Adnan hospital in Kuwait City and "left them on the cold floor to die"—was told to the U.S. Congress by a 15-year-old Kuwaiti girl who testified that she had been working as a volunteer at the hospital at the time. Nurses at this hospital later said not only that this never happened but also that they had never seen the girl before they saw her on CNN. It turned out that she was really Nayirah al-Sabah, the daughter of the Kuwaiti ambassador to the United States. She and six other "witnesses" had been coached by Hill & Knowlton, a public relations firm that had been given a $2 million contract by the Kuwaiti government to make the case for a U.S. war against Iraq. President Bush, who had a long-standing relationship with the al-Sabah family, cited this story at least five times in making the case for going to war.[32]

The president also lied about Saddam's invasion itself, claiming that it was "without provocation," whereas, as we have seen, it had been multiply provoked. Indeed, there is good reason to believe that the Bush administration knew that it would take great provocation to get Saddam to invade Iraq, because a study by the Strategic Studies Institute of the U.S. Army War College issued a report early in 1990 that said:

> Baghdad should not be expected to deliberately provoke military confrontations with anyone. Its interests are best served

30   Jean Heller, "Photos Don't Show Buildup," *St. Petersburg Times*, January 6, 1991.

31   Scott Peterson, "In War, Some Facts Less Factual," *Christian Science Monitor*, September 6, 2002.

32   See Chalmers Johnson, *The Sorrows of Empire: Militarism, Secrecy, and the End of the Republic* (New York: Henry Holt, 2004), 230; Maggie O'Kane, *The Guardian*, 5 February 2003; and, on the long-standing relationship between Bush and the al-Sabah family, see Craig Unger, *House of Bush, House of Saud: The Secret Relationship between the World's Two Most Powerful Dynasties* (New York & London: Scribner, 2004), 249.

now and in the immediate future by peace. . . . Force is only
likely if the Iraqis feel seriously threatened.[33]

And, indeed, it was only after two years of provocations from Kuwait,
which did seriously threaten the Iraqis, that they took action—and only
then after they thought they had America's blessing.

Bush's commitment to going to war was also shown by the fact
that he greatly exaggerated the seriousness of Iraq's invasion of Kuwait,
comparing it with Hitler's invasion of Poland and saying that it threatened world war. Bush even said that Saddam was "worse than Hitler."[34]

That the Bush administration was chomping at the bit to go to
war is shown, furthermore, by the fact that it used not only lies but
also threats and what William Blum calls "history's most spectacular
bribes"—thereby violating the rules of the UN Security Council, the
very institution whose rules it claimed to be enforcing. According to
Blum's summary statement, based on many reports, about bribes:

> Egypt was forgiven many billions of dollars in debt, while
> Syria, China, Turkey, the Soviet Union, and other countries
> received military or economic aid and World Bank and IMF
> loans, had sanctions lifted, not only from the U.S. but, un-
> der Washington's pressure, from Germany, Japan and Saudi
> Arabia. As an added touch, the Bush administration stopped
> criticizing the human rights record of any coalition member.[35]

According to the UN charter, nations, besides not bribing other
members of the Security Council, are also not supposed to punish or
threaten to punish them. And yet when the delegate from Yemen got

---

33 Quoted in Glenn Frankel, "Imperialist Legacy: Lines in the Sand," *Washington
    Post*, August 31, 1990, and in Ahmed, *Beyond the War on Terror*, 70.
34 *Los Angeles Times*, November 6, 1990: 4, quoted in Blum, *Killing Hope*, 27.
35 Blum cited the following sources for the bribery in general: *Wall Street Journal*,
    January 14, 1991; *Fortune Magazine*, February 11, 1991: 47; and Ramsey Clark, *The
    Fire This Time*, 153–56. For the IMF and World Bank loans, Blum cited *Washington
    Post*, January 30, 1991. He also cited these sources for particular countries: Daniel
    Pipes, *Foreign Affairs*, Fall 1991: 41–42 (Syria); *Los Angeles Times*, June 18, 1992
    (Turkey); Elaine Sciolino, *The Outlaw State: Saddam Hussein's Quest for Power
    and the Gulf Crisis* (New York: John Wiley, 1991), 237–39 (China & Russia).

some applause from the gallery for his vote against a U.S.-backed resolution to authorize the use force against Iraq, Secretary of State James Baker reportedly told the U.S. delegation: "I hope he enjoyed that applause, because this will turn out to be the most expensive vote he ever cast." Whether or not Baker actually made this comment, Yemen did learn, within a few days, that its U.S. aid was being sharply reduced.[36] Besides losing some $70 million, moreover, John Pilger reported, "Yemen suddenly had problems with the World Bank and the IMF, and 800,000 Yemeni workers were expelled from Saudi Arabia." Pilger reported, moreover, that economic threats were used by the U.S. delegation against Ecuador and Zimbabwe.[37]

The Bush administration also showed its desire for war by dismissing out of hand all offers by Saddam to negotiate a withdrawal. In August, shortly after his invasion, Saddam said he would withdraw in return for sole control of the Rumaila oil fields, Kuwait's agreement to abide by OPEC quotas, access to the Persian Gulf, and the lifting of the sanctions that had just been imposed. One Bush-administration Middle East specialist called this proposal "serious" and "negotiable," but it was summarily rejected.[38] Saddam got the same response from offers he made in October and yet another on January 2, in which he made fewer demands.[39] Finally, word was received on January 11 that Saddam was willing to pull out with even fewer conditions, insisting only on guarantees that his troops would not be attacked as they withdrew and that there would be negotiations to address the Iraq-Kuwait disputes and an international conference to address Palestinian grievances. He said only that he needed to wait until January 17 to withdraw so he could save face by showing that he had not been intimidated.[40] The U.S.-led coalition, however, began its attack as soon as the deadline of midnight on January 15 had passed.

---

36 Sciolino, *The Outlaw State*, 237–38; quoted in Blum, *Killing Hope*, 327.

37 John Pilger, cited in Norman Solomon and Reese Erlich, *Target Iraq: What the New Media Didn't Tell You* (New York: Context Books, 2003), 69–70.

38 Knut Royce, "Middle East Crisis Secret Offer: Iraq Sent Pullout Deal to US," *Newsday*, August 29, 1990.

39 Ahmed, *Behind the War on Terror*, 83–84, citing "Iraq Offers Deal to Quit Kuwait," *Newsday*, January 3, 1991; "Rumours of a Deal Emerge," *International Herald Tribunal*, January 4, 1991; Michael Emery, *Village Voice*, March 5, 1991.

40 *Guardian,* January 12, 1991: 2, cited in Blum, *Killing Hope*, 329.

Evidence of Collusion

In addition to all this circumstantial evidence suggesting that U.S. and Kuwaiti leaders had colluded to lure Saddam into invading Kuwait so that U.S. forces could come to the rescue, there is actual physical and testimonial evidence of this collusion.

After the invasion, Iraqis found a memo in a Kuwaiti intelligence file about a meeting in November of 1989 between CIA Director William Webster and the head of state security for Kuwait. This memo said, among other things:

> We agreed with the American side that it was important to take advantage of the deteriorating economic situation in Iraq in order to put pressure on that country's government to de-lineate our common border. The Central Intelligence Agency gave us its view of appropriate means of pressure, saying that broad cooperation should be initiated between us....

Although the CIA declared the document a "total fabrication," it did not, as the *Los Angeles Times* pointed out, *appear* to be a forgery. Its genu-ineness was suggested, furthermore, by the fact that when the Kuwaiti foreign minister was confronted with the document, he fainted.[41]

Additional evidence that "the American side" encouraged Kuwait's economic pressure and then encouraged its refusal to negotiate was pro-vided by Yasser Arafat, who said that at an Arab summit in May of 1990, Saddam had offered to negotiate a mutually acceptable border with Kuwait. However, "The U.S. was encouraging Kuwait not to offer any compromise."[42] We might, of course, be skeptical of such a statement coming from Arafat, an ally of Saddam, who himself had been badly treated by the United States.

But we have similar testimony from a long-time U.S. ally, King Hussein of Jordan. He later stated that, just before the invasion, the Kuwaiti foreign minister—the man who later fainted—had said: "We are not going to respond to [Iraq]. . . . [I]f they don't like it, let them

---

41   *Los Angeles Times*, November 1, 1990; *Washington Post*, August 19, 1990; both cited in Blum, *Killing Hope*, 323.

42   *Christian Science Monitor*, February 5, 1991, quoted in Blum, *Killing Hope*, 21.

occupy our territory.... [W]e are going to bring in the Americans." The king also reported that Kuwait's emir—the brother of the foreign minister—had told his military officers that if Iraq invaded, "American and foreign forces would land in Kuwait and expel them."[43]

Michael Emery, whose article "How Mr. Bush Got His War" contained these statements from his interview with King Hussein, further reported that:

> The evidence shows that President George Bush, British prime minister Margaret Thatcher, Egyptian president Hosni Mubarak, and other Arab leaders secretly cooperated on a number of occasions, beginning August 1988 [when the Iran-Iraq war ended], to deny Saddam Hussein the economic help he demanded for the reconstruction of his nation ... [and that] Washington and London encouraged the Kuwaitis in their intransigent insistence.[44]

Part of the evidence to which Emery refers is a note from Kuwait's emir to his prime minister, prior to the invasion. Pointing out that their policy of intransigence has support from Egypt, Washington, and London, he urges: "Be unwavering in your discussions [with the Iraqis about their financial demands].... We are stronger than they think."

In the light of this evidence, it seems impossible to interpret April Glaspie's statement to Saddam—"We have no opinion on ... your border disagreement with Kuwait"—as anything other than deliberate deception. This conclusion was reportedly reached, in fact, by Lee Hamilton, then a Democratic member of the U.S. House Committee on International Relations. According to former CIA agent John Stockwell, "Hamilton concluded, from hearings on this, that [America] had deliberately given Saddam Hussein the green light to invade Kuwait."[45]

---

43 Emery interviewed the king on February 19, 1991. Emery's article appeared in Greg Ruggiero and Stuart Sahulka, eds., *Open Fire* (New York: New Press, 1993), and in somewhat different form in *Village Voice*, March 5, 1991.

44 Michael Emery, "How Mr. Bush Got His War," *Village Voice,* March 5, 1991, quoted in Ahmed, *Beyond the War on Freedom*, 73.

45 John Stockwell, "The CIA and the Gulf War," a lecture given February 20, 1991. http://www.serendipity.li/cia/stock2.html

This conclusion was also reached by another member of the House of Representatives, Henry Gonzalez, who wrote:

> CIA representatives in Kuwait . . . encourag[ed] Kuwait to refuse to negotiate its differences with Iraq as required by the United Nations Charter, including Kuwait's failure to abide by OPEC quotas [and] its pumping of Iraqi oil from the Rumaila oil field.[46]

A similar conclusion was drawn by some newspapers. The *New York Daily News* wrote: "State Department officials . . . led Saddam Hussein to think he could get away with grabbing Kuwait. Bush and Co. gave him no reason to think otherwise."[47] Likewise, the *International Herald Tribune* published a story entitled "Setting the American Trap for Hussein."[48] That does seem to be what happened, making what came afterwards all the more despicable.

Crippling Sanctions, Continuing Attacks

Operation Desert Storm resulted, as we have seen, in perhaps 100,000 Iraqi deaths. That, however, was only the beginning. The United Nations, led by the United States, then imposed crippling sanctions, which prevented Iraq from getting enough food and also from receiving things such as vaccines, chemicals for water purification, and parts for sewage pumps, with the result that sewage spilled into the rivers from which most people got their drinking water. One can read the gruesome details in the first chapter of Dilip Hiro's *Iraq*, "Life in Iraq," which is oriented around the difference between what Iraqis called life "before the sanctions" and "after the sanctions."

These sanctions, first imposed during the Bush administration, were not lifted by the Clinton Administration. By 1996, as a result, evidently over 500,000 children had died from typhoid, dysentery, and other easily

---

46   House Resolution 86, February 21, 1991, quoted in Ahmed, *Beyond the War on Terror*, 77–78.

47   *New York Daily News*, September 29, 1991.

48   "Setting the American Trap for Hussein."

preventable diseases, leading one pair of authors to speak of "sanctions of mass destruction."[49]

When Clinton's ambassador to the UN, and soon to be Secretary of State, Madeleine Albright, was asked whether she thought this price was worth paying, she notoriously replied, similarly to President Bush's reply about Panama: "It is a difficult question. But, yes, we think the price is worth it."[50] An event causing a half million American lives would perhaps have been viewed somewhat differently.

In any case, Clinton also continued other policies of the Bush administration, most notably the so-called no-fly zones over both the northern and the southern parts of Iraq. These zones were established unilaterally by the United States, with no authorization from the Security Council—a fact seldom pointed out to the American public by the Fourth Estate.[51]

Clinton's administration also had U.S. planes attack Iraqi targets on a regular basis, compounding the illegality of these flights. The most intense attack was Operation Desert Fox, which occurred in December of 1998, while Clinton was facing impeachment hearings. This attack lasted for 100 hours, during which 415 cruise missiles and 600 laser-guided bombs were sent against Iraqi targets.[52]

Incessantly pounding Iraq had simply become a way of life for the U.S. military. In August of 1999, the Pentagon revealed that over the previous 8 months the Anglo-American air forces had attacked 359 Iraqi targets, firing some 1,100 missiles—almost three times the number fired during Operation Desert Fox.[53] It is not surprising, therefore, that after 9/11 the Iraqi foreign minister said: "All Muslim and Arab people consider America the master of terrorism, the terrorist power number one."[54]

---

49 John Mueller and Karl Mueller, "Sanctions of Mass Destruction," *Foreign Affairs*, May–June 1999: 43–53. They argued that, in addition to the other arguments against them, "economic sanctions may well have been a necessary cause of the deaths of more people in Iraq than have been slain by all so-called weapons of mass destruction throughout history" (51).

50 Hiro, *Iraq*, 18. On the impact of sanctions, including in later years, see Anthony Arnove, ed., *Iraq under Siege: The Deadly Impact of Sanctions and War*, updated edition (Cambridge: South End, 2002).

51 Hiro, *Iraq*, 147–49.

52 Hiro, 130.

53 Hiro, 147.

54 Hiro, 173–74.

11

The U.S./NATO
Destruction of Yugoslavia

At about the same time as the U.S. Gulf War, the George H.W. Bush administration started fighting wars in Europe. Explaining the primary motivation, William Engdahl said that because of the destruction of the Soviet Union,

> Washington faced an entirely new challenge. Suddenly, the rationale for permanent U.S. military and political control over the nations of the EU was under existential threat. Europe was beginning to sense its true independent power in the world as leading circles there contemplated life after NATO—Europeans would no longer have to bow to countless U.S. dictates merely because of a real or imagined threat of the Soviets.[1]

In 1991, the Maastricht Treaty (formally, the Treaty on European Unity) was signed by the heads of the states of the European Union. Forming the basis for a possible United States of Europe, the treaty authorized an independent European NATO, to be run by the EU states, not by the USA. Washington saw this development as a threat to America's global power.[2]

The response of the Bush administration, Engdahl added, "was to covertly trigger events in Yugoslavia that would explode in a violent war

---

1   F. William Engdahl, *Manifest Destiny: Democracy as Cognitive Dissonance* (Wiesbaden: mine.Books, 2018), 90.
2   Engdahl, *Manifest Destiny,* 91.

in the heart of Europe," thereby shattering the idea that European wars were a thing of the past and that therefore the European countries no longer needed a U.S.-led NATO.

Yugoslavia had been established in 1945 as a socialist federal republic consisting of six republics with different religions: Serbia, Macedonia, and Montenegro were primarily Orthodox Christian; Slovenia and Croatia were primarily Roman Catholic; and Bosnia-Herzegovina was primarily Muslim. The Bush administration's plan was to start wars to break up Yugoslavia into independent non-socialist countries.

The execution of the plan began by using the International Monetary Fund (IMF), which is controlled by the United States, to destroy Yugoslavia's economy. Predictably, "amid growing economic chaos, each region fought for its own survival against its neighbors."[3]

The Bush administration then made war inevitable by passing a Foreign Operations Appropriations Act, which said that any part of Yugoslavia that failed to declare independence within six months would lose all U.S. financial support. "The Act threw the Yugoslav federal government in Belgrade into existential crisis. It was unable to pay the enormous interest on its foreign debt or even to arrange the purchase of raw materials for industry. Credit collapsed and recriminations broke out on all sides."[4]

Bosnia-Herzegovina

Not relying on the Appropriations Act alone, the Bush administration had its Pentagon fly into Europe thousands of veterans of the Mujahideen operation in Afghanistan, where the U.S. had used them to defeat the Soviet Union. In 1992, these fighters were flown to Bosnia-Herzegovina (situated between Catholic Croatia and Orthodox Serbia), to help Bosnia's Muslims.[5] "Violent political Islamic fundamentalism," said

---

3   Engdahl, 93.
4   Engdahl, 94.
5   Professor Cees Wiebes of Amsterdam University later published a book entitled *Intelligence and the War in Bosnia: 1992–1995* (Studies in Intelligence History, 2003), in which he documented the secret alliance between the Pentagon and radical Islamic groups from the Middle East—including Osama bin Laden's Afghan Mujahideen networks—to assist Bosnia's Muslims.

Engdahl, "was suddenly at the heart of Europe and Washington made it happen."[6]

However, a plan was drafted in Lisbon that year to prevent a civil war in Bosnia-Herzegovina between Muslims, Catholics, and Orthodox Christians. The plan, conceived by Britain and Portugal, partitioned the country by religious concentration. All three leaders in Bosnia-Herzegovina signed the treaty.

But Secretary of State Lawrence Eagleburger instructed Warren Zimmermann, the U.S. ambassador to Yugoslavia, to convince Alija Izetbegović, the leader of the Bosnian Muslims, to renege on the Lisbon treaty. Zimmerman convinced Izetbegović by promising him political, diplomatic, and military aid if he would do so. The Lisbon Treaty likely could have avoided the Bosnian war, but "[a]voiding such a war was precisely what Washington wanted to prevent from happening. They wanted the Bosnian war for their larger geopolitical strategy in Europe and beyond."[7]

Because the Serbs were the ones most opposed to the breakup of the Yugoslav federation, they were America's main target. By demonizing the Serbs as Nazis and "portraying Bosnian Muslims as the hapless victims of Serbian atrocities" (even though the Bosnian Muslims were the aggressors), "the way was clear to blame the Serb forces in Bosnia for every imaginable crime."[8]

> While U.S. propaganda machinery turned out endless fake stories of Serbian bombings of civilian villagers and hospitals, attacks on UN so-called "safe zones," and fabricated accounts of tens of thousands of rapes of Muslim women in what the Western media, led by the *New York Times*, claimed were Serb-run "rape camps," the Muslim jihadist mercenaries working alongside Izetbegović's army created appalling atrocities against Bosnian Serbs that were blacked out of U.S. and Western media.[9]

---

6   Engdahl, *Manifest Destiny*, 96.
7   Engdahl, 97.
8   Engdahl, 101.
9   Engdahl, 105.

In that situation, Clinton was able to persuade allies to endorse an air campaign by NATO to undermine the military capabilities of the Bosnian Serb Army.

The most important demonization of the Serbs involved the "Srebrenica massacre" of innocent Bosnian Muslims in a UN "safe zone." Here is what happened: Prior to the massacre, Bosnian Muslim jihadists, under the leadership of one Naser Orić, used the safe haven in Srebrenica as an illegal base for attacks on Serbian villages, in violation of the UN humanitarian rules for safe havens. Orić's soldiers slaughtered over 3,500 Orthodox Christians, including women and children. These killings "created a rage and fury for revenge among the Bosnian Serb soldiers fighting to take control of Srebrenica away from the Bosnians." But when those soldiers entered Srebrenica, they encountered no opposition. After letting the women, children, and elderly go to safety, the Serbs shot the men.[10] The reason there was no opposition was explained later by Canadian Major General Lewis Mackenzie, who had been in command of Srebrenica. In an op-ed entitled "The Real Story behind Srebrenica," he wrote:

> [T]he man who led the Bosnian Muslim fighters [knew] that the Bosnian Serb army was going to attack Srebrenica to stop him from attacking Serb villages. So he and . . . his fighters slipped out of town. Srebrenica was left undefended with the strategic thought that, if the Serbs attacked an undefended town, surely that would cause NATO and the UN to agree that NATO air strikes against the Serbs were justified.[11]

In other words, said William Engdahl, "Washington wanted the Srebrenica massacre as casus belli it could use against the Serb population."[12] This plan worked.

The Clinton administration got what they wanted—the pretext for NATO to continue its existence as the controlling

---

10   Engdahl, 108–9.
11   Lewis Mackenzie, "The Real Story behind Srebrenica," *Globe and Mail*, July 14, 2005.
12   Engdahl, 109.

U.S.-run military organization in Western Europe. It also got a permanent 80,000-man NATO occupation force in Bosnia-Herzegovina to enforce "peace."[13]

The Bosnian War, which took place in Bosnia-Herzegovina between 1992 and 1995, ended up being the most devastating conflict in Europe since World War II, with more than 100,000 people killed and 2.2 million people displaced. But it achieved Clinton's purpose, beginning the breakup of Yugoslavia.[14]

Given Washington's hope that the dissolution of the Yugoslav Federation would "light the fuse to an explosive new series of Balkan wars," it provided finances for the wars:

> Washington's financial support was typically channeled into extreme nationalist or former fascist organizations that would guarantee a violent and bloody dismemberment of Yugoslavia. . . . Right-wing and fascist organizations [which had been maintained in exile by the CIA] were suddenly revived and began receiving covert support.[15]

Sir Alfred Sherman, an adviser to Prime Minister Margaret Thatcher, said in 1997: "The war in Bosnia was America's war in every sense of the word. The United States administration helped start it, kept it going, and prevented its early end."[16] As for keeping it going, Engdahl wrote: "The longer the war in Bosnia-Herzegovina raged, the better it was for Washington's attempt to revive the role of a U.S.-led NATO in the Balkans and Europe."[17]

But in 1995, America suddenly brought the war to an end. Why? Because Washington found it far more important to secure a permanent military base in Kosovo, in order to be able to control the entire region,

---

13   Engdahl, *Manifest Destiny*, 110.
14   Maria Markovic, "Are the Clintons Serbia's Most Hated Couple?" *Telesur,* March 24, 2016.
15   Engdahl, 95.
16   Engdahl, 94.
17   Engdahl, 104.

including the Middle East and the Caucasus.[18] The battle over Kosovo proved to be the most destructive part of the war.

Kosovo and Belgrade

In 1999, Clinton had NATO launch a second war on Yugoslavia, beginning with Serbia's province of Kosovo. This province was composed primarily of ethnic Albanians. The Clinton administration's main reasons for this war centered on Slobodan Milošević, who was the president of Yugoslavia from 1997 until he was persuaded to leave office in 2000. Engdahl wrote:

> By 1999, it was clear to Washington that the stubbornly popular Milošević had to go if they were to bring forward their agenda of NATO military domination of post-Soviet Europe. Washington was determined to construct a huge military air base in Kosovo, then an integral part of Serbia, in order to secure their control of the entire region of Southeast Europe and put the vital Russian Black Sea Fleet at Crimea within striking distance of a U.S. air attack.[19]

The fighting in Kosovo occurred primarily between Serbian troops and the Kosovo Liberation Army (KLA), whose fighters were trained by Mujahideen mercenaries recruited by the U.S. Although originally composed of Kosovars, the KLA was augmented by "former U.S. Pentagon special forces and retired military." In 1998, the KLA escalated its attacks on government officials in Belgrade, the capital of Yugoslavia. At the time, the KLA had only 500 trained fighters. But by providing the KLA with arms and training, by 1999 Western powers had built it into a major guerrilla army with perhaps 30,000 members.[20]

Having no interest in Kosovo moderates, who might be open to a diplomatic solution with the Serbian government, "Washington deliberately froze out the Kosovo moderates in favor of the jihadists of

---

18   Engdahl, 109.
19   Engdahl, 122.
20   Engdahl, 13–14.

the KLA mafia, who were guaranteed not to go for peace."[21] As for the term "mafia," former NSA official Wayne Madsen said that "the KLA was, in fact, a grouping of mafia clans in Kosovo who were known drug traffickers well before working for the U.S." In 1999, the *Washington Times* reported that the Clinton administration was fully aware of the KLA's heroin trafficking, but the mainstream press ignored this story. In fact, although the U.S. State Department had classified the KLA as a terrorist organization, the Clinton administration and the press began referring to its members as "democratic freedom fighters."[22]

In addition to supporting the KLA in Kosovo, Clinton's NATO began bombing Serbia and Yugoslavia's capital, Belgrade. Showing disdain for international law, "Clinton's bombing was done in violation of the UN Charter, the UN Security Council, and the NATO Charter itself."[23] This attack, which employed 2,300 missiles as well as 14,000 bombs, lasted 78 days, devastating Belgrade.

> The illegal bombing destroyed and damaged 25,000 homes, 300 miles of roads and close to 400 miles of railways. Many public buildings were damaged, including 14 airports, 19 hospitals, 18 kindergartens, 69 schools, 176 cultural monuments and 44 bridges. The attacks killed at least 5,000 people (some sources claim it was closer to 18,000), injured 12,500, and left the area contaminated with depleted uranium.[24]

Nevertheless, in spite of all of this death and destruction, defenders of the bombing continue to call it a "humanitarian intervention." The bombing was justified, they said, by the vast crimes that had occurred. However, Chomsky points out that "the vast crimes took place after the bombing began: they were not a cause but a consequence." It is absurd, he added, to argue that those crimes "provide retrospective justification for the actions that contributed to inciting them."[25]

21 Engdahl, *Manifest Destiny*, 111.
22 Engdahl, 111–12.
23 Engdahl, 114.
24 Markovic, "Are the Clintons Serbia's Most Hated Couple?"
25 Noam Chomsky, "A Review of NATO's War over Kosovo," *Z Magazine,* April–May 2001.

As the bombing began, General Wesley Clark, NATO's supreme commander, said: "We are going to systematically and progressively attack, disrupt, degrade, devastate, and ultimately…destroy [Milosevic's] forces and their facilities." Harold Pinter observed that Milošević's forces and facilities, "as we now know, included television stations, schools, hospitals, theatres, old people's homes."[26]

In any case, when the bombing was ended, Milošević, on the understanding that the UN would enforce order in Kosovo were he to remove Yugoslav troops, withdrew, ending the decade-long war. Nevertheless, in 2001, the United States pressured the Yugoslav government to extradite Milošević to a specially created International Criminal Tribunal in the Hague, on charges of "war crimes and crimes against humanity committed in Kosovo." The Yugoslav authorities acceded to this pressure because the United States had threatened to cut off financial aid from the IMF and World Bank if the extradition request was refused.[27]

At the Hague tribunal, Milošević was indicted for genocide. The main basis for the genocide charge was the Srebrenica massacre. But in 2004, a 7,000-page report by a team of specialists headed by Amsterdam University professor Cees Wiebes concluded that Milošević was innocent of genocide and the massacre. Weibes' team offered their evidence to the Hague tribunal chief prosecutor but were brushed off.

In 2006, Milošević was found dead in his cell. However, in 2016, ten years too late, the Hague Tribunal, in a trial of Bosnian Serb leader Radovan Karadžić, ruled that there was insufficient evidence to show that Milošević was guilty of the genocide charge, which had been used to justify "NATO military aggression against the people of Serbia."[28]

To summarize the human results of the plan to destroy Yugoslavia: it was "a gruesome series of regional, ethnic wars that would last a decade and result in the deaths of more than 133,000 people, with some estimates of over 200,000 dead."[29]

---

26   Harold Pinter, "Foreword," Philip Hammond and Edward S. Herman, ed., *Degraded Capability: The Media and the Kosovo Crisis* (Pluto Press, 2000), vii.

27   Engdahl, *Manifest Destiny*, 130.

28   Andy Wilcoxson, "Hague Tribunal Exonerates Slobodan Milosevic Again," *Strategic Culture*, July 12, 2017.

29   Wilcoxson, "Hague Tribunal Exonerates Slobodan Milosevic Again," 95.

12

The 2003 Attack on Iraq

Secretary of Defense Donald Rumsfeld and his assistant Paul Wolfowitz together argued that Iraq, under the control of Saddam Hussein, should be attacked in the first round of the war on terrorism after 9/11. There was quite a history behind that desire. This history shows, among other things, the truth of James Mann's statement: "The invasion of Iraq was in many ways Dick Cheney's war, just as the George W. Bush administration [was] in some respects Cheney's administration."[1]

Background

Several neocons, including some who became central members of the Bush-Cheney administration, had been wanting to bring about regime change in Iraq ever since Saddam Hussein's occupation of Kuwait in 1990. Leading voices for this policy included Cheney and Wolfowitz, who were then secretary and under-secretary of defense. But this idea was opposed by General Colin Powell, who was then chairman of the Joint Chiefs of Staff (JCS), and General Norman Schwarzkopf, the field commander. President George H.W. Bush agreed with them, saying that going to Baghdad would have gone beyond the UN authorization. This left many neocons with the determination to reverse the policy decision, which they considered a mistake.[2]

---

1   James Mann, *Rise of the Vulcans: The History of Bush's War Cabinet* (Viking, 2004), 369.
2   Stephen Sniegoski, "Neoconservatives, Israel, and 9/11," 86–87, citing Arnold Beichman, "How the Divide over Iraq Strategies Began," *Washington Times*, November 27, 2002.

From 1991 to 2001

In the decade prior to 9/11, the neocons took many steps to try to get Saddam Hussein removed from office (and perhaps from life):

- In 1992, Albert Wohlstetter, who had inspired Wolfowitz and other neocons, expressed exasperation that nothing had been done about "a dictatorship sitting on the world's second largest pool of low-cost oil and ambitious to dominate the Gulf."[3] (Wohlstetter's statement reflected his conviction, expressed back in 1981, that the United States needs to establish forces, bases, and infrastructure so as to enjoy unquestioned primacy in the region.[4])

- The 1996 paper "A Clean Break" proposed that Israel remove from power all of its enemies in the region, beginning with Saddam Hussein. This document, in the opinion of Arnaud de Borchgrave, president of United Press International, "provided the strategic underpinnings for Operation Iraqi Freedom seven years later."[5]

- In 1997, Wolfowitz and another neocon, Zalmay Khalilzad, published a statement arguing that "Saddam Must Go."[6]

- In 1998, William Kristol and Robert Kagan, in a *New York Times* op-ed headed "Bombing Iraq Isn't Enough," called for "finishing the job left undone in 1991." Wolfowitz told the House National Security Committee that it had been a mistake in 1991 to leave Saddam in power, and he wrote in the *New Republic*: "Toppling Saddam is the only outcome that can satisfy the vital U.S. interest in a stable and secure Gulf region."[7]

---

3   Albert Wohlstetter, "Help Iraqi Dissidents Oust Saddam," *Wall Street Journal*, August 25, 1992.

4   Albert Wohlstetter, "Meeting the Threat in the Persian Gulf," *Survey* 25 (Spring 1981): 128–88; discussed in Andrew J. Bacevich, *American Empire: The Realities and Consequences of U.S. Diplomacy* (Harvard University Press, 2002), 191.

5   Arnaud de Borchgrave, "All in the Family," *Washington Times*, September 13, 2004.

6   Paul D. Wolfowitz and Zalmay M. Khalilzad, "Saddam Must Go," *Weekly Standard*, December 1, 1997.

7   William Kristol and Robert Kagan, "Bombing Iraq Isn't Enough," *The New York Times*, January 30, 1998; "Prepared Testimony of Paul D. Wolfowitz," House National Security Committee, U.S. Congress, September 16, 1998; Paul Wolfowitz, "Iraqi Rebels with a Cause," *The New Republic*, December 7, 1998.

- Also in 1998 a PNAC letter to Clinton urged him to "take the necessary steps, including military steps," to "remov[e] Saddam's regime from power." Then, getting no agreement from Clinton, PNAC wrote a similar letter to Republicans Newt Gingrich and Trent Lott, who were at that time the leaders of the House and the Senate, respectively.[8]

- In 2000, PNAC's *Rebuilding America's Defenses*—pointing out that "the United States has for decades sought to play a more permanent role in Gulf regional security"—added: "While the unresolved conflict with Iraq provides the immediate justification, the need for a substantial American force presence in the Gulf transcends the issue of the regime of Saddam Hussein."[9]

The Bush-Cheney Administration

In light of this background, combined with the fact that central positions in the Bush administration went to Cheney, Libby, Rumsfeld, Wolfowitz, and other neocons, it is not surprising to learn, from two former members of this administration, that it had come into office intent on attacking Iraq.

Paul O'Neill, who was secretary of the treasury and hence a member of the National Security Council, said that within days of the inauguration, the main topic was going after Saddam, with the question being not "Why Saddam?" or "Why Now?" but merely "finding a way to do it." Richard Clarke, who had been the National Coordinator for Security and Counterterrorism during the first Bush-Cheney term, confirmed O'Neill's charge, saying: "The administration of the second George Bush did begin with Iraq on its agenda."[10]

---

8   "Letter to President Clinton on Iraq," Project for the New American Century [PNAC], January 26, 1998; "Letter to Gingrich and Lott on Iraq," PNAC, May 29, 1998.

9   *Rebuilding America's Defenses: Strategy, Forces and Resources For a New Century* (Project for the New American Century, September 2000), 14.

10 O'Neill is quoted to this effect in Ron Suskind, *The Price of Loyalty: George W. Bush, the White House, and the Education of Paul O'Neill* (Simon & Schuster, 2004). Suskind, whose book also draws on interviews with other officials, said that in its first weeks the Bush administration was discussing the occupation of Iraq and the question of how to divide up its oil; Richard Clarke, *Against All Enemies: Inside*

Until the attacks of 9/11, however, no one had found "a way to do it." Neocon Kenneth Adelman said: "At the beginning of the administration people were talking about Iraq but it wasn't doable.... That changed with September 11." Bob Woodward, in *Bush at War,* said: "The terrorist attacks of September 11 gave the U.S. a new window to go after Hussein." And John Mearsheimer and Stephen Walt, in their important essay "The Israel Lobby," wrote:

> The neo-conservatives had been determined to topple Saddam even before Bush became president. They caused a stir early in 1998 by publishing two open letters to Clinton, calling for Saddam's removal from power.... [They] had little trouble persuading the Clinton administration to adopt the general goal of ousting Saddam. But they were unable to sell a war to achieve that objective. They were no more able to generate enthusiasm for invading Iraq in the early months of the Bush administration. They needed help to achieve their aim. That help arrived with 9/11.[11]

But even 9/11, by itself, was not a sufficient basis for getting the American people's support for an attack on Iraq. Rumsfeld and Wolfowitz began immediately to turn 9/11 into a cause for such a war. On the afternoon of 9/11 itself, Rumsfeld said in a note to General Richard Myers—the acting head of the Joint Chiefs of Staff—that he wanted "best info fast. Judge whether good enough hit S.H. [Saddam Hussein] at same time. Not only UBL [Usama bin Laden]." In the following days, both Rumsfeld and Wolfowitz argued that Saddam's Iraq should be "a principal target of the first round in the war on terrorism."[12]

Despite the desire of Rumsfeld and Wolfowitz for this attack to be launched immediately, the attack had to be delayed. "[A]lthough the 9/11 atrocities psychologically prepared the American people for the war

---

America's War on Terror (Free Press, 2004), 264.

11   Adelman quoted in Elizabeth Drew, "The Neocons in Power," *New York Review of Books,* 50/10 (June 12, 2003); Bob Woodward, *Bush at War* (Simon & Schuster, 2002), 83; John Mearsheimer and Stephen Walt, "The Israel Lobby," *London Review of Books,* March 23, 2006.

12   Rumsfeld note reported by CBS News, September 4, 2002; Woodward, *Bush at War,* 48–49.

on Iraq," explained Stephen Sniegoski, "those horrific events were not sufficient by themselves to thrust America immediately into an attack on Iraq." Rather, a "lengthy propaganda offensive" would also be needed.[13]

The Administration's Propaganda Offensive

This propaganda offensive involved convincing a majority of the American people that Saddam Hussein was a threat to them—that Saddam Hussein was both able and willing to attack America.

Although this propaganda was necessary in order to get Americans to support an attack on Iraq, its success depended on 9/11. As Halper and Clarke affirmed, "it was 9/11 that provided the political context in which the thinking of neo-conservatives could be turned into operational policy."[14] Spelling out the point more fully, Sniegoski wrote:

> The 9/11 attacks made the American people angry and fearful. Ordinary Americans wanted to strike back at the terrorist enemy, even though they weren't exactly sure who that enemy was.... Moreover, they were fearful of more attacks and were susceptible to the administration's propaganda that the United States had to strike Iraq before Iraq somehow struck the United States.... It wasn't that difficult to channel American fear and anger into war against Iraq.[15]

The essence of this propaganda offensive was stated in the minutes of a briefing on July 23, 2002, provided to British Prime Minister Tony Blair by Richard Dearlove, the head of MI6 (the UK parallel to the CIA). Dearlove was reporting on meetings he had recently had with members of the Bush administration, especially CIA head George Tenet.

Dearlove's memo confirms the statements by O'Neill and Clarke quoted earlier that the Bush-Cheney administration began with a discussion of the need to remove Saddam. But these statements, which were

---

13   Sniegoski, "Neoconservatives, Israel, and 9/11," 101.
14   Stefan Halper and Jonathan Clarke, *America Alone: The Neo-Conservatives and the Global Order* (Cambridge University Press, 2004), 230.
15   Sniegoski, "Neoconservatives, Israel, and 9/11," 108–9.

published in books that appeared in 2004, said nothing about the pretext for removing him.

By contrast, Dearlove's memo, besides saying that the administration planned to use military force to remove Saddam, said that the war was to be "justified by the conjunction of terrorism and weapons of mass destruction." Saddam's possession of such weapons was prohibited by the U.N. Security Council in the settlement of Iraq's defeat in the Gulf War of 1991.

The U.S. plan, of course, presupposed that intelligence agencies would determine that Iraq did indeed have weapons of mass destruction (WMD)—a finding, Dearlove explained, that was guaranteed in advance: "The intelligence and facts are being fixed around the policy."[16]

The policy meant the plan to remove Saddam on the basis of terrorism and WMD. *Terrorism* was shorthand for saying that Saddam was capable of committing major acts of terrorism because he was affiliated with al-Qaeda. *WMD* (weapons of mass destruction) meant nuclear, biological, and chemical weapons.

Unfortunately, Dearlove's memo was not made public until over three years later, when London's *Sunday Times*, to which the memo had been leaked, published it on May 1, 2005. Had it been published much earlier, it might have prevented the long debate on whether Iraq really had WMD. In addition, once it was published, it should have prevented the other long debate over whether the Bush-Cheney administration was misled by faulty intelligence, or whether it simply lied. The memo shows that the administration had made its decision to invade Iraq before there was any intelligence about Iraq's WMD and connection to al-Qaeda.

Also unfortunately, the mainstream press in the United States devoted very little attention to this memo. For example, no American newspaper gave the story front-page coverage until 17 days later. The *New York Times* and *Washington Post* did finally run stories about it but buried them inside. The *Times* even ignored the most eye-popping fact—that the intelligence was to be "fixed."[17]

In any case, given the fear and anger that was evoked by the 9/11 attacks, it was not difficult, as Sniegoski pointed out, "to channel

---

16   Ray McGovern, "Proof Bush Fixed the Facts," *TomPaine.com,* May 4, 2005.

17   Robert Dreyfuss, "A Memo and Two Catechisms," *TomPaine.com,* May 23, 2005.

American fear and anger into war against Iraq." Some of this channeling was carried out by neoconservatives outside the government, who "linked their preexisting agenda (an attack on Iraq) to a separate event (9/11)." Through their propaganda—perhaps most widely spread in Lawrence Kaplan and William Kristol's *The War over Iraq: Saddam's Tyranny and America's Mission*—"Al-Qaeda and Saddam Hussein were morphed into the same enemy," said Halper and Clarke, and "the war on terror and war in Iraq were joined at the hip."[18]

But most of this channeling was carried out by people inside the Bush-Cheney administration, especially Bush and Cheney themselves, along with Donald Rumsfeld. The remainder of this chapter looks at their propaganda for the two major claims: (1) Saddam's Iraq had WMD of all three types: biological, chemical, and nuclear; (2) Saddam's Iraq was affiliated with al-Qaeda and was also involved in the 9/11 attacks.

The propaganda about these two points was incessant. In 2008, the Center for Public Integrity published a report on false statements about Saddam Hussein's Iraq made by leading members of the Bush administration during the two years following 9/11. The report enumerated 935 such statements.[19] Only a few examples will be quoted here.

Claims about Weapons of Mass Destruction (WMD)

With regard to weapons of mass destruction, there were charges of WMD in general, and also of biological, chemical, and nuclear WMD in particular.

WMD in General

"[T]here is no doubt," Cheney said in August 2002, "that Saddam Hussein now has weapons of mass destruction. There is no doubt he is amassing them to use against our friends, against our allies, and against us." The following month, Rumsfeld said: "There's no debate in the

---

18   Halper and Clarke, *America Alone*, 203, 209, 210 (see also their seventh chapter, "The False Pretenses").

19   Charles Lewis and Mark Reading-Smith, "The War Card: False Pretenses," Center for Public Integrity, January 23, 2008; updated June 30, 2014.

world as to whether they [the Iraqis] have those weapons. We all know that. A trained ape knows that."[20]

Biological WMD

The claim that Iraq had biological WMD originated from a low-level engineer who defected to Germany. Code-named "Curveball" by German intelligence, he said that Saddam had bioweapons in mobile weapons labs. There were many reasons why Curveball's claims should have been ignored: British and German intelligence agents considered him "crazy" and "probably a fabricator"; Tyler Drumheller, CIA's European operations chief, was so skeptical that he told George Tenet that all references to Curveball's claims should be deleted.

In spite of these red flags, U.S. agents never talked with Curveball or performed any background checks, and yet his claims were repeated by leading administration figures. In a presentation to the U.N. Security Council, shortly before the start of the war, Colin Powell said: "We have first-hand descriptions of biological weapons factories on wheels and on rails." Tyler Drumheller said, "My mouth hung open when I saw Colin Powell use information from Curveball." In any case, the following day Bush said: "Firsthand witnesses have informed us that Iraq has at least seven mobile factories for the production of biological agents, equipment mounted on trucks and rails to evade discovery."[21]

As Drumheller feared, the claim made by Powell turned out to be completely false. In fact, eight years after Powell's speech, Curveball—whose actual name was Rafid Ahmed Alwan al-Janabi—admitted that he had fabricated the story with the hope that it might help topple Saddam's regime.[22]

---

20 The White House, "Vice President Speaks at VFW 103rd National Convention," August 26, 2002; "Rumsfeld Comes Out Jabbing, Has No Regrets for Abu Ghraib, WMDs," *Bloomberg News,* February 4, 2011.

21 Colin Powell, "Remarks to the U.N. Security Council," February 5, 2003; Drumheller quoted in "War Card: Key false statements," *Center for Public Integrity,* January 23, 2008; updated June 26, 2015; "Bush: 'All the World Can Rise to This Moment,'" *CNN,* February 6, 2003.

22 Martin Chulov and Helen Pidd, "Defector Admits to WMD Lies that Triggered Iraq War," *The Guardian,* February 15, 2011.

How could such an error have been made? The fact is that, with the possible exception of Powell, the leading figures in the Bush administration, especially Cheney and Rumsfeld, were not concerned with having a report that would prove to be accurate. They were concerned only with persuading the American people to support an invasion of Iraq. This fact was shown not only by their use of Curveball's testimony, in spite of very good reasons not to trust it, but also by a report from the Joint Chiefs of Staff (JCS) entitled "Iraq: Status of WMD Programs." Part of the reason why Powell's speech was so terrible is that the JCS report was hidden from most people in the administration, including Powell.[23]

The JCS Report about WMD

This report had been prepared in response to Rumsfeld's question in August 2002 to the chairman of the Joint Chiefs of Staff's intelligence directorate, requesting "what we don't know" about the Iraqi WMD program. On September 5, this report was given to Rumsfeld, as well as to Richard Myers, the chairman of the Joint Chiefs of Staff.

In response, Rumsfeld sent a note to Myers, saying: "Please take a look at this material as to what we don't know about WMD. It is big." In calling the report "big," Rumsfeld evidently meant that it contradicted the case that was being made to attack Iraq. Accordingly, Rumsfeld and Myers did not publicize this report. Although Rumsfeld almost certainly would have sent it to Cheney, he did not send it to Powell or other people in the administration.[24]

As a general statement, the report said: "Our assessments rely heavily on analytic assumptions and judgment rather than hard evidence." Had Powell seen the report before addressing the UN Security Council, he probably would not have told it:

My colleagues, every statement I make today is backed up by sources, solid sources. These are not assertions. What

---

23   John Walcott, "What Donald Rumsfeld Knew We Didn't Know About Iraq," *Politico*, January 24, 2016.

24   Walcott.

we're giving you are facts and conclusions based on solid intelligence.[25]

Whereas Powell spoke confidently in his speech about evidence that Iraq was hiding biological weapons in mobile labs, the JCS report said: "We cannot confirm the identity of any Iraqi facilities that produce, test, fill, or store biological weapons."[26]

Chemical WMD

In June 2002, Rumsfeld said: "They have weaponized chemical weapons, we know that." In February 2003, Bush said: "Sources that tell us that Saddam Hussein recently authorized Iraqi field commanders to use chemical weapons—the very weapons the dictator tells us he does not have."[27] And in his U.N. Security Council statement, Powell said: "Our conservative estimate is that Iraq today has a stockpile of between 100 and 500 tons of chemical weapons agent."[28]

However, the ignored JCS report said: "We do not know if all the processes required to produce a weapon are in place," and "we cannot confirm the identity of any Iraqi sites that produce final chemical agent."

Both Biological and Chemical WMD

There were also statements claiming that Iraq had both biological and chemical WMD. For example, on September 26, 2002, Bush said: "The Iraqi regime possesses biological and chemical weapons." Two days later, he made an even more frightening claim:

The Iraqi regime possesses biological and chemical weapons, is rebuilding the facilities to make more, and, according to

---

25 Powell, "Remarks to the U.N. Security Council."
26 Walcott's article discussed this and all the other statements quoted from "Iraq: Status of Iraq WMD."
27 Rumsfeld, press conference, Kuwait City, June 11, 2002; "Bush to U.N.: We Will Not Wait," *CNN,* February 7, 2003.
28 Powell, "Remarks to the U.N. Security Council."

the British government, could launch a biological or chemical attack in as little as 45 minutes after the order is given.[29]

In crediting the British government with this information, Bush was referring to Tony Blair's foreword to the "September Dossier," which was the British government's assessment of Iraq's WMD. This foreword said that Saddam's "military planning allows for some of the WMD to be ready within 45 minutes of an order to use them."[30]

This statement resulted in panic-producing headlines, such as that of *The Sun*, Britain's biggest selling newspaper: "Brits 45 Minutes from Doom." It also led to a heated controversy between the British government and the BBC, after its defense correspondent, Andrew Gilligan, reported that a senior British official told the BBC that the September Dossier had been "sexed up."[31]

This official was later learned to be Dr. David Kelly, an authority on biological warfare who served as a weapons inspector in Iraq. In February 2003, Kelly said that if the U.S.-UK attack went ahead, he would "probably be found dead in the woods." After it became known that he had been the official to whom Gilligan referred, Kelly was brought before a parliamentary committee on July 15, 2003, but Geoff Hoon, the Defense Secretary, sought to prevent him from speaking about WMD. Two days later, Kelly was indeed found dead in the woods, with suicide-by-wrist-cutting being the official explanation.[32]

---

29 The White House, "Radio Address by the President to the Nation," September 28, 2002.
30 "Full Text of Tony Blair's Foreword to the Dossier on Iraq," *The Guardian*, September 24, 2003.
31 Steve Rendall, "'Sexed Up' After All," *FAIR,* April 1, 2008.
32 Even MasAskill et al., "Kelly's Chilling Words: 'I'll Be Found Dead in the Woods,'" *The Guardian*, August 23, 2003; "How Was Dr. Kelly Silenced," *The Insider,* August 21, 2003; Dr. David Halpin and James Corbett, "Ten Years Ago: The Death of Dr. David Kelly: Murder on the Orders of Her Majestry's Government?" *Global Research*, October 13, 2011. One reason many people doubt the official explanation is that the two paramedics, who were among the first to see the body, said that they did not believe that it was suicide, because there was not nearly enough blood (Antony Barnett, "Kelly Death Paramedics Query Verdict," *The Guardian,* December 11, 2004).

Nuclear WMD

Although the false reports about biological and chemical weapons played a role in creating fear of Saddam's Iraq, the greatest fear was created by claims about nuclear weapons. And these claims were abundant. For example:

- In March 2002, for example, Cheney called Saddam "a man of great evil" who is "actively pursuing nuclear weapons."[33]

- In June of that year, Rumsfeld said that Saddam Hussein, besides having chemical weapons, had "an active program to develop nuclear weapons," adding that Saddam's denial of this fact shows him to be a "world-class liar."[34]

- In September, Bush said to the UN General Assembly: "The first time we may be completely certain he has a nuclear weapon is when, God forbids, he uses one."[35]

- Having "experienced the horror of September the 11th," said Bush in October 2002, "America must not ignore the threat gathering against us. Facing clear evidence of peril, we cannot wait for the final proof—the smoking gun—that could come in the form of a mushroom cloud."[36]

- In March 2003, four days before the attack on Iraq, Cheney said: "We know he [Saddam Hussein] has been absolutely devoted to trying to acquire nuclear weapons. And we believe he has, in fact, reconstituted nuclear weapons." (Cheney surely meant, "reconstituted his nuclear weapons program.")[37]

Such claims to knowledge were not at all supported by the Joint Chiefs of Staff report about Iraqi WMD, which said:

---

33   "Vice President Dick Cheney Speaks with Wolf Blitzer," *CNN,* March 24, 2002.

34   Thom Shanker, "Rumsfeld Says Iraq Has Chemical Arms Ready," *The New York Times*, June 11, 2002.

35   Powell, "Remarks to the U.N. General Assembly."

36   The White House, "Remarks by the President on Iraq," October 7, 2002.

37   *Meet the Press,* "Transcript for September 14, 2003: Guest: Dick Cheney, Vice President."

The evidentiary base [for our assessments] is particularly sparse for Iraqi nuclear programs. . . . Our knowledge of the Iraqi (nuclear) weapons program is based largely—perhaps 90%—on analysis of imprecise intelligence.[38]

However, because Rumsfeld suppressed this report, the Bush-Cheney administration was able to fabricate reports saying that Iraq was seeking to develop nuclear weapons. These reports consisted of claims about Iraq's acquisition of (a) aluminum tubes and (b) yellowcake (uranium ore) from Niger.

Aluminum Tubes: On September 8, 2002, Michael R. Gordon and Judith Miller published a front-page story in the *New York Times* entitled "U.S. Says Hussein Intensifies Quest for A-Bomb Parts." It began:

More than a decade after Saddam Hussein agreed to give up weapons of mass destruction, Iraq has stepped up its quest for nuclear weapons and has embarked on a worldwide hunt for materials to make an atomic bomb, Bush administration officials said today. In the last 14 months, Iraq has sought to buy thousands of specially designed aluminum tubes, which American officials believe were intended as components of centrifuges to enrich uranium.[39]

"The first sign of a 'smoking gun,'" concluded Gordon and Miller, "may be a mushroom cloud," using the trope George Bush would echo on October 7.

The "administration officials" to whom the authors refer were Cheney's people, especially Cheney's chief of staff, Scooter Libby. Planning to use this story to begin their media blitz on the need to re-move Saddam, several members of the administration were set to be interviewed on Sunday morning talk shows the day the Gordon-Miller

38   As reported in Politico by John Walcott, "What Donald Rumsfeld Knew We Didn't Know About Iraq." https://www.politico.com/magazine/story/2016/01/iraq-war-wmds-donald-rumsfeld-new-report-213530/

39   Michael R. Gordon and Judith Miller, "U.S. Says Hussein Intensifies Quest for A-Bomb Parts," *The New York Times*, September 8, 2002.

story appeared. As James Bamford observed: "It was a perfect scheme—leak the secrets the night before so you can talk about them the next morning."[40] This scheme allowed these administrative officials to make their claims by attributing them to the authoritative *New York Times:* "[It's] now public," said Cheney on *Meet the Press*, that Saddam "has been seeking to acquire ... through this particular channel the kinds of tubes that are necessary to build a centrifuge."

On *Fox News,* Powell spoke of the "specialized aluminum tubing" that "we saw in reporting just this morning." Saying that the tubes "are only really suited for nuclear weapons programs," Condoleezza Rice told Wolf Blitzer's audience: "We don't want the smoking gun to be a mushroom cloud."

However, Rice's claim was untrue. State Department experts concluded that the tubes were *not* intended for use in Iraq's nuclear weapons program. Both the Department of Energy and Mohamed ElBaradei—the head of the International Atomic Energy Agency—said that the aluminum tubes were likely for artillery rockets, not centrifuges. Jonathan Landay of Knight Ridder Newspapers reported:

> Several senior administration officials and intelligence officers, all of whom spoke only on the condition of anonymity, charged that the decision to publicize one analysis of the aluminum tubes and ignore the contrary one is typical of the way the administration has been handling intelligence about Iraq.

In addition, Landay reported:

> [David] Albright, the director of the Institute for Science and International Security, a non-partisan think tank, said he has been told that scientists at the Lawrence Livermore National Laboratory in California and other U.S. nuclear weapons facilities disagreed with that assessment but have been ordered not to say anything.[41]

---

40   James Bamford, *A Pretext for War: 9/11, Iraq, and the Abuse of America's Intelligence Agencies* (Anchor Books, 2005), 324.

41   Jonathan S. Landay, "CIA Report Reveals Analysts' Split over extent of Iraqi Nuclear Threat," McClatchy, October 4, 2002.

With this dissent suppressed, Bush was able to say in his 2003 State of the Union address: "Our intelligence sources tell us that he [Saddam] has attempted to purchase high-strength aluminum tubes suitable for nuclear weapons production."[42]

Yellowcake from Niger: The Bush administration also claimed that Iraq had obtained hundreds of tons of yellowcake, an unprocessed uranium-rich ore. The claim was rooted in documents purportedly showing that Niger in 2000 had sold 500 tons of yellowcake. Upon learning of this story, Cheney asked the CIA to check out the story. The task was given to former ambassador Joseph Wilson, who had served in that region of Africa.

When Wilson arrived in Niger, he learned that the Niger story had been discredited by a four-star general, the ambassador to Niger, the CIA, the State Department, and the French, who said: "We told the Americans, 'Bullshit. It doesn't make any sense.'" Wilson also learned from experts that such a sale would have been improbable, likely impossible.[43]

When he returned to Washington, Wilson filed a report, which was circulated in the normal way, so he assumed that the president had seen it. He was shocked, therefore, to hear Bush utter these 16 words in his State of the Union address: "The British government has learned that Saddam Hussein recently sought significant quantities of uranium from Africa."[44]

Wilson spent some time trying to correct the story, but finally gave up, saying to Seymour Hersh: "I gave them months to correct the record, ...but they kept on lying." So he wrote a *New York Times* op-ed, "What I Didn't Find in Africa." As a result, there was much discussion about how those now notorious "16 words" got into Bush's talk. "Had there been even a peep that the agency did not want that sentence," Rice said on *Face the* Nation, "it would have been gone." But there had been far more than a peep: Rice's National Security Council assistant Stephen Hadley had received two CIA memos calling the intelligence dubious, one of which had gone directly to Rice.

---

42   The White House, "The 2003 State of the Union Address," January 28, 2003.
43   Craig Unger, "The War They Wanted, the Lies They Needed," *Vanity Fair*, October 17, 2006.
44   Bryan Burrough et al., "The Path to War," *Vanity Fair*, December 19, 2008.

A little later, but prior to the attack on Iraq, the International Atomic Energy Agency showed that the documents about the sale of many tons of yellowcake were obvious forgeries. For example, they referred to an organization that had gone out of existence in 1989, and they were signed by an official who had been out of office for a decade. The documents were so error-filled, said an IAEA official, that "they could be spotted by someone using Google on the Internet."[45]

Nevertheless, although Wilson was only one of many people who discredited the yellowcake story, Cheney singled him out to be discredited by having Libby and Karl Rove inform journalists that Wilson was married to an undercover CIA agent, Valerie Plame Wilson. The idea was evidently to discredit Joseph Wilson by falsely suggesting that his trip to Niger was a junket arranged by his wife. Because revealing the identity of an undercover agent is a federal crime, a special investigation resulted. The White House for many months categorically denied that Libby and Rove were responsible for the leak, but that was later shown to be untrue.[46] Libby was convicted of lying to the grand jury. Joe and Valerie Wilson concluded that he had lied to protect Cheney.[47]

In Sum

Every claim made by the Bush-Cheney administration about WMD proved to be false.

Claims about al-Qaeda and 9/11

In addition to the Bush-Cheney administration's claims about illegal WMD, its propaganda also argued that Saddam was linked to al-Qaeda terrorists. Indeed, there was a strong desire to link Saddam with the 9/11 attack, as shown by Rumsfeld note to General Myers quoted earlier, on

---

45 Bamford, *A Pretext for* War; Seymour Hersh, "Who Lied to Whom?" *New Yorker*, March 31, 2003.

46 Jim VandeHei and Walter Pincus, "Role of Rove, Libby in CIA Leak Case Clearer," *Washington Post*, October 2, 2005.

47 Nick Wing, "Joe Wilson, Husband of Valerie Plame: Dick Cheney Is a 'Traitor'(VIDEO)," *Huffington Post,* May 25, 2011.

the afternoon of 9/11, wanting to know whether the information was "good enough" to go after both Saddam Hussein and Osama bin Laden.[48]

Although Bush officials were not able to point to evidence that Saddam was involved in the attacks, they did claim that he and al-Qaeda were connected. A Congressional report of March 2004 found that the Bush Administration had made 237 misleading statements about the threat posed by Iraq, and that 61 of these "misrepresented Iraq's ties to al-Qaeda."[49] Here are three examples:

- Bush said: "We have learned that Iraq has trained al-Qaeda members in bomb-making and poisons and deadly gases."

- Bush also said that we "know that Iraq is harboring a terrorist network headed by a senior al-Qaeda terrorist planner."

- Cheney said: "If we're successful in Iraq. . . , we will have struck a major blow right at the heart of the base, if you will, the geographic base of the terrorists who have had us under assault now for many years, but most especially on 9/11."[50]

The claims about Iraq's WMD and Iraq's relation to al-Qaeda were equally important. The idea that Saddam had WMD would greatly increase the fear generated by his connections with al-Qaeda, the organization purportedly able to outwit the world's most sophisticated defense system, attack the Pentagon, and destroy the World Trade Center.

As Bush put it, "Imagine those 19 hijackers with other weapons and other plans—this time armed by Saddam Hussein."[51] The equal importance of WMD and al-Qaeda was also expressed by Rumsfeld when he said:

Iraq's weapons of mass terror and the terror networks to which the Iraqi regime are linked are not two separate themes—not two separate threats. They are part of the same threat.[52]

48   Reported by CBS News, September 4, 2002.
49   Congressional Record: March 16, 2004 (House), H1103–H1109. https://irp.fas.org/congress/2004_cr/h031604.html
50   "Bush: Don't Wait for Mushroom Cloud," *CNN,* October 8, 2002; *Meet the Press,* September 14, 2003; *Meet the Press,* March 14, 2003.
51   State of the Union Address, January 28, 2003.
52   Secretary of Defense Donald Rumsfeld, Speech to Council on Foreign Relations,

Connecting Iraq and al-Qaeda took some effort. Ten days after 9/11 Bush and Cheney were given a CIA briefing, at which they were told:

> [T]he U.S. intelligence community had no evidence linking the Iraqi regime of Saddam Hussein to the attacks and that there was scant credible evidence that Iraq had any significant collaborative ties with Al Qaeda.[53]

To deal with this problem, the Bush-Cheney administration tried to create the needed evidence. There were three major attempts:

Mohamed Atta in Prague

One claim of a link between Iraq and al-Qaeda involved Mohamed Atta. Two months after 9/11, Cheney was asked on *Meet the Press* whether Iraq was involved in 9/11. In response, Cheney referred to a story floating around about Atta meeting an Iraqi in Prague and said that has "been pretty well confirmed—[Mohamed Atta] did go to Prague and he did meet with a senior official of the Iraqi intelligence service in Czechoslovakia last April, several months before the attack."[54]

Cheney's assertion had actually been contradicted just the day before his interview, since the White House Situation Room had received this information from the CIA: "11 September 2001 Hijacker Mohammed Atta Did Not Travel to the Czech Republic on May 31, 2000."[55] But Cheney refused to give up the story.

This refusal resulted in a controversy while Secretary of State Powell was preparing his speech for the Security Council. Cheney's staff pressed Powell repeatedly to include the story about Atta in Prague. Powell would take it out of his speech, but Libby and others kept putting it back in. Powell finally "threw the paper down on the table and said, 'I'm not saying that.'"[56]

January 23, 2003.

53 Murray Waas, "Bush Told No Iraq-9/11 Connection 10 Days after Attack," *National Journal*, November 22, 2005.

54 The White House, "The Vice President Appears on NBC's Meet the Press," December 9, 2001.

55 Quoted in John Glaser, "9/11 and Iraq: The War's Greatest Lie," *Antiwar.com Blog*, March 18, 2013.

56 Bamford, *A Pretext for War*, 370.

Ibn al-Sheikh al-Libi

In 2001, a low-level Al-Qaeda operative named Ibn al-Sheikh al-Libi was captured in Pakistan and sent to the U.S. detention facility in Kandahar. A combination of torture and threats elicited from al-Libi the information that Iraq had provided training in chemical and biological weapons. Noting that his "information" contained no specific details, the DIA called it "likely" that "this individual is intentionally misleading the debriefers."

For the White House's purposes, however, the information was adequate. In a major speech just before Congress was to vote on the Iraq War resolution, Bush declared: "We've learned that Iraq has trained al-Qaeda members in bomb making and poisons and deadly gases." And although Colin Powell rejected the Atta story, he accepted this one. Speaking of a "sinister nexus between Iraq and the al-Qaeda terrorist network," he related the "story of a senior terrorist operative telling how Iraq provided training in [chemical and biological] weapons to al-Qaeda."[57]

Thanks to al-Libi's claims, he became, said Ray McGovern, "the poster boy for the success of the Cheney/Bush torture regime—that is, until he publicly recanted and explained that he only told his interrogators what he thought would stop the torture." To the Bush administration, however, this recantation was unimportant, because it did not come until after the invasion of Iraq was well underway.[58]

Cheney, of course, had long argued that torture, such as waterboarding, works. Most experts, however, accept the view of General John Kimmons, former head of Army intelligence, who said: "No good intelligence is going to come from abusive practices." However, added McGovern, "if it's bad intelligence you're after, torture works like a charm." That is, torture "induces those being tortured to fabricate answers that they think the torturers want to hear."[59]

Indeed, there is considerable evidence that the primary reason for torture after 9/11 was to produce false confessions. For example, Lawrence Wilkerson, Powell's chief of staff, said that the Bush-Cheney's

---

57   Powell, "Remarks to the U.N. General Assembly."
58   Ray McGovern, "What's the Next Step to Stop Torture?" *Consortium News*, December 11, 2014.
59   McGovern, "What's the Next Step to Stop Torture?"

administration's "principal priority for intelligence was not aimed at pre-empting another terrorist attack on the U.S. but discovering a smoking gun linking Iraq and al-Qaeda."[60]

Major Paul Burney, a U.S. Army psychiatrist sent to Guantanamo in 2002, indicated that torture was used at that facility in an effort to get the desired statements:

> A large part of the time we were focused on trying to establish a link between al-Qaeda and Iraq and we were not successful. The more frustrated people got in not being able to establish that link there was more and more pressure to resort to measures that might produce more immediate results.[61]

Tahir Jalil Habbush

Early in 2003, prior to the start of the war, Tahir Jalil Habbush, the head of Iraqi intelligence, had secret weekly meetings in Jordan with an official of British intelligence. Habbush told this official that Iraq had no WMD programs or stockpiles. Rob Richer, the head of the CIA's Near East division, said that the White House wanted to go to war. So the White House simply ignored the report by Habbush, gave him $5 million to keep quiet, and had him resettled in Jordan. And then, wrote Pulitzer Prize-winning journalist Ron Suskind in *The Way of the World*:

> The White House had concocted a fake letter from Habbush to Saddam, backdated to July 1, 2001. It said that 9/11 ringleader Mohammed Atta had actually trained for his mission in Iraq — thus showing, finally, that there was an operation link between Saddam and al-Qaeda. . . . A handwritten letter, with Habbush's name on it, would be fashioned by CIA and then hand-carried by a CIA agent to Baghdad for dissemination.[62]

---

60 Jonathan S. Landay, "Report: Abusive tactics used to seek Iraq-al Qaida link," McClatchy, April 21, 2009.

61 McGovern, "What's the Next Step to Stop Torture?"

62 Ron Suskind, *The Way of the World: A Story of Truth and Hope in an Age of Extremism* (Harper 2008), 371.

This fake letter appeared too late to help promote the drive to go to war but, being published on the day in December 2003 that Saddam was captured, it helped justify the war. On NBC, for example, journalist Con Coughlin called the letter "concrete proof that al-Qaeda was working with Saddam."[63]

Corruption of the CIA

Any discussion about how Cheney and Rumsfeld were able to sell their war against Iraq would be incomplete without a treatment of how Cheney, with the acquiescence of CIA director George Tenet,[64] corrupted the CIA's assessments. This corruption was a big factor in why Powell gave such an inaccurate presentation at the UN.

Powell had wanted to make a trustworthy presentation, one that would not ruin his reputation for truthfulness. After he had been persuaded to address the UN Security Council, he refused to base it on a dossier that had been prepared by Libby and other members of Cheney's team.[65] Assuming that the CIA analysis was carried out in a professional way, free from distortion by political goals (as it had been prior to 9/11),[66] he went to the CIA to get reliable information. But he ended up giving the United Nations a lecture that was, in James Bamford's words, "[m]ade up almost entirely of false charges."[67] The basic problem was that Powell did not realize how thoroughly Cheney had corrupted CIA analyses with regard to Iraq.

Given his plan to justify war on the basis of WMD and terrorism, Cheney had started traveling to CIA headquarters to talk to analysts. Some of them, reported the *Washington Post*, "felt they were being pressured to make their assessments fit with the Bush administration's

63 Bob Considine, "Author Claims Bush Knew Iraq Had No WMD," *Today*, August 5, 2008.
64 In a critique of Tenet's *At the Center of the Storm*, Sidney Blumenthal wrote that the book depicts Tenet "as feckless in defending [the men and women of the agency] from the intimidation of Cheney and the neoconservatives" (Blumenthal, "George Tenet, Spook for All Seasons," *Salon*, May 3, 2007).
65 Bryan Burrough et al., "The Path to War," *Vanity Fair*, December 19, 2008.
66 Melvin A. Goodman, "Dividing the CIA in Two," *Consortium News*, Dec. 23, 2014.
67 Bamford, *A Pretext for War*, 379.

policy objectives."[68] Some of the descriptions of the pressure were even stronger. One CIA official said:

> [T]here was a great deal of pressure to find a reason to go to war with Iraq. And the pressure was not just subtle; it was blatant. At one point in January 2003, the person's boss called a meeting and gave them their marching orders. And he said, "You know what—if Bush wants to go to war, it's your job to give him a reason to do so."[69]

In a report entitled "The Constitution in Crisis," Congressman John Conyers wrote:

> A former CIA analyst described the intense pressure brought to bear on the CIA by the Bush Administration in these terms: "The analysts at the C.I.A. were beaten down defending their assessments. And they blame George Tenet"—the CIA director—"for not protecting them ... from Dick Cheney, who with his sidekick I. Lewis Libby visited CIA headquarters about a dozen times to personally ensure that CIA analysts knew precisely what their instructions were—what conclusions their analysis should yield."[70]

The analysts were right to blame Tenet. Bamford wrote:

> Normally the CIA Director would protect his people from that kind of pressure. But ... Tenet decided against intervening directly whenever employees told him that they felt pressure while writing analytical papers on Iraq.... Ultimately Tenet lost sight of his role. Instead of the country's apolitical eyes

---

68   Walter Pincus and Dana Priest, "Some Iraq Analysts Felt Pressure from Cheney Visits," *Washington Post,* June 5, 2003.

69   Bamford, *A Pretext for War,* 333–34.

70   Quoted in David Swanson, "Pressuring the CIA to Lie, Calling Result an Accident," *Let's Try Democracy,* December 31, 2005.

and ears around the world, ...he simply became the President's cheerleader.[71]

In fact, Cheney and Bush likely retained Tenet from the Clinton administration because of what Sidney Blumenthal called "his chameleon-like quality of adapting to any environment."[72] It was this corrupted CIA to which Powell went to get reliable intelligence to use in his UN speech.

The Success of Bush-Cheney Propaganda

The Bush-Cheney administration's propaganda campaign was enormously successful. Shortly before the war on Iraq was launched, the idea that Iraq had weapons of mass destruction was accepted by 70 percent of the American people. That same percentage believed that Iraq was connected to al-Qaeda, and even that Saddam Hussein had played a direct role in the 9/11 attacks. Indeed, a 2006 poll showed that almost 90% of the U.S. troops in Iraq believed that the war was in "retaliation for Saddam's role in 9/11."[73]

As a result, as Stefan Halper and Jonathan Clarke point out, the Bush-Cheney administration was "able to build the environment surrounding the terrorist attacks of September 2001 into a wide moral platform from which to launch a preemptive strike."[74]

Incidentally, the success of this propaganda campaign could have been predicted, based on the observation of Hermann Göring, one of the top Nazi officials: "[I]t is the *leaders* of the country who determine the policy and it is always a simple matter to drag the people along," said Göring. "All you have to do is tell them they are being attacked."[75]

Accordingly, just as the propaganda offensive against Osama bin Laden, al-Qaeda, and the Taliban created almost unanimous acceptance of the war in Afghanistan, the propaganda offensive directed at Saddam

---

71   Bamford, *A Pretext for War*, 384–85.
72   Sidney Blumenthal, "George Tenet, Spook for All Seasons," *Salon*, May 3, 2007.
73   "U.S. Troops In Iraq: 72% Say End War in 2006," *Zogby,* February 28, 2006.
74   Halper and Clark, *America Alone*, 218.
75   Quoted in Gustave Gilbert, *Nuremberg Diary* (Farrar, Straus, & Co, 1947), 278. Gilbert was reporting a conversation he had with Hermann Göring on the evening of April 18, 1946, while the Nuremberg trials were going on.

Hussein was able to channel this fear, anxiety, and desire for revenge into a widespread feeling that a war to remove Saddam was justified.

However, this propaganda was based almost entirely on lies. On the last page of his *A Pretext for War*, James Bamford wrote:

> [T]he Bush administration's massive disinformation campaign, abetted by a lazy and timid press, succeeded spectacularly. In the end, it was the power of lies, not logic, that was the deciding factor.[76]

Although Republicans and the corporate media still commonly claim that the Bush administration was misled by faulty intelligence,[77] Paul Krugman, in an op-ed entitled "Errors and Lies," said that the invasion of Iraq "was worse than a mistake, it was a crime."[78]

Disastrous Consequences

Like the Afghanistan War, the Iraq War was disastrous for both the United State and the country it attacked.

Consequences for the USA

Although the negative consequences of the Iraq war were most serious for Iraq, this war was also very harmful to the United States.

Death and Injury: The war caused around 4,500 American deaths and hundreds of thousands of serious injuries, including over 320,000 brain injuries. In addition, as many as 35 percent of the returning veterans suffer from PTSD.[79]

76　Bamford, *A Pretext for War,* 377. (This is on the final page of the first [2004] edition; the 2005 edition has a new afterword.)

77　Ray McGovern, "The Phony 'Bad Intel' Defense on Iraq," *Consortium News,* May 15, 2015.

78　Paul Krugman, "Errors and Lies," *The New York Times*, May 18, 2015.

79　Margaret Griffis, "Military Casualties in Iraq: The Human Cost of Occupation," *AntiWar,* May 16, 2015; Dan Froomkin, "How Many U.S. Soldiers Were Wounded in Iraq? Guess Again," *Huffington Post,* February 29, 2012; "Iraq Troops' PTSD Rate as High as 35 Percent, Analysis Finds," *Science Daily,* September 15, 2009.

Economic Cost: Although the Bush administration predicted the war would cost a total of $50–60 billion, the war had cost $4 trillion by 2014 and may, counting interest to the national debt, come to more than $6 trillion over the following decades.[80]

Opportunity Costs: The devotion of these billions to the war meant that this money could not be used for many important matters, such as curing cancer, rebuilding infrastructure, and especially tackling climate change.

Loss of Respect and Status: Juan Cole has written:

> In the aftermath of the invasion and occupation of Iraq, the U.S. was widely seen as an international bully. . . . The U.S. invasion and occupation of Iraq harmed the U.S. in bringing into question its basic competency as a world leader. Almost everything the U.S. did in Iraq was a disaster. . . . It looked dishonest, bumbling. It went into the war having no plans, and the plans the Bush administration made on the fly were mostly poorly thought-out and doomed to fail.[81]

Fueling Islamophobia: Adding to the effect of 9/11, the Iraq war did much to fuel Islamophobia.

Consequences for Iraq

Whereas the Iraq War had negative consequences for the United States, it was *disastrous* for Iraq in many ways:

Iraqis Killed: Probably most surprising to Americans in general is the sheer number of Iraqis killed in the war, as the government and the media have not reported anything close to the truth. People were not told that

---

80   David M. Herszenhorn, *The New York Times,* March 19, 2008; "Estimates of War Cost Were Not Close to Ballpark," *The New York Times,* March 19, 2013; Daniel Trotta, "Iraq War Costs U.S. More Than $2 Trillion: Study," *Reuters*, March 14, 2013; Hayes Brown, "U.S. Wasted Billions Rebuilding Iraq," *Think Progress,* March 6, 2013.

81   Juan Cole, "What we Lost: Top Ten Ways the Iraq War Harmed the US," *Informed Comment,* March 18, 2013.

during the first month of the war, the U.S. and the UK unleashed over 29,000 bombs and missiles, which killed tens of thousands of civilians.

For the war as a whole, the mainstream media primarily use the Iraq Body Count, which estimates that the war caused 110,000 Iraqi deaths. However, this figure was reached by simply adding up media reports of civilian killings. In 2006, *The Lancet* published a scientific study, which combined violent deaths with deaths resulting from war-caused deprivation as well. This study, accepted by most epidemiologists, estimated that 655,000 Iraq deaths had already occurred by 2006. By 2008, a British study said that the figure had risen to over a million. And in 2015, Gideon Polya, using "UN and U.S. Just War Policy" figures, estimated that 2.3 million Iraqi deaths had been caused by the war.[82]

Murder and Genocide: According to Nicolas J. S. Davies (author of *Blood on Our Hands: The American Invasion and Destruction of Iraq*):

> The U.S. recruited, trained and deployed at least 27 brigades of Iraqi Special Police Commandos, who detained, tortured and murdered tens of thousands of men and boys in Baghdad and elsewhere in 2005 and 2006. At the peak of this campaign, 3,000 bodies per month were brought to the Baghdad morgue and an Iraqi human rights group matched 92% of the corpses to reported abductions by U.S.-backed forces. U.S. Special Forces officers in Special Police Transition Teams worked with each Iraqi unit, and a high-tech command center staffed by U.S. and Iraqi personnel maintained U.S. command and control of these forces throughout their reign of terror.... In 2006 and 2007, U.S. forces worked in tandem with the Special Police Commandos (by then rebranded "National Police") following the exposure of one of their torture centers ... to complete the ethnic cleansing of Baghdad. The U.S. occupation deliberately targeted the Sunni Arab minority in

---

82 Lt. Gen. T. Michael Moseley, USAF, "Operation Iraqi Freedom—By The Numbers," April 30, 2003; Nafeez Mosaddeq Ahmed, "Western Wars Have Killed Four Million Muslims since 1990," *Voltaire Network*, April 11, 2015; Les Roberts et al., "Mortality before and after the 2003 Invasion of Iraq: Cluster Sample Survey," *The Lancet*, October 11, 2006; Luke Baker, "Iraq Conflict Has Killed a Million Iraqis: Survey," Reuters, January 30, 2008.

Iraq, eventually killing about 10% of Sunni Arabs and driving about half of them from their homes. This clearly meets the definition of genocide in international treaties.[83]

Health Crisis: Dr. Margaret Chan of the World Health Organization said in 2015, "The situation [in Iraq] is bad, really bad, and rapidly getting worse." And according to international health consultant César Chelala, who quoted that statement, added:

> 2.9 million people have fled their homes, 6.9 million Iraqis need immediate access to essential health services, and 7.1 million need easier access to water, sanitation and hygiene assistance. Medical facilities, which in the 1980s were among the best in the Middle East, have deteriorated significantly after the 2003 invasion. As a result of the collapsed sanitation infrastructure, the incidence of cholera, dysentery and typhoid fever has increased. Malnutrition among children and other childhood diseases have also increased. . . . [It] is extremely difficult to find Iraqi doctors willing to work in certain areas because they fear for their security. . . . [P]eople's health [is] being seriously affected by the use of white phosphorus and depleted uranium by American and British forces. . . . We are facing nothing less than the almost total destruction of a country by an ill-advised invasion.[84]

Torture: Torture was more widespread than media reports about Abu Ghraib suggested. A leaked 2004 report from the Red Cross's International Committee documented torture of various types: mock executions, waterboarding, suffocation, electric shocks, beatings, burning, cutting with knives, deadly forms of hanging, injurious use of flexi-cuffs, extreme heat and cold, starvation and thirst, sleep deprivation, sensory deprivation, rape and sodomy, sexual humiliation, threats against family members, and withholding medical treatment.

---

83   Nicolas J.S. Davies, "10 Years after the Invasion: America Destroyed Iraq but Our War Crimes Remain Unacknowledged and Unpunished," *Alternet*, March 15, 2013.
84   César Chelala, "Iraq: A Nation Destroyed by American Contempt," Common Dreams, June 16, 2015.

This torture was carried out with virtual impunity: The most severe punishment was a five-month prison sentence, and even though torture was authorized from the highest levels, no criminal charges were brought against any officer above the rank of Major.[85]

Destruction of Cultural Heritage: In 2015, the Global Policy Forum said:

> The United States and its allies ignored the warnings of organizations and scholars concerning the protection of Iraq's cultural heritage, including museums, libraries, archaeological sites and other precious repositories. Arsonists badly burned the National Library and looters pillaged the National Museum. Looters also damaged or destroyed many historic buildings and artifacts.... Coalition forces destroyed or badly damaged many historic urban areas and buildings, while thieves have ruined thousands of incomparable, unprotected archeological sites.[86]

Insurgency and Civil War: Beyond the initial attack on Iraq, many of the consequences listed above resulted from an unbelievably stupid decision made by the Bush-Cheney administration three weeks after that initial attack. As described by Dexter Filkins of the *New York Times:*

> In 2003, the U.S. military, on orders of President Bush, invaded Iraq, and nineteen days later threw out Saddam's government. A few days after that, President Bush ... decreed the dissolution of the Iraqi Army.... Overnight, at least two hundred and fifty thousand Iraqi men—armed, angry, and with military training—were suddenly humiliated and out of work. This was probably the single most catastrophic decision of the American venture in Iraq. In a stroke, the Administration helped enable the creation of the Iraqi insurgency.... Many

---

85 Davies, "10 Years after the Invasion."
86 "Consequences of the War and Occupation of Iraq," Global Policy Forum, 2015.

of those suddenly unemployed Iraqi soldiers took up arms against the United States.[87]

Another disastrous decision by the Bush-Cheney administration was its choice of Nouri al-Maliki as the Prime Minister of Iraq in 2006. He was such a partisan Shiite that he made it difficult for Sunnis to get work, allotted less electricity to them, and transformed Baghdad into a largely Shiite city. His sectarianism led to violent conflict, with elements of a civil war between Sunnis and Shias. This conflict led to the rise of various insurgent groups, including al-Qaeda in Iraq.[88]

Conclusion

That the Iraq War was not based on faulty intelligence, but on lies, has been declared in the titles of many books and articles, such as: "Lie by Lie: A Timeline of How We Got into Iraq," "9/11 and Iraq: The War's Greatest Lie," and "*935 Lies.*"[89]

Once it is agreed that the Bush-Cheney administration lied us into war, one may be led to ask, with Joseph Wilson, noting in 2003 that the administration lied about an issue as fundamental as going to war: "[W]hat else are they lying about?"[90] In any case, the lies about Iraq led to the virtual destruction of that country.

---

87   Dexter Filkins, "Did George W. Bush Create ISIS?" *The New York Times*, May 15, 2015.

88   Juan Cole, "Top 10 Mistakes of Former Iraq PM Nouri al-Maliki (That Ruined His Country)," *Informed Comment,* August 15, 2014; "Elements of 'Civil War' in Iraq," BBC, February 2, 2007.

89   Jonathan Stein and Tim Dickinson, "Lie by Lie: A Timeline of How We Got Into Iraq," *Mother Jones,* September/October 2006; John Glaser, "9/11 and Iraq: The War's Greatest Lie," *Antiwar.com,* March 18, 2013; Charles Lewis, *935 Lies: The Future of Truth and the Decline of America's Moral Integrity* (Public Affairs, 2014).

90   Robert Scheer, "A Diplomat's Undiplomatic Truth: They Lied," *Salon*, July 9, 2003.

13

The U.S./NATO Destruction of Libya

Like Iraq, Libya was on the Bush-Cheney administration's list of countries to be targeted for regime change. But in 2003, the Libyan leader, Muammar Gaddafi (sometimes spelled Qaddafi), renounced terrorism and handed over all of his weapons of mass destruction. As a reward, the Bush-Cheney administration established full diplomatic relations with Libya. As *Time* magazine put it, "Gaddafi's Now a Good Guy."[1] However, the U.S. government's perception of him as a good guy did not last.

The Attack on Gaddafi

Although Gaddafi was supported by many Libyans—for one thing, he had given them the highest standard of living in Africa and shared profits from his country's oil with them—he did have enemies. In 2010, some of these enemies began protests against him, and these protests soon turned into an insurrection, led by Islamic extremists, including al-Qaeda's North African affiliate. In response, Gaddafi in 2011 counter-attacked and, within a month, had almost completely defeated the rebels, with remarkably little loss of life. He needed only to defeat the rebels in Benghazi, which was the stronghold of the anti-Gaddafi forces. However, anti-Gaddafi rebels, neocons, and members of the Obama administration began making false claims, especially the claim that Gaddafi had pledged to create a bloodbath in Benghazi.[2]

---

1 Elise Labott, "U.S. to Restore Relations with Libya," *CNN,* May 15, 2006; Scott MacLeod, "Why Gaddafi's Now a Good Guy," *Time,* May 16, 2006.
2 Alan J. Kuperman, "Obama's Libya Debacle," *Foreign Affairs*, March/April 2015.

Neocons and others began pressuring President Obama to take action. A letter demanding immediate military action to depose Gaddafi was signed by 40 members of the neocon Foreign Policy Initiative (which succeeded the Project for the New American Century).[3] The *Washington Post* supported this demand. "Clearly pining for the days of George W. Bush's muscular unilateralism," wrote Robert Parry, "the [Washington] *Post's* editors demanded that Obama take the lead in implementing a military strategy that ensures regime change in Tripoli."[4]

The drive to remove Gaddafi was led by Secretary of State Hillary Clinton, who was sometimes labeled a "humanitarian interventionist" but was also considered a neocon by many political thinkers. Robert Parry concluded, "Yes, Hillary Clinton Is a Neocon," and several others have said the same.[5] That claim may be too strong: She was surely not a card-carrying neocon, but her policies show her to be a fellow traveler. (Parry at one time referred to her as "a neocon-lite."[6]) One of the founders of the Project for the New American Century, Robert Kagan, endorsed her presidential bid, saying: "If she pursues a policy which we think she will pursue it's something that might have been called neocon." (By contrast, Donald Trump, said Parry, had "disdain for neocon strategies that he views as simply spreading chaos around the globe.")[7]

In any case, Clinton in 2011 argued strongly for a R2P ("Responsibility to Protect") intervention. Speaking on ABC News, with a reference to the Rwanda massacre (which her husband had allowed to happen), Clinton said:

---

3   Jim Lobe, "U.S. Neo-Cons Urge Libya Intervention," *Al Jazeera,* February 27, 2011.

4   Robert Parry, "The Neocons Regroup on Libyan War," *Consortium News,* March 24, 2011; "President Obama's Muddled Libya Policy," Editorial, *Washington Post,* March 22, 2011

5   Robert Parry, "Yes, Hillary Clinton Is a Neocon," *Consortium News,* April 16, 2016; Gabby Morrongiello, "Rand Paul: 'Hillary Clinton Is a Neocon,'" *Washington Examiner,* November 6, 2015; Webster G. Tarpley wrote an article entitled "Hillary Clinton: The International Neocon Warmonger" (*Voltaire Network,* April 13, 2015); in "Hillary's Neocon Problem," Gerald Sussman called Clinton "a good neocon soldier for American exceptionalism" (*Counterpunch,* April 15, 2016).

6   Robert Parry, "What Neocons Want from Ukraine Crisis," *Consortium News,* March 2, 2014.

7   Parry, "Neocon Kagan Endorses Hillary Clinton," *Consortium News,* February 25, 2016; Jason Horowitz, "Events in Iraq Open Door for Interventionist Revival, Historian Says," *The New York Times,* June 15, 2014.

> Imagine we were sitting here and Benghazi had been overrun,
> a city of 700,000 people, and tens of thousands of people had
> been slaughtered, hundreds of thousands had fled.... The cries
> would be, "Why did the United States not do anything?"[8]

Accepting this argument, Obama asked the UN Security Council to authorize a military intervention in order to save the lives of peaceful, "pro-democracy" protesters, because Gaddafi was poised to commit a "bloodbath" in Benghazi.[9]

Although the case for a R2P intervention was also made to Obama by Susan Rice (then the U.S. ambassador to the UN) and Samantha Power (then serving on the National Security Council), it is widely agreed that Clinton's argument was so pivotal in persuading the president that it is sometimes known as "Hillary's War."

In any case, the Security Council gave the authorization for the use of force, with NATO providing air support for the rebels. (Although it was officially a NATO operation, the United States provided all of the planes and drones.[10]) After a seven-month battle, the rebels, with continued Western support, conquered the country and killed Gaddafi (with Clinton crowing on CBS, "We came, we saw, he died").[11]

Another Attack Based on Lies

However, the attack was based on lies. There were claims that large numbers of peaceful citizens were targeted; that Gaddafi's air force had bombed and strafed civilians in Tripoli and Benghazi; that Gaddafi "adopted a rape policy, and even distributed Viagra to troops." All of these claims proved to be false. Although there was some indiscriminate violence, most of those killed or injured were fighting-age males; few women and children were killed.[12]

---

8   Hillary Rodham Clinton, "Interview with Jake Tapper of ABC's This Week," March 27, 2011.

9   Kuperman, "Obama's Libya Debacle."

10   Charlie Savage, *Power Wars: Inside Obama's Post-9/11 Presidency* (Little, Brown, & Co., 2015), 640.

11   Kuperman, "Obama's Libya Debacle" ; "Clinton on Qaddafi: 'We Came, We Saw, He Died,'" *CBS News,* October 20, 2011.

12   Robert Parry, "What Hillary Knew about Libya," *Consortium News,* January 12,

Most important, the claim about an impending bloodbath had no basis. Whereas a Saudi news channel claimed that Gaddafi had killed 10,000 people in the first few days, Human Rights Watch documented only 233 deaths. Also, far from promising a bloodbath, Gaddafi had pledged to protect Benghazi's citizens; he even promised that no harm would come to rebels who disarmed. Gaddafi's warning about his impending violence was directed only at rebels who refused to disarm—rebels who, Gaddafi had warned, were mainly al-Qaeda terrorists.[13]

"Obama's Libya Debacle," as Alan Kuperman has called it, was even more deplorable because of the reports given by objective witnesses monitoring the situation. The Defense Intelligence Agency, besides calling it highly unlikely that Gaddafi would have risked alienating the international community with a bloodbath, also reported that there was no evidence to support the fear of such an outcome. Rather, said the DIA, Clinton's case for intervention rested "more on speculative arguments of what might happen to civilians than on facts reported from the ground."[14]

In the same vein, Human Rights Watch said: "Our assessment was that up until that point, the casualty figures—around 350 protesters killed by indiscriminate fire of government security forces—didn't rise to the level of indicating that a genocide or genocide-like mass atrocities were imminent."[15]

It later turned out, moreover, that the claim that the U.S. attacked Libya for humanitarian reasons was a lie. The goal was to bring about regime change, as was confirmed by then-Secretary of Defense Leon Panetta, who stated that "our goal in Libya was regime change."[16]

It seems that what really happened was that Clinton wanted Gaddafi out of the way so that the CIA, then under the leadership of its

---

2016; Kuperman, "Obama's Libya Debacle."

13   Kuperman, "Obama's Libya Debacle."

14   Kelly Riddell and Jeffrey Scott Shapiro, "Hillary Clinton's 'WMD' Moment: U.S. Intelligence Saw False Narrative in Libya," *Washington Times*, January 29, 2015; Gareth Porter, "U.S. 'Regime Change' Madness in the Middle East," Middle East Eye, January 4, 2016.

15   Joel Gillin, "Benghazi Won't Stick to Hillary Clinton, But the Disastrous Libyan Intervention Should," *New Republic*, May 27, 2015.

16   Kelly Riddell and Jeffrey Scott Shapiro, "Exclusive: Secret Tapes Undermine Hillary Clinton on Libyan War," *Washington Times*, January 28, 2015.

new director, General David Petraeus, could have a free hand to send Gaddafi's weapons to the anti-Assad "rebels" in Syria (see below).[17] At least this was one of the reasons. Another major reason was to forestall Gaddafi's plan to use his gold to create a single African currency, which would be needed to buy Libyan oil, thereby threatening the dollar.[18]

Overall Consequence of the Attack: Chaos

With the operation seeming like a success, Clinton and her people were anxious to brag that it was her operation. A *New York Times* account said: "Mrs. Clinton had taken a triumphal tour of the Libyan capital, Tripoli, and for weeks top aides had been circulating a 'ticktock' that described her starring role." The timeline, said her top policy aide, demonstrated Mrs. Clinton's "leadership/ownership/stewardship of this country's Libya policy from start to finish."[19]

However, this operation worked out no better than the neocons' regime changes in Afghanistan[20] and Iraq. The term most commonly used for post-Gaddafi Libya is *chaos*.

- Ellen Brown, pointing out that Clinton's victory lap was premature, said that "as the country dissolved into chaos, leading to a civil war that would destabilize the region," the State Department relegated Libya to the back burner.[21]

- Ralph Nader wrote: "Gates had warned about the aftermath. He was right. Libya has descended into a ghastly state of chaotic violence that has spilled into neighboring African nations."[22]

---

17 Damien McElroy, "CIA 'Running Arms Smuggling Team in Benghazi When Consulate Was Attacked," *Telegraph,* August 2, 2013; "Pulitzer-Prize Winning Reporter Sy Hersh: Benghazi Is a Huge Scandal . . . But Not for the Reason You Think," *Washingtons Blog,* April 15, 2014.

18 Alex Newman, "Gadhafi's Gold-Money Plan Would Have Devastated Dollar," *New American,* November 11, 2011; Brad Hoff, "Hillary Emails Reveal True Motive for Libya Intervention," *Foreign Policy Journal,* January 6, 2016.

19 Scott Shane and Joe Becker, "The Libya Gamble, Part 2: A New Libya, With 'Very Little Time Left,'" *The New York Times*, February 27, 2016.

20 A failed regime-change war that lasted twenty years, cost over $2 trillion, and caused an estimated 240,000 direct fatalities.

21 Ellen Brown, "Exposing the Libyan Agenda: A Closer Look at Hillary's Emails," March 13, 2016.

22 Ralph Nader, "Hillary Clinton Sugarcoating Her Disastrous Record," *Huffington*

- "[T]he cascading Libyan chaos has turned the 'regime change' from a positive notch on Clinton's belt," said Robert Parry, "into a black mark on her record."[23]

- Jo Becker and Scott Shane of the *New York Times* wrote: "Libya's descent into chaos began with a rushed decision to go to war, made in what one top official called a 'shadow of uncertainty' as to Colonel Qaddafi's intentions."[24]

- With Gaddafi's death, "A peaceful and prosperous country descended into chaos," wrote Diana Johnstone in her book about Hillary Clinton, *Queen of Chaos*.[25]

- Finally, a 2016 book, entitled *Sowing Chaos: Libya in the Wake of Humanitarian Intervention,* was written by an Italian author, who referred to the "ever-destructive Hillary Clinton."[26]

Without using the term "chaos," Glenn Greenwald gave a similar verdict in a comment about a *New York Times* story entitled "U.S. Tactics in Libya May Be a Model for Other Efforts," which appeared just after the killing of Gaddafi.[27] Writing in 2016, Greenwald said:

> Libya—so predictably—has all but completely collapsed, spending years now drowning in instability, anarchy, fractured militia rule, sectarian conflict, and violent extremism.... This was supposed to be the supreme model of Humanitarian Intervention. It achieved vanishingly few humanitarian benefits, while causing massive humanitarian suffering.[28]

Post, February 12, 2015.

23 Robert Parry, "Hillary Clinton's Failed Libya 'Doctrine,'" *Consortium News,* July 1, 2015.

24 Jo Becker and Scott Shane, "Hillary Clinton, 'Smart Power' and a Dictator's Fall," *The New York Times,* February 27, 2016.

25 Diana Johnstone, *Queen of Chaos* (CounterPunch Books, 2016), 123.

26 Paolo Sensini, *Sowing Chaos: Libya in the Wake of Humanitarian Intervention* (Clarity Press), 2016.

27 Helene Cooper and Steven Lee Myers, "U.S. Tactics in Libya May be a Model for Other Efforts," *The New York Times,* August 28, 2011.

28 Glenn Greenwald, "The U.S. Intervention in Libya Was Such a Smashing Success That a Sequel Is Coming," *The Intercept,* January 27, 2016.

Particular Consequences for Libya of NATO's Attack

In addition to the general chaos created by the attack on Gaddafi, the attack resulted in many particular consequences.

- When NATO intervened, the civil war was about to end, as Gaddafi had the rebels in retreat. But thanks to NATO's intervention, the rebels regained the offensive and the war continued for another eight months. As a result, although only about 1,000 people had been killed before NATO intervened, at least 10,000 more people were killed after the intervention.[29]

- Arguing that Clinton's NATO intervention was not really "humanitarian intervention," Dan Kovalik, a professor of international rights law, said: "[T]he human rights situation in Libya is a disaster, as 'thousands of detainees [including children] languish in prisons without proper judicial review,' and 'kidnappings and targeted killings are rampant.'"[30]

- Libya quickly became a failed state, having two warring governments with roughly 400,000 Libyans fleeing their homes.[31]

- Greenwald wrote, "Just as there was no al Qaeda or ISIS to attack in Iraq until the U.S. bombed its government, there was no ISIS in Libya until NATO bombed it." The chaos in Libya, moreover, allowed ISIS to establish its most important outpost there.[32] Indeed, "The branch in Libya," said CIA Director John Brennan in 2016, "is probably the most developed and the most dangerous."[33]

- Whereas Gaddafi had been effective in limiting the territory controlled by terrorists, the militants by 2016 were trying to take control of the entire country.[34]

---

29 Kuperman, "Obama's Libya Debacle."
30 Dan Kovalik, "Clinton Emails on Libya Expose the Lie of 'Humanitarian Intervention,'" *Huffington Post,* January 22, 2016.
31 Kuperman, "Obama's Libya Debacle."
32 Greenwald, "The U.S. Intervention in Libya Was Such a Smashing Success."
33 Andrea Germanos, "CIA Chief Just Confirmed 'War on Terror' Has Created a Lot More Terrorists," *Common Dreams,* June 16, 2016.
34 Germanos, "CIA Chief…"; Kovalik, "Clinton Emails on Libya."

- After having attained, through Gaddafi's leadership, the highest standard of living in all of Africa, after the NATO attacks Libya went into free fall, leaving cities with power outages much of the time, along with other problems.[35]

- Gaddafi had created the world's largest irrigation system, the Great Man-Made River. Called by Libyans the "eighth wonder of the world," it was built to provide free fresh water to all Libyans and to make their country self-sufficient in food production. Committing a war crime, the U.S.-led NATO destroyed it, leaving Libya with a national water crisis.[36]

Consequences of NATO's Attack for the Region

Just as the U.S. intervention created chaos in Libya, complete with a host of ruinous internal consequences, the intervention was also ruinous for the larger region.

- When Gaddafi was taken out, his enormous arsenal of arms was not secured, with the result that the weapons started "turning up in Syria, Tunisia, Algeria, Mali, Niger, Chad, Nigeria, Somalia, Sudan, Egypt and Gaza, often in the hands of terrorists."[37]

- The effort to reduce the world's nuclear and chemical weapons programs was undermined by the fact that Gaddafi was attacked after he had voluntarily given up these programs. For example, North Korea said that having learned from Libya's experience, it would not fall for the U.S. attempts to get it to abolish its own programs.[38]

- By 2016, about 100,000 Libyans left Libya for Europe, thereby adding to its refugee crisis. By August of that year, "Obama's Libya Debacle" led him to authorize a month-long bombing campaign against ISIS in the formerly "peaceful and prosperous country" of Libya.[39]

---

35 Kuperman, "Obama's Libya Debacle."
36 Nafeez Ahmed, "War Crime: NATO Deliberately Destroyed Libya's Water Infrastructure," *Ecologist*, May 14, 2015.
37 Shane and Becker, "The Libya Gamble, Part 2."
38 Kuperman, "Obama's Libya Debacle."
39 Jamie Merrill, "Obama Authorizes 30 Days of Air Strikes on Libya," *Middle East Eye*, August 4, 2016.

Conclusion

The idea of removing Gaddafi from power was advocated by the same mindset that was behind the removal of Saddam. And the result was the same: Disaster, chaos.

14

How the U.S. Protects Israel from International Law

Today's chaos in the Middle East is rooted, Arabs and impartial scholars agree, in what Palestinians call the "catastrophe," when in 1947 the UN partitioned Mandate Palestine into Arab and Jewish states, allocating over half of the land to the Jewish state, which then began forcibly taking more and more of the land. Within three years, more than a quarter of a million Arabs became refugees, having been forced by the onslaught of Israeli fighters to flee for their lives. By now, there are over 7 million refugees (in other countries) and internally displaced persons, who according to international law have the right to return. But Israel has passed laws forbidding them to return. Although the United States has never officially endorsed Israel's position, it has tried to convince the refugees that they should settle for a symbolic return.[1]

Terrorism and the Occupation

The fact that Palestine has long been occupied is considered by many people, both Arab and not, to be the main source of instability in the region and terrorism. For example, this view was stated in 2015 by speakers at the UN's annual International Day of Solidarity with the Palestinian People.

---

1   "The Nakba, 65 Years of Dispossession and Apartheid," Institute for Middle East Understanding, May 8, 2013; "Palestinian Refugees and the Right or Return," American Friends Service Committee.

- "The continued Israeli occupation of Arab and Palestinian territory," said Nabil al-Arabi (Secretary-General of the Arab League), "represents the main cause for the spread of terrorism and extremist ideology in the region."

- "Failure to find a just solution to the Palestinian cause—as the core issue in the Middle East"—has been fueling conflicts in the region, threatening to affect international peace and security," said Iyad Ameen Madani (Secretary-General of the Organization of Islamic Cooperation)[2]

For a long time, writers seldom commented on the connection between and terrorism and the occupation, except for Arabs and Muslims. "It is simply extraordinary," remarked Palestinian-American Edward Said in 1996,

> that Israel's history, its record—from the fact that it is a state built on conquest, that it has invaded surrounding countries, bombed and destroyed at will, to the fact that it currently occupies Lebanese, Syrian, and Palestinian territory against international law—is simply . . . never addressed as playing any role at all in provoking "Islamic terror."[3]

However, increasingly Americans have been speaking out. For example, the website If Americans Knew says: "The Israeli-Palestinian conflict is one of the world's major sources of instability."[4] Francis Boyle, University of Illinois professor of international law, writes:

> As matters of fact and of law, the gross and repeated violations of Palestinian rights by the Israeli army and Israeli settlers living illegally in occupied Palestine constitute war crimes.[5]

---

2   Patrick Goodenough, "At UN, Israel Blamed for Spread of Terror Across the Region," CNSNews.com, November 24, 2015.

3   Edward Said, *The Progressive*, May 30, 1996.

4   If Americans Knew: What Every American Needs to Know about Israel/Palestine (website).

5   Francis A. Boyle, "The International Laws of Belligerent Occupation" (a segment of Boyle's *Palestine, Palestinians and International Law* [Clarity Press, 2011]).

Richard Falk, in his final report as UN Special Rapporteur on Human Rights in the Palestinian Territories, said:

> Through prolonged occupation, with practices and policies of apartheid and segregation, ongoing expansion of settlements, and continual construction of the wall arguably amounting to de facto annexation of parts of the occupied Palestinian territory; the denial by Israel of the right to self-determination of the Palestinian people is evident.

In this report, Falk charged Israel with apartheid, inhuman and degrading treatment, torture, systematic oppression, and murder.[6]

However, what provokes terrorism against the United States is not simply Israel's policies, but the fact that the United States allows these policies and even finances them.

American Support for the Occupation

In 2006, the University of Chicago's John Mearsheimer and Harvard University's Stephen Walt published a major study entitled "The Israel Lobby," in which they say that "the centrepiece of U.S. Middle Eastern policy has been its relationship with Israel." Its "unwavering support for Israel," they wrote, has "inflamed Arab and Islamic opinion and jeopardized not only U.S. security but that of much of the rest of the world."[7]

In explaining how it has jeopardized U.S. security, they wrote:

> Support for Israel is not the only source of anti-American terrorism, but it is an important one.... [M]any al-Qaeda leaders

---

6   Richard Falk, "December 2013 Report to UN Human Rights Council on Occupied Palestine." A collection of such reports by a succession of UN special rapporteurs can be found in Richard Falk, John Dugard, and Michael Lynk, *Protecting Human Rights in Occupied Palestine: Working Through the United Nations* [Clarity Press, 2023].

7   John Mearsheimer and Stephen Walt, "The Israel Lobby," *London Review of Books*, March 23, 2006. A slightly revised version was later published as a book, *The Israel Lobby and U.S. Foreign Policy* (Farrar, Straus and Giroux, 2007). As shown by the title of Mearsheimer and Walt's study, their major focus is on how the Israel Lobby has been effective in persuading the U.S. government to give so much to Israel for so little in return.

. . . are motivated by Israel's presence in Jerusalem and the plight of the Palestinians. Unconditional support for Israel makes it easier for extremists to rally popular support and to attract recruits.

Moreover, although during the Clinton administration "Middle Eastern policy was largely shaped by officials with close ties to Israel," the situation was "even more pronounced in the Bush administration."[8]

In illustrating how decisions of the Bush-Cheney administration were influenced by its complete support for Israel, Mearsheimer and Walt quoted a statement by Philip Zelikow, explaining why Iraq was attacked. Pointing out that Iraq was no threat to America, Zelikow said that the "real threat" was "the threat against Israel."[9]

Alison Weir, who runs the above-mentioned website If Americans Knew, pointed out that the case for which Mearsheimer and Walt argued was stated matter-of-factly by Daniel Shapiro, the Obama-appointed Ambassador to Israel. Speaking to a Jewish institute, Shapiro said:

> The test of every policy the Administration develops in the Middle East is whether it is consistent with the goal of ensuring Israel's future as a secure, Jewish, democratic state. That is a commitment that runs as a common thread through our entire government.

Giving an example of America's support for Israel, Shapiro said:

> Israel will receive over $3 billion in U.S. funding for training and equipment in the coming fiscal year. This assistance allows Israel to purchase the sophisticated defense equipment it needs to protect itself, by itself, including the world's most advanced fighter aircraft, the F-35 Joint Strike Fighter.

---

8   Mearsheimer and Walt, "The Israel Lobby,"
9   Mearsheimer and Walt, discussed more fully in Emad Mekay, "Iraq Was Invaded 'to Protect Israel' – US Official," *Asia Times*, March 31, 2004.

Currently, he said [in 2011], the administration is "doing everything we can" to oppose the Palestinian bid for UN membership to come later this month.[10]

Using Its UN Security Council Veto

One of the main ways in which the United States supports Israel's continued oppression of Palestinians is by using its veto power to block resolutions critical of Israel or otherwise opposed by it. Here is the list of such blocked resolutions since the beginning of the Bush-Cheney administration:

2001   To send unarmed monitors to the West Bank and the Gaza Strip.

2002   Condemns the killing of a UN worker from the United Kingdom by Israeli forces.

2003   Condemns a decision by the Israeli parliament to "remove" the elected Palestinian president, Yasser Arafat.

2003   Condemns the building of a wall by Israel on Palestinian land.

2004   Condemns the assassination of Hamas leader Sheik Ahmad Yassin.

2004   Condemns the Israeli incursion and killings in Gaza.

2006   Calls for an end to Israeli military incursions and attacks on Gaza.

2007   Calls for the right of self-determination for the Palestinian people.

2008   Calls for a treaty on children's rights.

2008   Condemns racial discrimination.

2008   Affirms the sovereignty of Palestinians over the occupied territories and their resources.

2008   Affirms the right of the Palestinians to self-determination.

2008   Calls on Israel to pay the cost of cleaning up an oil slick off the coast of Lebanon caused by its bombing.

---

10   Alison Weir, "US Ambassador: Support for Israel Drives All US Policies," *Antiwar. com*, September 14, 2011.

2008   Resolutions concerning Palestine, its people, their property, and Israeli practices in Palestine, including settlements.

2009   Calls for an end to the twenty-two-day-long Israeli attack on Gaza.

2011   Calls for a halt to the illegal Israeli West Bank settlements. Prime Minister Netanyahu said, "Israel deeply appreciates the decision by President Obama to veto the Security Council Resolution."[11]

The list of Obama's vetoes need not be further pursued, given a *New York Times* story of 2016 saying: "Over seven years, Mr. Obama has not permitted passage of any Security Council resolution specifically critical of Israel."[12]

In vetoing resolutions critical of Israel, the United States allows Israel to violate international law with impunity. For example, the Fourth Geneva Convention of 1949, which deals with "belligerent occupation," applies to the West Bank, the Gaza Strip, and the entire City of Jerusalem, in order to protect the Palestinians living there. In 2000—just before the installation of the Bush-Cheney administration—the Security Council passed a resolution that:

> Calls upon Israel, the occupying Power, to abide scrupulously by its legal obligations and its responsibilities under the Fourth Geneva Convention relative to the Protection of Civilian Persons.

The vote, said Boyle, "was 14 to 0, becoming obligatory international law."[13]

The Palestinian People living in this Palestinian Land, Boyle continues, are "protected persons," whose "rights are sacred under international law." The Fourth Geneva Convention has 149 articles spelling

---

11   "Israel 'Deeply Appreciates' U.S. Veto on UN Resolution Condemning Settlements," *Haaretz,* February 19, 2011.

12   Lara Friedman, "Israel's Unsung Protector: Obama," *The New York Times*, April 10, 2016.

13   Boyle, "The International Laws of Belligerent Occupation," op. cit.

out these rights. However, although violations of the Fourth Geneva Convention are war crimes,

> The Israeli Government is currently violating, and has since 1967 been violating, almost each and every one of these sacred rights of the Palestinian People recognized by the Fourth Geneva Convention.[14]

And yet, the United States has continued to protect Israel from needing to abide by any such obligations under international law. One can see why Palestinians, both within and without the country, and other Arabs and Muslims, are enraged by both Israel and the United States.

Comparisons

Israel, to be sure, says that its actions against Palestinians are justified as self-defense. But it takes only a few comparisons (up to 2015) to see the ridiculousness of this claim:

- Between 2000 and 2015: There were 1,224 Israelis killed by Palestinians, while 9,370 Palestinians were killed by Israelis.

- During that same period, 139 Israeli children were killed by Palestinians, while 2,112 Palestinian children were killed by Israelis.

- Between 1967 and 2015: At least 48,888 homes of Palestinians were demolished by Israelis, while 0 Israeli homes were demolished by Palestinians.

- During that same period, 11,755 Israelis were injured by Palestinians, while 87,305 Palestinians were injured.

- Israel currently has 261 (illegal) settlements and outposts on confiscated Palestinian land, whereas Palestinians have no settlements on Israeli land.

- Currently, no Israelis are imprisoned by Palestinians, while 7,000 Palestinians are imprisoned by Israel.

14　Boyle, "The International Laws of Belligerent Occupation."

- The Israeli unemployment rate is 5.6%, while the Palestinian unemployment in the West Bank is 17.7% and 44% in Gaza.

- During Fiscal Year 2014, the U.S. provided Israel with at least $10.2 million in military aid per day, while it provided $0 to Palestinians.[15]

- Reflecting the differences of their military budgets: Palestinian weapons are limited to stones, knives, rockets, and a few guns, whereas Israel has one of the best-equipped militaries in the world, having up-to-date pistols, rifles, assault weapons, grenade launchers, missiles, artillery, drones, fighter planes, and nuclear weapons, as well as its Iron Dome, which intercepts rockets.[16]

---

15   If Americans Knew: What Every American Needs to Know about Israel/Palestine: Statistics.

16   Jeremy Bender, "The 11 Most Powerful Militaries in the World," *Business Insider,* April 23, 2014; "Military Equipment of Israel," *Wikipedia.*

The War in Ukraine

Seeing Russia as a major obstacle, along with China, to establishing an all-inclusive global empire, America wants to bring about regime change in Russia. It has sought to do this by expanding NATO, despite multiple warnings not to do this.

Background

Warnings Against Expanding NATO

In February 1990, James Baker, President George H. W. Bush's secretary of state, told Soviet leader Mikhail Gorbachev that NATO would not expand "one inch eastward." And as Iain Davis pointed out,

> Baker's words weren't the only reassurances the Russians received. In 1990, West German Foreign Minister Hans-Dietrich Genscher gave a keynote speech with regard to German reunification, during which he said:
>
> > [T]he changes in Eastern Europe and the German unification process must not lead to an "impairment of Soviet security interests." Therefore, NATO should rule out an "expansion of its territory towards the east, i.e. moving it closer to the Soviet borders."

Furthermore, wrote Davis,

Russia was offered assurances by political leaders from the U.S., France, the UK, Germany and other NATO aligned states. Russia agreed to German reunification only after German Chancellor Helmut Kohl convinced Gorbachev that NATO would not expand toward Russian borders.

Nevertheless,

[f]rom 1991 onwards NATO completely ignored both the assurances it had given and Russia's security concerns. It systematically rolled eastward, and by 2005 Estonia, Latvia, Lithuania, Slovakia, Poland, the Czech Republic, Hungary, Slovenia, Romania and Bulgaria had become members of NATO.[1]

In 1994 Ted Galen Carpenter wrote:

It would be extraordinarily difficult to expand NATO eastward without that action's being viewed by Russia as unfriendly. Even the most modest schemes would bring the alliance to the borders of the old Soviet Union. Some of the more ambitious versions would have the alliance virtually surround the Russian Federation itself.

Carpenter wrote those words in in his book *Beyond NATO: Staying Out of Europe's Wars*. He added that such an expansion "would constitute a needless provocation of Russia."[2]

The next year, in 1995, Russia's president, Boris Yeltsin, told U.S. President Bill Clinton that NATO expansion would result in "nothing but humiliation for Russia" and could provoke a new Cold War. Yeltsin also said:

---

1   Iain Davis, "Ukraine War! What Is It Good For? The Nationalist Agenda," *OffGuardian*, May 23, 2022.
2   Ted Galen Carpenter, *Beyond NATO: Staying Out of Europe's Wars* (Cato Institute, 1994).

How do you think it looks to us if one bloc [from the Cold War] continued to exist when the Warsaw Pact has been abolished? It's a new form of encirclement if the one surviving Cold War bloc expands right up to the borders of Russia.[3]

George F. Kennan, who was credited with being the architect of the "containment" of the Soviet Union and was one of America's greatest experts on Russia, said in 1997:

Expanding NATO would be the most fateful error of American policy in the post-Cold War era. Such a decision might be expected to inflame the nationalistic, anti-Western and militaristic tendencies in Russian opinion; to have an adverse effect on the development of Russian democracy; and to empower Russian foreign policy in directions decidedly not to our liking.[4]

In 1998, after the Clinton administration got Senate approval to add Poland, Hungary, and the Czech Republic to NATO, Kennan was asked about the Senate's ratification. Kennan stated:

I think [NATO expansion] is the beginning of a new cold war. . . . I think the Russians will gradually react quite adversely and it will affect their policies. I think it is a tragic mistake. There was no reason for this whatsoever. No one was threatening anybody else. . . . I was particularly bothered by the references to Russia as a country dying to attack Western Europe. Don't people understand? Our differences in the Cold War were with the Soviet Communist regime. And now we are turning our backs on the very people who mounted the greatest bloodless revolution in history to remove that Soviet regime. Of course there is going to be a bad reaction from

---

3   "Summary Report on One-on-One Meeting Between Presidents Clinton and Yeltsin, May 10, 1995, 10:10 a.m.–1:19 p.m., St. Catherine's Hall, The Kremlin," National Security Archive. https://nsarchive2.gwu.edu//dc.html?doc=4950563-Document-04-Summary-report-on-the-one-on-one

4   George F. Kennan, "A Fateful Error," *The New York Times*, February 5, 1997.

Russia, and then [the NATO expanders] will say that we always told you that is how the Russians are—but this is just wrong.[5]

In 1999, NATO added Poland, Hungary and the Czech Republic to its membership.

In 2016, Bill Clinton's former secretary of defense, William Perry, told the London *Guardian*:

> In the last few years, most of the blame can be pointed at the actions that Putin has taken. But in the early years I have to say that the United States deserves much of the blame. Our first action that really set us off in a bad direction was when NATO started to expand, bringing in Eastern European nations, some of them bordering Russia. At that time, we were working closely with Russia and they were beginning to get used to the idea that NATO could be a friend rather than an enemy. . . but they were very uncomfortable about having NATO right up on their border and they made a strong appeal for us not to go ahead with that.[6]

Indeed, Bill Clinton himself penned an essay titled, "I Tried to Put Russia on Another Path."[7] This was later countered by Jeremy Kuzmarov's 2022 article, "Bill Clinton Makes a Pathetic Attempt to Retroactively Justify His Decision to Expand NATO." Kuzmarov wrote:

> Clinton's essay erroneously makes it seem that NATO expansion was purely defensive and in reaction to potential future Russian aggression—rather than rooted in any U.S. imperial designs. Clinton also omits the role of military lobbies.[8]

---

5   George L. Friedman, "Foreign Affairs; Now a Word from X," *The New York Times*, May 2, 1998.

6   Quoted in Thomas L. Friedman, "This Is Putin's War. But America and NATO Aren't Innocent Bystanders," *The New York Times,* February 21, 2022.

7   Clinton, "I Tried to Put Russia on Another Path," *The Atlantic*, April 7, 2022.

8   *CovertAction Magazine,* April 6, 2022.

In March 2007, Putin addressed the annual Munich security conference. Putin complained: "NATO has put its frontline forces on our borders." NATO expansion, he continued,

> represents a serious provocation that reduces the level of mutual trust. And we have the right to ask: Against whom is this expansion intended? And what happened to the assurances our western partners made after the dissolution of the Warsaw Pact?

On February 1, 2008, amid rumors that NATO planned to offer membership to Ukraine, Russian Foreign Secretary Sergei Lavrov warned U.S. Ambassador William Burns that "Nyet Means Nyet."[9] Burns then cabled a memo to Washington with the title, "Nyet means Nyet: Russia's NATO Enlargement Redlines."[10]

Later that year, there was the 2008 NATO Bucharest Summit, for which the concluding statement said, "NATO welcomes Ukraine's and Georgia's Euro-Atlantic aspirations for membership in NATO. We agreed today that these countries will become members of NATO." And in 2019, Davis further points out, "then-President of Ukraine Petro Poroshenko signed a constitutional amendment committing Ukraine to membership in both the EU and NATO."

Forebodingly, in 2014, Henry Kissinger said: "If Ukraine is to survive and thrive, it must not be either side's outpost against the other—it should function as a bridge between them."[11] In 2022 Andrew Bacevich concluded that "Ukraine is Paying the Price for the U.S. 'Recklessly' Pushing NATO Expansion."[12]

Cheney and Russia

Major Todd E. Pierce, who retired as a defense counsel in the Army's Judge Advocate General Corps, argued that "Dick Cheney's ideology of

---

9   Ray McGovern, "Ukraine For Dummies," *Consortium News,* November 14, 2019.
10   https://wikileaks.org/plusd/cables/08MOSCOW265_a.html#efmBTnBfi
11   Kissinger, "To Settle the Ukraine Crisis, Start at the End," *Washington Post*, March 5, 2014.
12   *Democracy Now!,* March 11, 2022. https://www.democracynow.org/shows/2022/3/11

U.S. global domination has become an enduring American governing principle regardless of who is sitting in the Oval Office."[13]

This ideology was first fully stated in the 1992 draft of the Defense Planning Guidance (DPG), which was to describe "American foreign policy after the Cold War." Although this draft was attributed primarily to Cheney's assistant, Paul Wolfowitz, the ideas were primarily Cheney's.[14] Indeed, one critic called it "Dick Cheney's Song of America."[15]

In speaking of this ideology as "enduring," Pierce said that "President Obama has cemented Cheney's ideological legacy by continuing his unilateralism and even expanding it." Although there have been changes in the details, "there is virtually no deviation in the United States from the core of Cheney's ideology," namely, the "unrelenting pursuit of total U.S. global military domination as outlined in the Defense Planning Guidance."[16]

Referring to this ideology as "Cheneyism," Pierce entitled his essay "We're All Cheneyites Now." In describing Cheneyism, Pierce said that it combines "an un-American, anti-constitutional authoritarianism" with "militarism under a state of permanent war" and "an aggressiveness toward past, present and possibly future adversaries, especially Russia."[17] With regard to Russia in particular, Pierce quoted former CIA director Bob Gates' memoir, *Duty*, which said: "[Cheney] wanted to see the dismantlement not only of the Soviet Union and the Russian Empire but of Russia itself."[18]

The double-cross of Russia is central to the drive of the Bush-Cheney administration to bring about regime change there. In 1989, the first President Bush negotiated with Mikhail Gorbachev about the dissolution of the Soviet Union and the unification of Germany. Gorbachev was fearful that allowing East Germany to be absorbed by West Germany would simply be the first step of the movement of NATO towards Russia, but he nonetheless accepted the unification on the basis of a deal suggested by Bush's secretary of state, James Baker: that on

---

13 Todd E. Pierce, "We're All Cheneyites Now," *Consortium News,* April 1, 2004.

14 Nicholas Lemann, "The Next World Order: The Bush Administration May Have a Brand-New Doctrine of Power," *The New Yorker,* April 1, 2002.

15 David Armstrong, "Dick Cheney's Song of America," *Harper's*, October 2002.

16 Pierce, "We're All Cheneyites Now."

17 Pierce.

18 Robert M. Gates, *Duty: Memoirs of a Secretary at War* (Knopf, 2014), 97.

the one hand, Moscow would not use force to re-impose control over Eastern Europe, and on the other hand, NATO would not—in Baker's words—"leapfrog" eastward over Germany. In fact, promised Baker, NATO would not expand "one inch" eastward. Various people have testified that they knew about this promise. One of these was West German Chancellor Helmut Kohl, who had intended to keep the promise. But Bush Senior said: "To hell with that! We prevailed, they didn't." On that basis, his and subsequent administrations acted as if that promise had never been made.[19]

Although Cheney was Bush's Secretary of Defense from 1989 to 1993 and must have known about the agreement not to expand NATO eastward, he later spoke as if it had never happened. In 2008 he said:

> [T]he Russian government is increasingly antagonistic toward the enlargement of NATO and the advance of democracy.... Moscow has opposed every eastward addition to NATO.... Russia strongly protested membership in the Alliance for Georgia and Ukraine, now and forever.... [But Cheney said:] Let us make clear that the enlargement of NATO will continue as and where the Allies decide.[20]

The following day, Cheney stated this policy in relation to Ukraine in particular, saying: "Ukrainians have a right to choose whether they wish to join NATO, and NATO has a right to invite Ukraine to join the alliance when we believe they are ready and that the time is right."[21]

At its Bucharest Summit of 2008, NATO opted not to invite Ukraine into the alliance at that time but still acknowledged the idea as a possibility, even though the government of Victor Yanukovych (2010–2014) elected to remain non-aligned.

After the United States engineered regime change there in 2014, the new West-leaning government of Ukraine took steps to overturn the

---

19 Ray McGovern, "Rebuilding the Obama-Putin Trust," *Consortium News,* January 3, 2015; Eric Zuesse, "How America Double-Crossed Russia and Shamed West," Strategic Culture Foundation, October 9, 2015.

20 The White House, "Vice President's Remarks at the Ambrosetti Forum," Office of the Vice President, September 6, 2008.

21 John D. McKinnon, "Cheney Chides Russia in Speech to European Security Conference," *Wall Street Journal,* September 7, 2008.

non-alignment policy. The fateful consequences of this change in policy must be considered in the historical context.

The Context of the 2014 Coup in Ukraine and Its Aftermath

Neocon Plans for Regime Change in Russia

Russian leaders have believed the United States wants to bring about regime change in Russia since at least 2014. Russia's foreign minister Sergey Lavrov said in 2014 that the U.S. "wants to secure regime change." Likewise, President Putin has said that Moscow must guard against a "color revolution."[22]

Although this has been portrayed in the West as Russian paranoia, many commentators believed there were good grounds for these fears.

- Robert Parry wrote in 2014 that the financial crisis being imposed on Russia appears to be another neocon-driven "regime change" scheme, this time focused on Moscow with the goal to take down Russian President Vladimir Putin and presumably replace him with some U.S. puppet.[23]

  - In 2015, in "Regime Change in Russia?" Neil Clark noted that:

    > Russia is the biggest block on the endless war-lobby's plans for world domination, which is why the removal of Putin and his replacement with a marionette who will do exactly what the neocons want is their overriding objective.

    Clark added that this scheme was hatched back when Cheney was in charge:

---

22 Polina Devitt, "Lavrov Accuses West of Seeking 'Regime Change' in Russia," *Reuters*, November 22, 2014.

23 Robert Parry, "The Crazy US 'Group Think' on Russia," *Consortium News,* December 18, 2014.

The neocon plans for regime change in Russia can be traced back to 2003 when it became clear that Vladimir Putin would (unlike Boris Yeltsin) stand up for Russia's legitimate interests.[24]

As to how the regime change would be engineered, there is a consensus that the plan is for a hybrid war against it—one employing the use of both military and nonmilitary means. In this case, the approach would be to combine both military and economic means.

The Military Route to Regime Change

The following facts could reasonably make Russia fear that the United States is planning to use military means to bring about regime change in Russia.

- Since the latter part of 2014, as John Pilger has pointed out, "the greatest build-up of military forces since World War II—led by the United States—[has been] taking place along Russia's western frontier."[25] Hardly anyone believes that Russia would attack America (unless, at least, it feared that the United States was intending to preemptively attack it). So, what could be the purpose of this build-up, Russia can reasonably ask, unless it was for the purpose of attacking Russia?

- Second, the United States and NATO have been encircling Russia, so that Russia will be surrounded on virtually all sides by former Warsaw Pact countries that are now members of NATO. In 2016, Philip Giraldi, in an essay titled "How the World Ends: Baiting Russia Is Not Good Policy," said that "the Obama Administration is already treating Georgia and Ukraine as if they were de facto members of NATO." In the same year, Hillary Clinton, while she was running for the presidency, pledged to bring both of these nations into the alliance.[26]

---

24 Neil Clark, "Regime change in Russia? Think Again, Neocons," *RT*, July 25, 2015.
25 John Pilger, "A World War Has Begun: Break the Silence," *teleSUR*, March 25, 2016.
26 Philip Giraldi, "How the World Ends: Baiting Russia Is Not Good Policy," *Unz Review*, May 24, 2016.

- Third, in addition to encircling Russia with NATO allies, the United States is putting missiles in these countries. Let us recall how the Soviet Union's placing of missiles in Cuba during the Kennedy administration almost resulted in a nuclear war. The United States seems to believe that Russia will accept a situation that the U.S. itself would not.

- The U.S. has installed an anti-missile shield in Romania, which it could do because President George W. Bush unilaterally withdrew from the ABM treaty in June 2002. Russia has denounced this shield as a threat because it undermines the mutually-assured-destruction (MAD) system, which had provided an effective deterrence against nuclear war since WW II.[27] This development seems to reflect a switch in the final years of the Bush-Cheney administration from the policy of MAD to a policy of nuclear primacy. The development of this "shield" understandably infuriated the Russians, because these "defensive" missile systems can be easily and quickly converted into offensive systems, and thus pose an existential threat to their national security. According to *Reuters*:

  > Russia is incensed at such a show of force by its Cold War rival in formerly communist-ruled eastern Europe where it once held sway. Moscow says the U.S.-led alliance is trying to encircle it close to the strategically important Black Sea, home to a Russian naval fleet.[28]

  The United States claims that Russia has nothing to fear, because the "system is not aimed against Russia," but at Iran.[29] But this claim is absurd: Iran has no nuclear missiles and would not have them for some time if the U.S. remained a signatory to the JCPOA treaty (made possible partly by Putin himself). The Kremlin noted: "[T]he missile shield's real aim

---

27 Ryan Browne, "U.S. Launches Long-Awaited European Missile Defense Shield," CNN, May 12, 2016; Andrew E. Kramer, "Russia Calls New U.S. Missile Defense System a 'Direct Threat,'" *The New York Times*, May 12, 2016.

28 Robin Emmott, "U.S. to switch on European missile shield despite Russian alarm," *Reuters*, May 11, 2016.

29 Robin Emmot.

is to neutralize Moscow's nuclear arsenal long enough for the United States to make a first strike on Russia in the event of war."[30] The issue could hardly be more existential. Moreover, the United States argued that Russia should not fear an attack because the missiles are purely defensive. However, Putin countered, these defense positions being installed near Russia's borders can "inconspicuously" be transformed into offensive weapons.[31]

Still another dimension of the military threat to Russia is the fact that the United States is developing new nuclear weapons which could make a nuclear strike seem more doable. One of these weapons is a tiny nuclear bomb—a new model (Model 12) of the long-existing B61. It has a "dial-a-yield" feature, which allows the yield to be dialed down to the level at which it would be only two percent as powerful as the Hiroshima bomb. The B61-12 also has moveable fins, which allow the bomb to be guided much more precisely to the target, so the bomb does not need to be terribly powerful to take the target out.[32]

One of the reasons why America has never used nuclear weapons since Hiroshima and Nagasaki is that they would have been devastating not only to an enemy but also to America itself and its allies. The use of powerful nuclear weapons would also likely result in a "nuclear winter," which could bring all life to an end. But the B61-12 could entice American leaders to believe that they could launch a crippling nuclear attack on Russia with only an "acceptable" level of collateral damage to the U.S., its allies, and the environment.[33] In announcing the 2010 Nuclear Posture Review (which includes the B61-12), President Obama said: "My Administration is taking a significant step forward by fulfilling another pledge that I made in Prague—to reduce the role of

---

30 Emmott, "U.S. to Switch on European Missile Shield Despite Russian Alarm."

31 "Putin: 'We Know When US Will Get New Missile Threatening Russia's Nuclear Capability,'" *RT,* June 18, 2016.

32 William J. Broad and David E. Sanger, "As U.S. Modernizes Nuclear Weapons, 'Smaller' Leaves Some Uneasy," *The New York Times,* January 11, 2016; Julian Borger, "America's New, More 'Usable', Nuclear Bomb in Europe," *The Guardian,* November 10, 2015.

33 Broad and Sanger, "As U.S. Modernizes Nuclear Weapons, 'Smaller' Leaves Some Uneasy."

nuclear weapons in our national security strategy and focus on reducing the nuclear dangers of the 21st century."[34]

However, many experts draw the opposite conclusion. For example:

- Gen. James E. Cartwright, who as vice chairman of the Joint Chiefs of Staff was an influential nuclear strategist for Obama, likes the fact that precise targeting allows the United States to hold fewer weapons. But "what going smaller does," he added, "is to make the weapon more thinkable."[35]

- Hans M. Kristensen, the director of the Nuclear Information Project, said that he included himself among the critics who say that "the increased accuracy and lower yield options could make the B61-12 more attractive to use because of reduced collateral damage and radioactive fallout."[36]

The most important objection to these new weapons, however, came from Moscow. The Obama administration defended the development of the B61-12 by saying that it "creates more strategic stability."[37] Russia's deputy defense minister, Anatoly Antonov, condemned a (warheadless) test of the B61-12, which used an F-15E fighter-bomber to carry the bomb as "irresponsible" and "openly provocative," giving "grounds to believe that the test was conducted in order to examine the possibility of using the B61-12 atomic bomb by NATO fighter-bombers stationed in Europe." In addition, Russia's Security Council Secretary Nikolay Patrushev said that the test showed that the U.S. missile shield is intended for use against Russia.[38]

Accordingly, Russians are not paranoid if they fear that the United States is preparing to launch a first strike. American leaders might believe that they could take out virtually all of Russia's nuclear weapons

---

34 The White House, "Statement by President Barack Obama on the Release of Nuclear Posture Review," April 6, 2010.

35 Broad and Sanger, "As U.S. Modernizes Nuclear Weapons, 'Smaller' Leaves Some Uneasy."

36 Hans M. Kristensen, "General Confirms Enhanced Targeting Capabilities of B61-12 Nuclear Bomb," in *NATO, Nuclear Weapons, United States*, January 23, 2014.

37 Broad and Sanger, "As U.S. Modernizes Nuclear Weapons."

38 "Russia Slams US Test of B61-12 Atomic Bomb as 'Provocative,'" Press TV, July 13, 2015.

in a first strike by using the B61-12 (possibly along with other low-yield nuclear weapons), while producing relatively little collateral damage. And thanks to the missile shield, they may believe that they can destroy any remaining Russian weapons that survived the first strike. Given how rabid the neocons are in their pursuit of a completely global empire—Robert Parry spoke of their "madness," another critic calls them "psychopaths"[39]—they may believe the so-called collateral damage to be worth the price, especially because taking over Russia would give America control of Russia's unequaled natural resources.

Given Russia's legitimate fear that the U.S. may be preparing for a first strike against it, Russia's leaders might well decide to launch a pre-emptive first strike themselves, believing that it would have a better chance of surviving an American counterstrike than a first strike.

This returns us to Philip Giraldi's essay entitled "How the World Ends" and the essay's subtitle, "Baiting Russia Is Not Good Policy." As those of us old enough to remember, America's new "nuclear posture" will bring us back to the kinds of debates about nuclear strategy that we had in the 1980s, which were brilliantly described in Fred Kaplan's 1984 book, *The Wizards of Armageddon*.

The Economic Route to Regime Change

The second way for the United States to attempt to bring about regime change in Russia is to use economic power. America has been engaged, as Mahdi Darius Nazemroava has emphasized, in a "multi-spectrum war."[40]

We now focus on one aspect of the economic war: the placing of sanctions on Russia's economy. Neil Clark gave this brief explanation of the rationale:

> The neocon plan is for the Russian economy to be weakened by sanctions, which they hope will lead to a reduction in support for Putin and make it easier for them to destabilize the

---

39   Robert Parry, "What Neocons Want from Ukraine Crisis," *Consortium News,* March 2, 2014; Zuesse, "US Elite Wants to Destroy Russia at Any Price."

40   Mahdi Darius Nazemroava, "From Energy War to Currency War: America's Attack on the Russian Ruble," Strategic Culture Foundation, December 26, 2014.

country and bring about a "regime change" in Moscow. They want a compliant stooge in the Kremlin who will surrender all of Russia's natural resources, and allow them to get rid of President Assad and the Baathists in Syria—an essential prerequisite before any attack on Iran.[41]

In other words, the White House has been following the approach taken in 1973 by President Nixon in bringing about a coup in Chile: "Make the economy scream."[42]

The Russian leaders are, of course, fully aware of this strategy. "Now public figures in Western countries say there is a need to impose sanctions that will destroy the economy and cause public protests," noted Foreign Minister Lavrov.[43]

The Obama administration did not try to hide its intentions. At the end of 2014, top White House economist Jason Furman said that the West's sanctions on Russia, combined with the falling price of oil, have "put their economy on the brink of crisis." White House press secretary Josh Earnest added: "As long as that sanctions regime remains in place, the costs on the Russian economy will continue to increase."[44]

In 2014, U.S. Assistant Secretary of State Victoria Nuland, the wife of neocon Robert Kagan, told the House's Foreign Affairs Committee that—in Nazemroava's paraphrase—"the objectives of the U.S. economic sanctions strategy against the Russian Federation was not only to damage the trade ties and business between Russia and the EU, but to also bring about economic instability in Russia and to create currency instability and inflation." The aims of the U.S., added Nazemroava, do not "appear to be geared at coercing the Russian government to change its foreign policy, but to incite regime change in Moscow."[45]

Two ways in which Putin could be removed from power were suggested by Herbert E. Meyer, who had been a special assistant to the CIA

---

41   Neil Clark, "Putin Demonized for Thwarting Neocon Plan for Global Domination," *RT,* November 8, 2014.

42   Jonathan Marshall, "Risky Blowback from Russian Sanctions," *Consortium News,* January 19, 2015.

43   Devitt, "Lavrov Accuses West of Seeking 'Regime Change' in Russia."

44   David Jackson, "Obama Aides Say Sanctions Are Biting Russia's Economy," *USA Today*, December 16, 2014.

45   Nazemroava, "From Energy War to Currency War."

director in the Reagan administration. The goal of U.S. sanctions against Russia, said Meyer, "should be to get the Russians who've been keeping Putin in power, or tolerating Putin in power, to throw that knockout punch." Alternatively, he added:

> If Putin is too stubborn to acknowledge that his career is over, and the only way to get him out of the Kremlin is feet-first, with a bullet hole in the back of his head—that would also be okay with us.[46]

In any case, the Obama administration's approach was to put the screws on Russia's economy and then progressively tighten them with a series of sanctions.

The 2014 Regime Change in Ukraine

Ukraine had long been divided between the Russian-speaking East and the Ukrainian-speaking West. Historically, Ukraine had been associated with Russia, but in 2013–14, there was an insurrection that replaced the Russia-friendly president Victor Yanukovych. How and why this occurred is contentious. According to Western politicians and media, the standard account of what happened goes something like this:

The Yanukovych government was presented with a proposal that it sign an association agreement with the European Union. Although Yanukovych originally intended to do this, he changed his mind at the last moment, partly because Russia offered a $15 billion loan, which would allow Ukraine to maintain closer economic ties with Russia (which was Yanukovych's preference). This decision, which caused great anger, sparked a wave of protests in Kiev's central square (so the protest became known as the Euromaidan movement—"maidan" being the Ukrainian word for "square"). The protests were peaceful until the Yanukovych government sent in police to use violence to disperse the protestors. Then pro-Russian groups joined in and soon more than 100 people were killed, many of them by unidentified snipers, probably hired by Yanukovych. In February 2014, Yanukovych suddenly fled to Russia

---

46 Carol Adl, "Ex-CIA Official Proposes Assassination of Putin," YourNewsWire. com, August 28, 2014.

for some unknown reason. Arseniy Yatsenyuk was then named the new prime minister, and he signed the agreement to join Europe. Eventually, a civil war between the new Ukrainian government and pro-Russian separatists broke out in the southeast region of Ukraine, known as the Donbass, consisting of the Donetsk and Luhansk oblasts (provinces), which came to call themselves people's republics (DPR and LPR).

The Minsk Protocol, detailing conditions for a ceasefire, was signed in 2014, but it did not hold; in 2015, Minsk II was signed, but it also did not hold. By 2016, over 9,000 people had been killed, and this tragedy is Russia's fault for funding the separatists. In the midst of these developments, Putin used the crisis as an occasion to take over Crimea in order to begin rebuilding the Russian empire. On the basis of this account, the U.S. and European governments leveled sanctions on Russia for provoking the conflict, for extending the civil war by funding the separatists, and for invading Ukraine to occupy Crimea.

This is the story the Biden administration wanted people to believe. However, the true story begins with a statement by Carl Gersham, the long-time director of the National Endowment for Democracy (NED). Writing in 2013, before the Kiev coup, Gersham said: "Ukraine is the biggest prize." If it could be pulled away from Russia and into the West, then "Putin may find himself on the losing end not just in the near abroad but within Russia itself."[47] Consistent with that motivation for the Ukraine crisis, the facts about what happened were stated by John Mearsheimer, one of America's leading political scientists, who wrote an article in the fall of 2014 for *Foreign Affairs* titled "Why the Ukraine Crisis Is the West's Fault." Mearsheimer wrote:

> According to the prevailing wisdom in the West, the Ukraine crisis can be blamed almost entirely on Russian aggression. Russian President Vladimir Putin, the argument goes, annexed Crimea out of a long-standing desire to resuscitate the Soviet empire, and he may eventually go after the rest of Ukraine, as well as other countries in eastern Europe. In this view, the ouster of Ukrainian President Viktor Yanukovych in February

---

47 Quoted in Joe Lauria, "Biden Confirms Why the US Needed This War," *Consortium News,* March 27, 2022.

2014 merely provided a pretext for Putin's decision to order Russian forces to seize part of Ukraine.

But this account is wrong: the United States and its European allies share most of the responsibility for the crisis. The taproot of the trouble is NATO enlargement, the central element of a larger strategy to move Ukraine out of Russia's orbit and integrate it into the West.... Since the mid-1990s, Russian leaders have adamantly opposed NATO enlargement, and in recent years, they have made it clear that they would not stand by while their strategically important neighbor turned into a Western bastion. For Putin, the illegal overthrow of Ukraine's democratically elected and pro-Russian president—which he rightly labeled a "coup"—was the final straw. He responded by taking Crimea, a peninsula he feared would host a NATO naval base.... Putin's pushback should have come as no surprise. After all, the West had been moving into Russia's backyard and threatening its core strategic interests, a point Putin made emphatically and repeatedly.[48]

In the same vein, a 2014 *Guardian* article by Seumas Milne declared: "The story we're told about the protests gripping Kiev bears only the sketchiest relationship with reality."[49]

In fact, reality-based reports show that virtually every element in the Western narrative is false, as facts from several sources have shown:

- What happened at Maidan "was not a peaceful democratic regime change, as it was presented in Western media, but a violent putsch complete with murderous acts by hired assassins," reported professor Vlad Sobell of New York University's campus in Prague. He said that there were some 20 snipers, who killed both policemen and demonstrators on both sides to provoke chaos.[50]

---

48   John J. Mearsheimer, "Why the Ukraine Crisis Is the West's Fault. The Liberal Delusions That Provoked Putin," *Foreign Affairs* (Sept-Oct. 2014).

49   Seumas Milne, "In Ukraine, Fascists, Oligarchs and Western Expansion Are at the Heart of the Crisis," *The Guardian*, January 29, 2014.

50   "Washington Was Behind Ukraine Coup: Obama admits that US 'Brokered a Deal' in Support of 'Regime Change,'" *Global Research*, February 3, 2015.

- The coup was not provoked by outrage about Yanukovych's refusal to sign the agreement with the EU. Rather, the coup was planned by Victoria Nuland, the wife of neocon Robert Kagan and sister-in-law of Frederick Kagan, who had strongly advocated for Ukraine's reorientation toward Europe. Nuland had been made Assistant Secretary of State for European Affairs by Hillary Clinton. To indicate that she was to be in charge, Nuland reminded Ukrainian business leaders that America had invested $5 billion in their "European aspirations," and at the beginning of the coup, she was even at the Maidan passing out cookies to the anti-Yanukovych agitators.[51]

- Three weeks before the coup, Nuland told Geoffrey Pyatt, the U.S. Ambassador in Kiev, that when Yanukovych is replaced by a new president, the new prime minister should be Arseniy Yatsenyuk. In a four-minute intercepted phone call between Nuland and Pyatt, she can be heard saying (on You Tube), "Yats is the guy who's got the economic experience."[52]

- Catherine Ashton, the EU's foreign-affairs chief, had asked Urmas Paet to investigate the cause of the violence that brought down Yanukovych's government. Although she had assumed that the snipers had been sent by Yanukovych, Paet told her in a phone conversation that "behind the snipers, it was not Yanukovych, but it was somebody from the new coalition." This conversation, which was hacked by security service officers loyal to Yanukovych, can be heard on You Tube.[53]

- The coup, said former CIA officer Ray McGovern, was "spearheaded by well-organized neo-Nazi militias."[54] For the months of the Euromaidan conflict, added the late Robert Parry, the commandant

---

51 Parry, "The Whys Behind the Ukraine Crisis," *Consortium News,* September 3, 2014.

52 Ray McGovern, "Rebuilding the Obama-Putin Trust," *Consortium News,* January 3, 2015.

53 Eric Zuesse, "The Paet-Ashton Transcript," *Fort Russ,* February 3, 2015; Michael Bergman, "Breaking: Estonian Foreign Minister Urmas Paet and Catherine Ashton Discuss Ukraine over the Phone," video clip, 10:50, March 5, 2014. https://www.youtube.com/watch?v=ZEgJ0oo3OA8

54 Ray McGovern, "Rebuilding the Obama-Putin Trust."

was Andriy Parubiy, a well-known neo-Nazi, who directed the acts of neo-Nazi storm troopers, including the snipers.[55]

- In an essay on the "snipers'" massacre, Ivan Katchanovski of the University of Ottawa pointed out that the conclusion "that the massacre was perpetrated by government snipers and special police units on a Yanukovych order had been nearly universally accepted by the Western governments [and] the media." However, Katchanovski said:

> This academic investigation concludes that the massacre was a false flag operation, which was rationally planned and carried out with a goal of the overthrow of the government and seizure of power.... Concealed shooters and spotters were located in at least 20 Maidan-controlled buildings or areas. The various evidence that the protesters were killed from these locations include some 70 testimonies, primarily by Maidan protesters; there are several videos of "snipers" targeting protesters from these buildings.[56]

- Contrary to the claim that Russia was behind the breakout of civil war in the Donbass, Russia scholar Paul Robinson said: "No plausible evidence has been produced to indicate that members of the Russian army were involved at the start of the uprising."[57]

- With regard to Crimea: Putin knew immediately that the regime change in Ukraine was illegal, and Russian intelligence knew quickly, as correspondent Pepe Escobar said, "that Maidan would be replicated in Crimea, so the Kremlin acted swiftly."[58] Naturally, Putin was not going to allow an illegal coup to take over Crimea,

---

55 Robert Parry, "Ukraine, Through the US Looking Glass, *Consortium News,* April 16, 2014.

56 Ivan Katchanovski, "The 'Snipers' Massacre' on the Maidan in Ukraine," *Social Science Research Network,* September 5, 2015.

57 Paul Robinson, "Vladimir Putin Not Responsible for Ukrainian Civil War, Expert Says," *Truthdig,* March 21, 2015.

58 "Washington Was Behind Ukraine Coup: Obama admits that US 'Brokered a Deal' in Support of 'Regime Change.'"

which had been part of Russia since the 18th century and provides its only warm-water port. Contrary to the claim that Putin had "invaded" Ukraine, Russian troops were already stationed inside Crimea at the Russian naval base at Sevastopol. But Putin did not annex Crimea until a referendum was held, which showed that 97% percent of the Crimeans wanted to remain with Russia.[59]

Certainly, Putin would be concerned about an anti-Russian, neo-Nazi government in Ukraine, particularly considering its demonstrated antagonism towards the large populations of Russian-speaking people. "[T]he consistent pattern of the mainstream U.S. news media," wrote Robert Parry, has been "to whiteout the role of Ukraine's brownshirts." However, a few comments did make it through the U.S. and UK censors.[60]

- A *New York Times* article cited a leader of the neo-Nazi Right Sector, who bragged that Ukraine's revolution would never have happened without the Right Sector.[61]

- A *Telegraph* article reported that the Kiev regime recruited neo-Nazis to serve as storm troopers, some of whom carried banners with the Wolfsangel symbol, which the German SS had had on its banners.[62]

- The BBC provided a video showing how neo-Nazis spearheaded the seizure and occupation of government buildings, then forced Yanukovych and his aides to flee for their lives. (Accordingly, it is not true that Yanukovych fled for "some unknown reason.")[63]

---

59 Alan Yuhas, "Ukraine Crisis: An Essential Guide to Everything that's Happened So Far," *The Guardian*, April 13, 2014.

60 Robert Parry, "NYT Discovers Ukraine's Neo-Nazis at War," *Consortium News,* August 10, 2014.

61 Andrew Higgins, "Mystery Surrounds Death of Fiery Ukrainian Activist," *The New York Times*, April 12, 2014.

62 Tom Parfitt, "Ukraine Crisis: The Neo-Nazi Brigade Fighting Pro-Russian Separatists," *Telegraph*, August 11, 2014.

63 "Neo-Nazi Threat in New Ukraine: NEWSNIGHT," BBC, February 28, 2014, news broadcast, 6:48, https://youtu.be/5SBo0akeDMY; see also Robert Parry, "What Neocons Want from Ukraine Crisis," March 2, 2014.

- The UK *Independent* reported: "The military action is accompanied by stridently aggressive rhetoric from politicians in Kiev who are crowing about the numbers of 'terrorists' killed and threatening further lethal punishment."

But there were several significant events that the U.S. and UK censors did not allow their people to know, if they were depending on mainstream sources. For example, Robert Parry reported in Consortium News that on May 2, in the port city of Odessa, pro-regime militants chased dissidents into the Trade Unions Building and then set it on fire.

> As some 40 or more ethnic Russians were burned alive or died of smoke inhalation, the crowd outside mocked them as red-and-black Colorado potato beetles, with the chant of "Burn, Colorado, burn." Afterwards, reporters spotted graffiti on the building's walls containing Swastika-like symbols.... However, the coup regime found itself unable to count on regular Ukrainian troops to fire on civilians. Thus, its national security chief Andriy Parubiy, himself a neo-Nazi, turned to the intensely motivated neo-Nazi shock troops who had been battle-tested during the coup. These extremists were reorganized as special units of the National Guard and dispatched to the east and south to do the dirty work that the regular Ukrainian military was unwilling to do. [They] dream of a racially pure Ukraine, free of Jews, ethnic Russians and other "inferior" beings.[64]

Months later, Parry published a more general essay entitled "Ignoring Ukraine's Neo-Nazi Storm Troopers."[65]

> You might think a story about modern-day Nazi storm troopers attacking a European city without mercy would merit front-page coverage in the U.S. press, but not when the Nazi

---

64   Robert Parry, "Burning Ukraine's Protestors Alive," *Consortium News*, May !0, 2014. https://consortiumnews.com/2014/05/10/burning-ukraines-protesters-alive/
65   Robert Parry, "NYT Discovers Ukraine's Neo-Nazis At War," *Consortium News*, August 10, 2014.

paramilitaries are fighting for the U.S.-backed Ukrainian government and are killing ethnic Russians.

The U.S.-backed Ukrainian government is knowingly sending neo-Nazi paramilitaries into eastern Ukrainian neighborhoods to attack ethnic Russians who are regarded by some of these storm troopers as "Untermenschen" or subhuman. . .

[H]ypocrisy has permeated nearly everything said by the U.S. State Department and reported by the mainstream U.S. news media since the Ukraine crisis began last year. There was fawning coverage of the Maidan protesters who sought to overthrow Yanukovych and then an immediate embrace of the "legitimacy" of the regime that followed the Feb. 22 coup. As part of this one-sided U.S. narrative, reports about the key roles played by neo-Nazi activists and militias were dismissed as "Russian propaganda". . . .

But the ugly reality has occasionally broken through the blinders of the Western press. . . . [as reported in the *New York Times*] "Officials in Kiev say the militias and the army coordinate their actions, but the militias, which count about 7,000 fighters, are angry and, at times, uncontrollable. One known as the Azov Battalion flies a neo-Nazi symbol resembling a Swastika as its flag.[66]

Parry elaborated on the Nazi presence a week later:

Actually, the Azov fighters do more than wave a Swastika-like flag; they favor the Wolfsangel flag of Hitler's SS divisions, much as some of Ukraine's neo-Nazis still honor Hitler's Ukrainian SS auxiliary, the Galician SS. A Ukrainian hero hailed during the Maidan protests was Nazi collaborator Stepan Bandera whose paramilitary forces helped exterminate Jews and Poles.

Yet, this dark side of the Kiev regime generally gets ignored by the mainstream U.S. media despite the fact that the

---

[66] "Ukraine Strategy Bets on restraint by Russia," *The New York Times*, August 9, 2014. https://www.nytimes.com/2014/08/10/world/europe/ukraine.html?ref=world&_r=0

idea of modern-day Nazi storm troopers wreaking havoc on Slavic "Untermenschen" would seem like a very juicy story.

But it would destroy the white-hat/black-hat narrative that the State Department and the MSM have built around the Ukraine crisis, with the Kiev regime in the white hats and the ethnic Russian rebels and Russian President Vladimir Putin wearing the black hats. It might be hard to sell the American people on the notion that neo-Nazis waving an SS flag and ranting about "Untermenschen" deserve white hats.[67]

Despite the overwhelming evidence that the regime change in Ukraine was organized by the Obama administration, the G7 countries used the 2013–14 events in Ukraine as an excuse to put sanctions on Russia.[68]

Ukraine: Coup, Lies, and Sanctions

The Euromaidan affair had a double benefit for the United States: Besides reorienting Ukraine's government from the East to the West, it provided an excuse for imposing economic sanctions on Russia. But the claim against Russia was contrary to the evidence, as was the case with U.S. claims that Saddam Hussein was involved in 9/11 and had weapons of mass destruction, that Gaddafi was planning to launch a bloodbath in Libya, and that Assad had used chemical weapons. And yet European countries continued to echo U.S. claims that were devoid of evidence and even contrary to the evidence. The entire G7 endorsed a U.S. document stating that: "Sanctions can be rolled back when Russia meets these commitments," meaning the commitments the U.S. demands that Russia make, based on the assumption that the U.S. charges against Russia were correct.[69]

---

67 Parry, "Ignoring Ukraine's Neo-Nazi Storm Troopers," *Consortium News,* August 13, 2014.
68 Eric Zuesse, "G7 Boldly Displays Its Lies Regarding Anti-Russia Economic Sanctions," *Global Research,* June 3, 2016; "G7 Foreign Ministers' Meeting, April 10–11, 2016 in Japan: Extracts of the Joint Communiqué (12/04/2016)."
69 Giraldi, "How the World Ends: Baiting Russia Is Not Good Policy."

Conclusion as of 2016

As many astute commentators have pointed out, America's pressuring of Russia, both militarily and economically, had no rational basis. As Robert Parry said, the neocon desire for an all-inclusive empire has caused Washington and the American press to go mad.

In his 2014 essay "How the World Ends," Philip Giraldi wrote that, according to Mearsheimer, "if the United States has but a single foreign policy imperative it would be to maintain a solid working relationship with Russia [one would now add, "and China"]."[70] But the United States has been doing the opposite, seemingly doing everything it can to humiliate and anger Russia. Putin wrote:

> [T]here is a limit to everything. And with Ukraine, our Western partners have crossed the line.... If you compress the spring all the way to its limit, it will snap back hard.[71]

Russia has its own national interests that need to be taken into account and respected. Speaking to this point, Giraldi added:

> No one but Victoria Nuland and the Kagans actually want a war but Moscow is being backed into a corner with more and more influential Russian voices raised against détente with a Washington that seems to be intent on humiliating Russians at every turn as part of a new project for regime change. Many Russian military leaders have quite plausibly come to believe that the continuous NATO expansion and the stationing of more army units right along the border means that the United States wants war.[72]

This dynamic, Giraldi pointed out, has "the potential to become the greatest international catastrophe of all time." The "nearly constant animosity directed against Russia by the Obama Administration," Giraldi

---

70   Quoted in Ray McGovern, "Rebuilding the Obama-Putin Trust," *Consortium News,* January 3, 2015.
71   Vladimir Putin, Speech to Kremlin on Annexaton of Crimea, March 18, 2014.
72   Giraldi, "How the World Ends."

added, "should be seen as madness as the stakes in the game, a possible nuclear war, are, or should be, unthinkable."[73]

In his essay "A World War Has Begun," John Pilger referred to fact that "the U.S. military is deploying combat troops, tanks, [and] heavy weapons" in "Latvia, Lithuania and Estonia—next door to Russia." This is, Pilger pointed out, "extreme provocation of the world's second nuclear power."[74] Similarly, Robert Parry, referring to the coup in Ukraine, stated that this risk "occurred on the border of Russia, a nuclear-armed state that—along with the United States—could exterminate all life on the planet."[75] Insofar as the potential cost of "thermo-nuclear warfare that could end all life on the planet is so high," wrote Parry, "the motivation must be commensurate. And there is logic behind that thinking." However, he added, "it's hard to conceive what financial payoff is big enough to risk wiping out all humanity including the people on Wall Street."

In an essay entitled "The Looming U.S. War on Russia," Irish journalist Finian Cunningham wrote of the "burgeoning U.S.-led aggression towards Russia—in the form of provocative political campaigns to demonize and vilify with false accusations, economic sanctions and the spurning of diplomacy and dialogue, as well as the expansion of military forces, including the deployment of missile systems." Cunningham's essay was published in the context of the U.S.'s provocative war games in June 2016, the "largest war games since Soviet Russia dissolved in 1991," Stephen Lendman pointed out.[76]

In Richard Sakwa's 2014 book, *Frontline Ukraine: Crisis in the Borderlands*, he described a "fateful geographical paradox: that NATO exists to manage the risks created by its existence."

Robert Bridge, an American journalist living in Moscow, wrote in RT:

73   Eric Zuesse, "G7 Boldly Displays Its Lies Regarding Anti-Russia Economic Sanctions," *Global Research,* June 3, 2016.

74   Giraldi, "How the World Ends."

75   Robert Parry, "Ukraine, Through the US Looking Glass, *Consortium News,* April 16, 2014.

76   Stephen Lendman, "Threatening Russia: Reckless US-NATO War Games in Poland," *Global Research,* June 8, 2016.

For those who still aren't convinced that Russia has some serious grounds for concern as the U.S.-led war machine grinds ever closer, let's put the situation into its proper perspective. Let's imagine that the geopolitical chessboard were suddenly flipped and it is Russia that is now busy hatching a 28-member military alliance near America's border, for example, in Latin America. . . . But why stop there? Let's roll the dice and see what Washington's reaction would be if Russia had just dispatched three TU-160 Blackjack bombers to South America to participate in war games with the likes of Cuba, Venezuela and Brazil, for example, just weeks after Moscow dropped a missile defense system—which could go offensive with the flick of a switch—in, say, Colombia. Yikes! I dare say there's not a straitjacket in the world that could restrain the writhing neocon convulsions that would break out across the Beltway.[77]

Does anyone believe that neocons and many others in Washington, if convinced that Russia was getting ready to launch a nuclear attack on America, would not argue that we should strike first? Can anyone be certain that this not what the Kremlin will do, if we continue to threaten and humiliate Russia?

Dick Cheney famously said that, if there is even a 1% chance that something truly awful will happen, one should act as if it were a certainty.[78] This doctrine should be applied to the possibility that America's aggressiveness towards Russia might result in nuclear holocaust that might bring about the end of human life. "But the neocons," said Parry, "apparently think the risks are well worth it." This is, as he observes, madness. But what is particularly shocking, he added, "is how virtually everyone in U.S. officialdom and across the mainstream media spectrum has bought into this madness."[79]

---

77   Robert Bridge, "With NATO Knocking, It's Time for Russian Military Games in Latin America," *RT,* June 4, 2016.

78   See Ron Suskind, *The One Percent Solution: Deep Inside America's Pursuit of Its Enemies since 9/11* (Simon & Schuster, 2006).

79   Parry, "What Neocons Want from Ukraine Crisis."

The Trump Interlude

After Donald Trump beat Hillary Clinton in the 2016 race for the presidency, there was a break from the U.S. attempt to destroy Putin. Trump was a terrible president and did lots of horrible things, including to Russia. But there was at least an absence of any apparent attempt to bring about regime change in Russia.

Yet, as Caitlin Johnstone reported on March 28, 2022, Trump "spent his term pouring weapons into Ukraine, shredding treaties with Russia and escalating cold war tensions with Moscow which helped lead us to where we're at now, and yet liberals spent that whole time calling him a Putin puppet"…it was actually the Trump administration that began the U.S. policy of arming Ukraine in the first place."[80] The Obama administration did provide more than $100 million in security assistance, as well as a significant amount of non-lethal defense and military equipment."[81]

Making sense of this—that Trump was considered a "Putin Puppet" but in reality, he shredded treaties with Russia and increased tensions with Moscow—has been aided by learning that the Russia-Trump collusion narrative was, as Ray McGovern said, "a dirty trick for the ages." McGovern noted:

> Clinton campaign manager Robbie Mook … admitted under oath that prior to the 2016 election Mrs. Clinton personally approved feeding the media a bogus story that Donald Trump had a back channel to Alfa Bank in Moscow.

In addition, "Shawn Henry, the head of the cyber-sleuth firm CrowdStrike, … promoted the fiction of Russian 'hacking,' until he was put under oath," whereupon he admitted that "there is no technical evidence that the DNC emails were hacked by Russia or anyone else." But then "House Intelligence Committee chair Adam Schiff kept Shawn Henry's Dec. 5, 2017, testimony locked up for two and a half years. He was forced to

---

80 Caitlin Johnstone, "Re-Visiting Russiagate in Light of the Ukraine War," *Daily Writings about the End of Illusions* (blog), March 28, 2022.

81 Ryan Browne and Holmes Lybrand, "Fact-checking Trump's claim that Obama gave Ukraine 'pillows and sheets'," *CNN,* September 26, 2019, https://www.cnn.com/2019/09/26/politics/donald-trump-barack-obama-ukraine-military-aid-sheets-pillows-fact-check/index.html

release it on May 7, 2020." McGovern concluded by saying: "A large majority of Americans have been brainwashed to hate Russians."[82]

The Ukraine War of 2021–2022

With the election to the presidency of Joseph Biden, who hired Victoria Nuland to be Under Secretary for Political Affairs, the demonizing of Vladimir Putin resumed.

Writer and journalist Diana Johnstone, an American long living in Paris, wrote such a good two-part essay about this that no summary or paraphrase would do it justice. Johnstone's first essay is called "U.S. Foreign Policy Is a Cruel Sport." She wrote on February 23, 2022, one day before the Russia invasion:

> In the time of the first Queen Elizabeth, British royal circles enjoyed watching fierce dogs torment a captive bear for the fun of it. The bear had done no harm to anyone, but the dogs were trained to provoke the imprisoned beast and goad it into fighting back. Blood flowing from the excited animals delighted the spectators. This cruel practice has long since been banned as inhumane.
>
> And yet today, a version of bear baiting is being practiced every day against whole nations on a gigantic international scale. It is called United States foreign policy. It has become the regular practice of the absurd international sports club called NATO.
>
> United States leaders, secure in their arrogance as "the indispensable nation," have no more respect for other countries than the Elizabethans had for the animals they tormented. The list is long of targets of U.S. bear baiting, but Russia stands out as prime example of constant harassment. And this is no accident. The baiting is deliberately and elaborately planned.[83]

---

82 Ray McGovern, "Lies about Russia Still Matter—a Lot," *Antiwar.com,* June 7, 2022.

83 Diana Johnstone, "US Foreign Policy Is a Cruel Sport," *Consortium News,* February 23, 2022.

As evidence, Johnstone called attention to a 2019 report by the RAND corporation entitled "Extending Russia." The RAND corporation is hired to figure out ways to lure other nations into troubles U.S. leaders hope to exploit.

The U.S. argues publicly that the Kremlin threatens Europe by its aggressive expansionism. But when the strategists talk among themselves, they talk about using sanctions, propaganda, and other measures to provoke Russia into taking these steps that America can then exploit to Russia's detriment. One effect might be to cause "the regime to lose domestic and/or international prestige and influence." Johnstone pointed out that this describes the operation in Ukraine: "advancing a hostile military alliance onto its doorstep, while describing Russia's totally predictable reactions as gratuitous aggression."

"Diplomacy," Johnstone added, "involves understanding the position of the other party. But verbal bear-baiting requires total refusal to understand the other." She commented:

> For a generation, Russian leaders have made extraordinary efforts to build a peaceful partnership with "the West," institutionalized as the European Union and above all, NATO. They truly believed that the end of the artificial Cold War could produce a peace-loving European neighborhood. But arrogant United States leaders, despite contrary advice from their best experts, rejected treating Russia as the great nation it is, and preferred to treat it as the harassed bear in a circus.

Eventually, Russia realized that the West would accept it only as an adversary. But it still advocated the 2015 Minsk II agreement, which was endorsed by a UN Security Council resolution.

The Minsk agreement set out a few steps to end the Ukrainian crisis, which was caused by the 2014 Maidan coup, which got rid of the president for whom the Russian-speaking Ukrainians had voted and which threatened to outlaw the Russian language.[84] The Minsk

---

84 It was not simply the language. As Sonja van den Ende pointed out: "All their values, norms, culture and language had to be thrown overboard," U.S. Media Are Lying About Russian Atrocities in Mariupol," *CovertAction Magazine,* April 23, 2022.

agreement called for local elections on self-governance in the eastern Russian-speaking regions of Donetsk and Lugansk, to be held under the supervision of the OSCE (Organization for Security and Co-operation in Europe), with these regions to remain within the state borders of Ukraine, and with reform of the Ukrainian constitution to include provisions on decentralization. A general amnesty was to be granted to soldiers on both sides.

However, although it signed the agreement, Kiev never implemented any of these points and refused to negotiate with the eastern rebels. Having signed on as guarantors of Minsk II, France and Germany were expected to put pressure on Kiev to accept this peaceful settlement, but they did not. In a December 2022 interview with *Der Spigel*, former German Chancellor Angela Merkel revealed that with the Minsk negotiations "she was able to buy the time Ukraine needed to better fend off the Russian attack," whereas before that, "she is certain, it would have been overrun by Putin's troops."[85] In other words, there was no honest intention to implement the agreement by the German government. Later, Francois Hollande similarly confirmed that intent on the part of France. Effectively, from the Russian perspective, this put the viability of good faith negotiations with NATO countries in doubt.

Furthermore, Diana Johnstone wrote,

> Kiev officials regularly reiterate their refusal to negotiate with the rebels, while demanding more and more weaponry from NATO powers in order to deal with the problem in their own way.[86]

The second part of Diana Johnstone's essay was entitled, "For Washington, War Never Ends." In WWII, "the Russian war and the American war were very, very different," she explained:

> For Russians, the war was an experience of massive suffering, grief and destruction. The Nazi invasion of the Soviet Union was utterly ruthless, propelled by a racist ideology of contempt

---

85   Alexander Osang, "A Year with Ex-Chancellor Angela Merkel, *Spiegel International,* December 1, 2022.

86   Diana Johnstone, op. cit.

for the Slavs and hatred of "Jewish Bolsheviks." An estimated 27 million died, about two thirds of them civilians. . . . This gigantic struggle to drive the German invaders from their soil is known to Russians as the Great Patriotic War.[87]

America's World War II was very different:

It enabled the United States to emerge as the richest and most powerful nation on earth. . . . Military Keynesianism emerged as the key to prosperity. The Military-Industrial Complex was born. To continue providing Pentagon contracts to every congressional constituency and guaranteed profits to Wall Street investors, it needed a new enemy. The Communist scare—the very same scare that had contributed to creating fascism—did the trick.[88]

What happened next, Johnstone wrote, proved that the whole "communist scare" justifying the Cold War had been false. There was no longer any Soviet Union; no more Soviet communism; no Warsaw Pact. NATO no longer had a reason to exist. But in 1999, NATO started bombing Yugoslavia, transforming itself from a defensive to an aggressive military alliance. Yugoslavia had been non-aligned; it threatened nobody. Without justification for self-defense or authorization from the Security Council, the NATO aggression violated international law. The Yugoslavian war made it clear that NATO, under U.S. command, felt it could authorize itself to bomb, invade or destroy any country it chose. With NATO spreading its tentacles, nobody was safe. Libya provided another example.

NATO continued to expand eastward. The encirclement of Russia took a qualitative leap with the 2014 U.S. seizure of Ukraine through the engineering of the Maidan coup.

By the end of 2014, the government of "democratic Ukraine" was largely in the hands of U.S.-approved foreigners.[89] The anti-Russian

---

87 Diana Johnstone, "For Washington, War Never Ends," *Consortium News,* March 16, 2022.

88 Johnstone, "For Washington, War Never Ends."

89 Bohdana Kostyuk, "Foreigners in the Ukraine Government," *Euromaidan Press,*

thrust of this regime-change aroused resistance in the southeastern parts of the country, largely inhabited by ethnic Russians. Shortly after more than 40 protesters were burned alive in Odessa, the provinces of Lugansk and Donetsk moved to secede in resistance to the coup. The U.S.-installed regime in Kiev then launched a war against the provinces that continued for eight years, killing thousands of civilians.

A referendum returned Crimea to Russia. The peaceful return of Crimea was obviously vital to preserve Russia's main naval base at Sebastopol from a threatened NATO takeover. While the population of Crimea had never approved the peninsula's transfer to Ukraine by Nikita Khrushchev in 1954, its 2014 return was accomplished by a democratic vote, without bloodshed. But the West called this an unforgivable aggression. All the while, Russia kept warning that NATO enlargement must not encompass Ukraine, while the West called Kiev's war against Donetsk and Lugansk "Russian aggression."

Putin was asked by Russia's State Duma (Assembly) to stop the genocide in Donetsk and Lugansk. Having tried other options such as Minsk to no avail, Putin regarded the "military operation" in Ukraine as a necessity.

For the Americans, whose strategist Zbigniew Brzezinski boasted of having lured the Russians into the Afghanistan trap (giving them "their Vietnam"), this has been a psychological victory. The Western world is united as never before in hating Putin—even more than against Saddam or Gaddafi, his similarly Hitler-labeled precursors. The Americans rejected any effort to prevent this war, did everything to provoke it, and will extract whatever advantages they can from its continuation.

Diana Johnstone ended her second essay with these words: "The American war aim is not to spare Ukraine, but to ruin Russia. That takes time."[90]

Although Diana Johnstone's two-part essay covered most of the essential points, it may be helpful to draw attention to some issues that have been emphasized by other authors.

December 15, 2014. https://euromaidanpress.com/2014/12/15/foreigners-in-the-ukrainian-government/

90 Johnstone, "For Washington, War Never Ends."

Counternarratives

Who Is Primarily to Blame for the War?

It remains the case, as John Mearsheimer stated in 2014 and repeated in 2022, that the crisis in Ukraine is the West's fault.

Phyllis Bennis, who directs the New Internationalism Project at the Institute for Policy Studies, argued in the journal *Foreign Policy*:

> The illegal Russian invasion of Ukraine is already causing enormous suffering.... As for resolving the conflict, that requires understanding its causes—which has everything to do with when we start the clock. If we start the clock in February 2022, the main problem is Russia's attack on Ukraine. If we start the clock in 1997, however, the main problem is Washington pushing NATO—the Cold War-era military alliance that includes the United States and most of Europe—to expand east, breaking an assurance the U.S. made to Russia after the Cold War.[91]

Bennis's statement about the starting date is necessary in light of American and European television coverage of the war that has assumed that the war started in February of 2022 with the start of Russia's Special Military Operation, and that it was unprovoked. There is no talk about the fact that NATO has been expanding despite its assurances not to do so, that there was a coup in 2014 that led to a Russia-hating regime, and that this regime had been systematically killing Ukrainian Russian-speaking citizens in the Donbass region.

Speaking also to this issue, Noam Chomsky said:

> The Iraq War was totally unprovoked. . . . In contrast, the Russian invasion of Ukraine was most definitely provoked....
> A host of high-level U.S. diplomats and policy analysts have been warning Washington for 30 years that it was reckless and

---

91   Phyllis Bennis, "Respond to Putin's Illegal Invasion of Ukraine with Diplomacy, Not War," *Foreign Policy*, February 25, 2022.

needlessly provocative to ignore Russia's security concerns, particularly its red lines: No NATO membership for Georgia and Ukraine, in Russia's geostrategic heartland.[92]

The issue of who started the war was clearly stated by Richard Ochs in his essay titled, "The United States and Ukraine Started the War—Not Russia." Ochs wrote that after the U.S.-sponsored coup, Ukraine started the war, killing thousands of Russian-speakers and violating the Minsk ceasefire agreements. Then in February of 2022, "Ukraine attacked a kindergarten in Donetsk (as reported by the Organization for Security & Co-operation in Europe [OSCE]), blaming Donbass separatists," and "increased its shelling of Donbass by a factor of 100 within four days." Next, "Donetsk reported intelligence that said that Ukraine planned an invasion of Donbass." Finally, "Russia blocked that with the incursion on February 24."

What exactly happened was more fully explained by Bernard at the Moon of Alabama website:

> When during the winter of 2021 Biden warned of an "imminent Russian invasion" of Ukraine he did not know what Russia's plans were. What he did know was that the Ukraine was planning, with U.S. help, for an all-out attack on the Donbass republics in February 2022. Biden knew that no Russian politician could stand back if that were to happen. When you know on what date a war will start it is of course easy to predict when the response to it will happen.

Starting on February 16 Ukrainian artillery attacks on Donbass increased from a few dozen per day to more than 2,000 per day, as was duly noted and reported by the OSCE special observer mission. It was these artillery preparations for a full-blown attack that pushed Russia into the preemptive operation in Ukraine.[93]

---

92 C.J. Polychroniou, "Noam Chomsky: Propaganda Wars Are Raging as Russia's War on Ukraine Expands," *Truthout,* April 28, 2022.

93 "No, the Ukraine War Has Not Stoked a Global Food Crisis," *Moon of Alabama,* May 21, 2022.

So, whereas Biden publicly portrayed Putin's attack on Ukraine as a terrible thing, that attack was precisely what Biden wanted.

Also showing that NATO provoked the war, British blogger Philip Roddis often included what he called his "most overused map" showing how NATO has been regularly enlarged since its founding, and especially since 1989, after U.S. Secretary State James Baker promised Gorbachev that NATO would move "not one inch" eastward. Roddis also has a hypothetical map showing an alliance involving Mexico, Central America, and Cuba and controlled by Russia or China. Roddis commented that this was something that "Washington would never for a moment tolerate—both Monroe Doctrine and Latin America's bloody history testifies."

In the same vein, CIA and State Department veteran Larry C. Johnson wrote:

> I think Putin's demands are quite reasonable. The problem is that 99% of Americans have no idea of the kind of military provocation that NATO and the U.S. have carried out over the last 7 years. The public was always told the military exercises were "defensive." That simply is not true. . . . I guess Putin could agree to allow U.S. nuclear missile systems in Poland and Romania if Biden agrees to allow comparable Russian systems to be deployed in Cuba, Venezuela and Mexico. When we look at it in those terms we can begin to understand that Putin's demands are not crazy nor unreasonable.[94]

Incidentally, Pope Francis said that NATO's barking at Russia's door may have been the reason for Russia's invasion. He said that "while he might not go as far as saying NATO's presence in nearby countries 'provoked' Moscow, it 'perhaps facilitated' the invasion."[95]

---

94   Larry C. Johnson: "The Ukrainian Army Has Been Defeated. What's Left Is Mop-Up," *Unz Review,* March 21, 2022.

95   Hannah Roberts, "Pope says NATO May Have Caused Russia's Invasion of Ukraine," Politico, May 3, 2022.

Did the U.S. Want to Cancel Nord Stream 2?

In 2011, Russia and Germany opened the first Nord Stream pipeline. Nord Stream 2 was to follow. As Iain Davis said,

> The purpose of Nord Stream pipelines was to enable Russia to sell much cheaper gas to the EU, via Germany, while eliminating both the EU's and Russia's 80% reliance on the precarious Ukrainian pipelines. For obvious reasons, this aim had wide support among other EU member states.[96]

However, said Davis,

> The Nord Stream pipelines were not in the interest of the U.S.... Consequently, its foreign policy objectives were to stop Nord Stream 2 (which would double the pipelines' gas flow to Europe from Russia) and install a Ukrainian government amenable to Washington's demands. If the U.S. could break the EU's blossoming trade relationship with Russia, it would not only secure U.S. dominance over Europe, both in economic and collective defence terms, but would also open up the EU market to the U.S.'s pricier Liquefied Natural Gas (LNG) exports—an added bonus.[97]

In a State Department press briefing on January 27, 2022, Ned Price said: "If Russia invades Ukraine ... Nord Stream 2 will not move forward."

Mike Whitney published an article entitled "The Crisis Is Not about Ukraine. It's about Germany," stating:

> The Ukrainian crisis has nothing to do with Ukraine. It's about Germany and, in particular, a pipeline that connects Germany to Russia called Nord Stream 2. Washington sees the pipeline

---

96 Iain Davis, "Ukraine War! What Is It Good For? The Nationalist Agenda," *OffGuardian,* May 23, 2022.
97 Davis, "Ukraine War! What Is It Good For?"

as a threat to its primacy in Europe and has tried to sabotage the project at every turn.[98]

Whitney explained why:

> The U.S. Foreign Policy establishment is not happy about these developments. They don't want Germany to become more dependent on Russian gas because commerce builds trust and trust leads to the expansion of trade. As relations grow warmer, more trade barriers are lifted, regulations are eased, travel and tourism increase, and a new security architecture evolves. In a world where Germany and Russia are friends and trading partners, there is no need for U.S. military bases, no need for expensive U.S.-made weapons and missile systems, and no need for NATO....
>
> That's where Ukraine comes into the picture. Ukraine is Washington's "weapon of choice" for torpedoing Nord Stream and putting a wedge between Germany and Russia.... Washington needs to create the perception that Russia poses a security threat to Europe. That's the goal. They need to show that Putin is a bloodthirsty aggressor with a hair-trigger temper who cannot be trusted.[99]

At a press conference with President Biden and German Chancellor Olaf Scholz: "Everything was orchestrated to manufacture a 'crisis atmosphere' that Biden used to pressure the chancellor in the direction of U.S. policy."

It worked. Scholz did not certify Nord Stream 2. And to make up for the lost natural gas, Biden "graciously" offered to sell Europe U.S. liquid natural gas.[100] It will be sold, of course, at America's higher

---

98   Mike Whitney, "The Crisis Is Not about Ukraine. It's about Germany," *Unz Review,* February 11, 2022.

99   Whitney, "The Crisis Is Not about Ukraine. It's about Germany."

100 Clifford Krauss, "Europe and the U.S. Make Ambitious Plans to Reduce Reliance on Russian Gas," *The New York Times,* March 25, 2022.

price—3 to 7 times more than they had been paying, Michael Hudson pointed out.[101]

In a piece entitled "How Europe Was Pushed Towards Economic Suicide," Bernard at Moon of Alabama began by saying: "With the active help from Europe's 'leadership' the U.S. is succeeding in ruining Europe." In support of this claim, he quoted economist Michael Hudson, who before the February intervention in Ukraine had said:

> America no longer has the monetary power and seemingly chronic trade and balance-of-payments surplus that enabled it to draw up the world's trade and investment rules in 1944–45. The threat to U.S. dominance is that China, Russia and Mackinder's Eurasian World Island heartland are offering better trade and investment opportunities than are available from the United States with its increasingly desperate demand for sacrifices from its NATO and other allies.
>
> The most glaring example is the U.S. drive to block Germany from authorizing the Nord Stream 2 pipeline to obtain Russian gas for the coming cold weather.... The only way left for U.S. diplomats to block European purchases is to goad Russia into a military response and then claim that avenging this response outweighs any purely national economic interest.... As ... explained in a State Department press briefing on January 27: "If Russia invades Ukraine one way or another Nord Stream 2 will not move forward." The problem is to create a suitably offensive incident and depict Russia as the aggressor.[102]

Michael Hudson expressed a similar view in an article called "America Defeats Germany for the Third Time in a Century." Hudson argued that "preventing European countries, particularly Germany, from developing deeper economic ties with China and Russia is what's really at stake." Pointing out that Biden had been demanding that

---

101 "Sociopath Neocons Sacrifice Ukrainians and Global Poor—Economist Michael Hudson," *Useful Idiots,* April 29, 2022.

102 "How Europe Was Pushed Toward Economic Suicide," *Moon of Alabama,* May 18, 2022.

Germany prevent the Nord Stream 2 pipeline from supplying its industry and housing with low-priced gas and turn to the much higher-priced U.S. suppliers. . . . [T]he most pressing U.S. strategic aim of NATO confrontation with Russia is soaring oil and gas prices. In addition to creating profits and stock-market gains for U.S. companies, higher energy prices will take much of the steam out of the German economy. . . . Will European nationalist leaders . . . ask why their countries should pay for U.S. arms that only put them in danger, pay higher for U.S. LNG and energy, pay more for grain and Russian-produced raw materials, all while losing the option of making export sales and profits on peaceful investment in Russia–and perhaps losing China as well.[103]

Writing for the Saker blog, Jorge Vilches pleaded with Europeans to reverse the policy of reducing the oil from Russia. He wrote:

Europe should already have learned from history books and its generals not to underestimate or discriminate against Russia. Let alone cheat on it repeatedly as Europe has done since the downfall of the former Soviet Union. Yet again, history will not be kind to anyone directly or indirectly involved, including yourselves. Equivalent events took place in Europe not that long ago and winter will not care what was said where or why or by whom. It will just freeze and starve Europeans to death with no mercy. . . . Please do not waste any more precious time with forever failed attempts to find substitutes of any kind. Quite simply it is very easy to prove in a matter of minutes . . . that God Almighty has no adequate oil available for you in large enough quantities anywhere on planet Earth other than Russia, let alone deliverable at refineries and processing plants per your own needs and capabilities. You simply cannot dismiss one full third of your oil supplies in

103 Michael Hudson, "America Defeats Germany for the Third Time in a Century: The MIC, BARE and OGAM Conquer NATO," *Naked Capitalism,* February 28, 2022. https://www.nakedcapitalism.com/2022/02/america-defeats-germany-for-the-third-time-in-a-century-the-mic-bare-and-ogam-conquer-nato.html

one sudden stroke of a pen and assume that nothing important will happen including a very negative direct impact upon the price YOU pay.... Besides, in case you didn't notice, Russia is winning on all fronts, militarily, geopolitically, logistically, socially, economically, and financially. The Ruble is as strong as it cares to be and Russia is the only world power able to self-sustain independently from what happens in the rest of the world. After many years of trying to accommodate your requirements, Russia simply does not care anymore what the West thinks, does, or threatens to do. It can now beat you at any of the three at any time. Your sanctions work against Europe, not Russia.

In late September 2022, the stated American policy of not allowing Russian gas to flow to Europe received a boost when undersea explosions breached the Nord Stream 1 and 2 pipelines. Though no gas was flowing, the pressurized gas contained in them was released into the atmosphere. Western propaganda, of course, sprang into action and blamed Russia, which owns a controlling stake in the pipelines. It could shut them off at will; so why blow them up? Russia claimed to have evidence of U.S. and British involvement, and we can note, per above, that the West has both a strong motive and a stated intent as in Biden's statement at a press conference that "we will bring an end to it,"[104] and the State Department assurance cited above that "...Nord Stream 2 will not move forward."

Then, on February 8, 2023, Pulitzer prize–winning investigative journalist Seymour Hersh published a Substack article detailing U.S. planning and execution of the sabotage, citing an inside source. He reported that some involved in the planning were "dismayed" by Biden's and Under Secretary of State Nuland's public announcements of intent, but that the CIA used these statements as cover for going ahead with the operation without congressional approval.[105] Craig Murray comments thus at Consortium News:

---

104 "President Biden on Nord Stream 2 Pipeline if Russia Invades Ukraine: 'We will bring an end to it,'" C-SPAN, February 7, 2022, video news clip, 3:42. https://www.youtube.com/watch?v=OS4O8rGRLf8

105 Seymour Hersh, "How America Took Out the Nordstream Pipeline," February

For the executive branch to commit what is an act of war without the approval of the legislature is fundamentally unconstitutional. But that is one of those quaint remnants of democracy that the neoliberal elite consensus can quietly sidestep nowadays.[106]

The mainstream media, of course, would have us turn away entirely from the suggestion of American responsibility. Murray continues,

The media line, parroted here relentlessly by the BBC and corporate media, was that the Russians had probably them-selves blown up the pipeline on which they had expended such great resources and three decades of intense diplomatic activity, and which was to be the key to Russia's single most valuable source of income for the next 40 years.

That the U.S. would act unilaterally to destroy a piece of international infrastructure of importance to our ally Germany as well as to our sup-posed adversary, with whom we claim we are not at war, is emblematic of the U.S. attitude toward the rest of the world that is amply illustrated in this book.

Have the U.S. and NATO Used Ukraine Against Russia?

There has been much discussion in the American press about the at-tempts by Ukraine to convince NATO or the U.S. (it is the same thing, because the Supreme Allied Commander of NATO is always a U.S. 4-star general) to provide more lethal aid.

First the Ukrainian president, Volodymyr Zelensky, tried to con-vince NATO to install a no-fly zone, but this request was denied on the grounds that this could lead to air battles with Russia, and this could lead to World War III. Zelensky then asked for fighter planes, but this was also denied on the grounds that it too would be too dangerous.

8, 2023. https://seymourhersh.substack.com/p/how-america-took-out-the-nord-stream

106 Craig Murray, "Sy Hersh and the Way We Live Now," *Consortium News* 28, no. 41 (February 10, 2023).

Near the end of March 2022, when President Biden went to Poland, a senior aide to President Zelensky said officials were "very disappointed" in the outcome of the series of summits among NATO and European Union leaders in Brussels. "We expected more bravery. We expected some bold decisions," Andriy Yermak, Zelensky's chief of staff, told the Washington-based Atlantic Council via live video March 25.

Various other suggestions have been made on how the war could be ended, but as Diana Johnstone has said, "The American war aim is not to spare Ukraine, but to ruin Russia."

In her blog, Daily Writings about the End of Illusions, Caitlin Johnstone alluded on March 6, 2022, to Zbigniew Brzezinski's image of the "grand chessboard."[107] In an essay entitled "Pawn on the Imperial Chessboard," she wrote:

> Zelensky is now raging at NATO powers for refusing to intervene militarily against Russia, apparently having previously been given the impression that the U.S.-centralized empire might risk its very existence defending its dear friends the Ukrainians from an invasion.... It must be hard, the process of learning that you were never actually a valued partner in western civilization's fight for freedom and democracy. That you were always just one more sacrificial pawn on the imperial chessboard.... [A]ll the self-righteous posturing by the western political/media class about the need to pour weapons into Ukraine is not really about saving Ukrainian lives (only negotiating a ceasefire can do that), but about seizing this golden opportunity to hurt Russia's geostrategic interests as much as possible.... [W]eapons can be used to fight a "long, bloody insurgency" ... which costs many more lives, keeps Moscow militarily preoccupied and hemorrhaging money, and ultimately hurts Putin's popularity at home.... That's a whole lot of potential benefit to the U.S. empire just for losing Ukraine. Kind of like sacrificing a pawn to get the queen in chess.[108]

---

107 Zbigniew Brzezinski, *The Grand Chessboard: American Primacy and Its Geostrategic Imperatives* (Basic Books, 1997).

108 Caitlin Johnstone, "Pawn on the Imperial Chessboard," *Daily Writings about the*

The idea that Ukraine is just a pawn on Brzezinski's Grand Chessboard was also expressed by Rick Sterling in a piece posted by Antiwar.com. Sterling concluded:

> As with Afghanistan, the U.S. "didn't push Russia to intervene" but "knowingly increased the probability that they would." The purpose is the same in both cases: to use a pawn to undermine and potentially eliminate a rival. We expect the U.S. will make every effort to prolong the bloodshed and war, to bog down the Russian army and prevent a peaceful settlement. The U.S. goal is just what Joe Biden said: regime change in Moscow.[109]

On March 25, 2022, Caitlin Johnstone wrote an essay entitled "More Evidence that the U.S. Is Trying to Prolong this War." In it, she cited a revelation in the *Washington Post*, which reported:

> Secretary of State Antony Blinken has not attempted any conversations with his counterpart, Russian Foreign Minister Sergei Lavrov, since the start of the conflict, according to U.S. officials, *The Washington Post* reports.

So, said Caitlin Johnstone,

> the U.S. government is continuing its policy of refusing to attempt any high-level diplomatic resolutions to this war despite its public hand-wringing about the horrific violence that's being inflicted upon the people of Ukraine. This revelation fits nicely with a recent report by Bloomberg's Niall Ferguson that sources in the U.S. and UK governments have told him the real goal of western powers in this conflict is not to negotiate peace or end the war quickly, but to prolong it in order "bleed Putin" and achieve regime change in Moscow.[110]

End of Illusions (blog), March 6, 2022.
109 Rick Sterling, "Ukraine Is a Pawn on the Grand Chessboard," *Antiwar.com,* April 25, 2022.
110 Caitlin Johnstone, "More Evidence that the US Is Trying to Prolong this War,"

In a later piece, "They're Just Outright Telling Us that Peace in Ukraine Is Not an Option," Johnstone wrote: "As Chris Hedges recently explained,"

> war is the only path the empire has left open to itself. I've seen some cute kids in my time, but nobody's as adorable as people who think the U.S. pours weapons into foreign nations in order to achieve peace.[111]

Walt Zlotow drew the same conclusion in an essay entitled "Billions in Weapons, Zero Negotiations, Reveal Real U.S. Agenda in Ukraine." Commenting about Defense Secretary Austin's pledge that "[t]he U.S. is ready to move heaven and earth to help Ukraine win the war against Russia," Zlotow observed that Austin's statement "contains no goal of saving Ukrainian lives. That is because saving Ukrainians is not a major focus of U.S. war aims in Ukraine." The pledge to move "heaven and earth" apparently

> includes billions in weaponry, but not a single pair of U.S. boots on the ground. Nor does it include American war planes; even a no-fly zone to counter Russian air superiority. That telegraphs America does not consider the Ukraine war critical to America's national self-interests that risks a single American life. U.S. policy boils down to: Ukraine does the dying; America does the supplying.[112]

Glenn Greenwald agreed, saying:

Daily Writings on the End of Illusions (blog), March 25, 2022; referring to Niall Ferguson, "Putin Misunderstands History. So, Unfortunately, Does the U.S.," *Bloomberg Opinion,* March 21, 2022.

111 Caitlin Johnstone, "They're Just Outright Telling Us that Peace in Ukraine Is Not an Option," *Daily Writings about the End of Illusions* (blog), May 24, 2022.

112 Walt Zlotow, "Billions in Weapons, Zero Negotiations, Reveal Real US Agenda in Ukraine," *Antiwar.com,* April 29, 2022.

[T]he only goal that the U.S. and its allies have when it comes to the war in Ukraine is to keep it dragging on for as long as possible.[113]

As photojournalist Patrick Lancaster said, "NATO seems to be gearing up to keep weapons and ammo flowing to fight to the last Ukrainian."[114]

Were the United States and NATO Seeking Regime Change in Russia?

The idea that the U.S. was seeking regime change in Russia, which Caitlin Johnstone suggested, was given added fuel when President Biden, while speaking in Poland about Putin on March 26, 2022, blurted, "For God's sake, this man cannot remain in power." Ray McGovern called this the Mother of All Faux Pas,[115] probably having in mind the convention that a faux pas is when one mistakenly speaks the truth. The national director of RootsAction.org, Norman Solomon, writing about "Biden's Unhinged Call for Regime Change in Russia," said that "Administrative officials scurried to assert that Biden didn't mean what he said." But, he added, "no amount of trying to 'walk back' his unhinged comment at the end of his speech in front of Warsaw's Royal Castle can change the fact that Biden had called for regime change in Russia." As Solomon added, the *New York Times* asked on March 26 whether "Biden's barbed remark" was "A Slip or a Veiled Threat?" But, said Solomon, whether Biden's comment was a "slip and/or threat," it was "mind-blowingly irresponsible, endangering the survival of humanity on this planet."[116]

---

113 Glenn Greenwald, "Western Dissent from US/NATO Policy on Ukraine is Small, Yet the Censorship Campaign is Extreme," *Glenn Greenwald* (blog), April 13, 2022. https://greenwald.substack.com/

114 Patrick Lancaster reporting from Mariupol region, *Veterans Today,* March 24, 2022.

115 Ray McGovern, "Biden Slips: Calls Openly for Removal of Putin," *Antiwar.com,* March 26, 2022.

116 Norman Solomon, "Biden's Unhinged Call for Regime Change in Russia," *Reader Supported News,* March 29, 2022; Glenn Greenwald, "Western Dissent from US/NATO Policy on Ukraine is Small, Yet the Censorship Campaign is Extreme," *Glenn Greenwald* (blog), April 13, 2022. https://greenwald.substack.com/

Is George Soros Implicated in the Effort to Use Ukraine Against Russia?

According to Veterans Today, billionaire George Soros, "an integral part of the American intelligence agencies," sponsored the Orange Revolution of 2004–05 and the 2014 Euromaidan coup in Ukraine. Soros said: "We need Ukraine as a torpedo in the war with Russia. The fate of the citizens of this country does not concern us at all."

Why did he invest in these projects? To make money. He said: "I'm just making money there. I cannot and will not look at the social consequences of what I do." The George Soros Foundation successfully promoted "'European values and democracy' among young people. The result was a jumping Maidan and the unleashing of genocide in Donbass."

What did Soros get in return? "Experts believe that the international speculator expects to become one of the main beneficiaries of the sale of Ukraine." But the really big prize would be "a new Russia without Putin," because with such a Russia, he could make an enormous amount of money.[117]

Did Ukraine Enable Nazis?

When Putin launched his "special military operation," he said he sought the "demilitarization and denazification of Ukraine." The American media ridiculed this latter goal, saying that Ukraine could hardly harbor Nazis, given that its president, Volodymyr Zelensky, is Jewish. For example, on Fox & Friends, former CIA officer Dan Hoffman said, "it's the height of hypocrisy to call the Ukrainian nation to denazify—their president is Jewish after all." And NPR said, "Putin's language [about denazification] is offensive and factually wrong."

Zelensky's self-identification as Jewish is a recent addition. He was raised in a non-religious family, and as late as 2019 he joked: "The fact that I am Jewish barely makes 20 in my long list of faults." But today, said Max Blumenthal of The Grayzone and Alex Rubenstein, "the

---

117 "George Soros: From All His Projects, He is 'Most Proud' of His Work in Ukraine," *Veterans Today,* April 20, 2022.

president's Jewish background has become an essential public relations tool."

Moreover, although he had begun his presidency with the intention of de-escalating the hostility with Russia, his attempt to do this led to his being threatened by the neo-Nazis, and he ended up collaborating with them.[118]

We can also add the voice of Scott Ritter, who had been the chief weapons inspector in Iraq under President Bill Clinton and had testified that Iraq was not in violation of its obligation to eschew weapons of mass destruction. But his fact-based argument conflicted with the regime-change policies of the Bush-Cheney administration. He fears that fact-based arguments were once again being dismissed in the U.S. mania to destroy Russia, writing that

> NATO expansion has been consistently identified by Russia as an existential threat. The domination of the hate-filled neo-Nazi ideology of the Ukrainian far-right is well documented, up to and including their threat to kill the incumbent president, Volodymyr Zelensky, if he did not do their bidding. And the fact that the former president of Ukraine, Petro Poroshenko, promised to make the Russian-speaking population of the Donbass cower in the basements under the weight of Ukrainian artillery fire is well documented.

But these facts, said Ritter, are inconvenient from the point of view of the American "government, and mainstream media today."[119]

Laura Ruggeri, a former academic who has recently been studying color revolutions, wrote an essay entitled "Is Russia Losing the Information War?," which had some illuminating things to say about Neo-Nazi tendencies. She wrote:

> After the 2014 bloody coup, with the removal of any counterweight, U.S.-NATO influence turned into full control and violent repression of dissent: those who had opposed Maidan

---

118 Alex Rubinstein and Max Blumenthal, "How Zelensky Made Peace with Neo-Nazis," *The Grayzone,* March 4, 2022.

119 Scott Ritter, "Pity the Nation," *Consortium News,* March 7, 2022.

lived in fear—the Odessa massacre being a constant reminder of the fate that would befall anyone who dared to resist the new regime. The promotion of Neo-Nazi tendencies intensified, together with the cult of Nazi collaborationist Stepan Bandera; members of terrorist organizations such as the Azov Battalion and other ultranationalist groups joined the government and the Ukrainian National Guard, the past was erased and history re-written, Soviet monuments were destroyed, Russian-speakers faced daily threats and discrimination, pro-Russian parties and information outlets were banned, and Russophobia was inculcated in children starting from kindergarten. In 2020 alone ultranationalist projects, such as the "Young Banderite Course," the "Banderstadt Festival of Ukrainian Spirit," etc. received almost half of all the funds allocated by the Ukrainian government for children's and youth organizations. Ukrainians who lived in the separatist People's Republics of Donetsk and Lugansk and couldn't be targeted by influence operations were targeted by rockets, bombs, and bullets: these former compatriots had been recast as enemies almost overnight.[120]

The fact that Neo-Nazis have played a prominent role in Ukraine, at least since the violent coup in 2014, is well documented in mainstream articles. The Moon of Alabama website provided a list of 30-some mainstream press stories between 2014 and 2022 in which the Nazi problem in Ukraine was recognized. Here are six:

- "Analysis: U.S. Cozies Up to Kiev Government Including Far Right," *NBC,* March 30, 2014.
- "German TV Shows Nazi Symbols on Helmets of Ukraine Soldiers," *NBC,* September 9, 2014.
- Lev Golinken, "The Reality of Neo-Nazis in Ukraine is Far from Kremlin Propaganda," *The Hill,* November 9, 2017.

---

120 Laura Ruggeri, "Is Russia Losing the Information War?" https://laura-ruggeri.
medium.com/is-russia-losing-the-information-war-79016e0ee32e

- Josh Cohen, "Commentary: Ukraine's Neo-Nazi Problem," *Reuters*, 19 March 2018.

- "Ultranationalism in Ukraine," *The Guardian,* April 11, 2019.

- "Like, Share, Recruit: How a White-Supremacist Militia Uses Facebook to Radicalize and Train New Members," *Time*, January 7, 2021.

As Patrick Lawrence pointed out, prior to the Russian invasion acknowledgements of neo-Nazi prominence in the Ukrainian government and military could be found in mainstream media, but after that time, any such claim was dismissed as pure Russian propaganda:

> Prior to the war, *The [New York] Times* and its pilot fish among the American dailies reported often enough on the neo–Nazi character of the Azov Battalion and other Ukrainian nationalists. Now they never do.[121]

In 2018, the late Stephen F. Cohen, America's recognized expert on Russia, published an essay entitled "America's Collusion with Neo-Nazis." (Although Cohen's essay chronologically belongs in the pre-2022 period, it substantially belongs with the later period.) It began:

> The orthodox American political-media narrative blames "Putin's Russia" alone for the new U.S.-Russian Cold War. Maintaining this (at most) partial truth involves various mainstream media malpractices, among them lack of historical context; reporting based on unverified "facts" and selective sources; editorial bias; and the excluding, even slurring, of proponents of alternative explanatory narratives as "Kremlin apologists" and carriers of "Russian propaganda".... Among the omissions, few realities are more important than the role played by neofascist forces in U.S.-backed, Kiev-governed Ukraine since 2014.... Not even many Americans who follow

---

121 "Patrick Lawrence: The Pathology of Ukrainian Nationalism," *Scheerpost* (blog), February 1, 2023. https://scheerpost.com/2023/02/01/patrick-lawrence-the-pathology-of-ukrainian-nationalism/

international news know the following, for example: That the snipers who killed scores of protestors and policemen on Kiev's Maidan Square in February 2014, thereby triggering a "democratic revolution" that overthrew the elected president, Viktor Yanukovych, and brought to power a virulent anti-Russian, pro-American regime—it was neither democratic nor a revolution, but a violent coup unfolding in the streets with high-level support—were sent not by Yanukovych, as is still widely reported, but instead almost certainly by the neofascist organization Right Sector and its co-conspirators.

Cohen continued his account of what most Americans did not know in 2018 (as remains true today):

> That the pogrom-like burning to death of ethnic Russians and others in Odessa shortly later in 2014 reawakened memories of Nazi extermination squads in Ukraine during World War II has been all but deleted from the American mainstream narrative even though it remains a painful and revelatory experience for many Ukrainians.
>
> That the Azov Battalion of some 3,000 well-armed fighters, which has played a major combat role in the Ukrainian civil war and now is an official component of Kiev's armed forces, is avowedly "partially" pro-Nazi, as evidenced by its regalia, slogans, and programmatic statements, and well-documented as such by several international monitoring organizations.

In 2018, Cohen also reported that "Congressional legislation recently banned Azov from receiving any U.S. military aid," but now, in 2022, Congress is working overtime to send as much money and weapons as possible to Ukraine.

This fact raises the question, as the title of a 2022 article by John Potash asks: "Do Americans Really Want to Support the Neo-Nazi Filled Western Ukrainian Government?" Potash wrote:

> On March 10, Congress passed a $13.6 billion aid package to Ukraine, half of which is being directed by the Pentagon.

Ukraine is presented as some great moral beacon when its government has been acquiescent to the rise of neo-Nazism since a February 2014 coup backed by the Obama/Biden administration. As the battle of Mariupol comes to an end with Russian forces securing the city, reports are coming out of wide-scale atrocities carried out by the neo-Nazi Azov battalion, including firing on civilians. Residents said that members of the battalion were real Nazis who walked around with swastikas and other Nazi symbols clearly visible on them.

Potash followed this report with a suggestion:

Given...the dirty war that western Ukraine's coup regime has waged on its eastern regions for eight years now, Americans should ask their government to cease supporting Ukraine's western government.[122]

A similar account is given by Sonja Van den Ende, the woman from the Netherlands who was embedded with the Russian army in Donetsk. The headline of her account stated, frankly, "U.S. Media Are Lying About Russian Atrocities in Mariupol." The lie in the U.S. propaganda war is that the Russian army had bombed the Donetsk Regional Drama Theater in Mariupol. "On the day of the destruction, March 16, 2022," she said:

[A]ccording to eyewitnesses, there were no bombings, but heavy rocket attacks. Ammunition and explosives from the Ukrainian army and its battalions were stored in the cellars. The Ukrainian army and battalions heard that the Russians were coming and detonated the explosives in the shelters, where many people still took refuge from the ongoing fighting. This is not new for the Ukrainians to perform such deeds, especially the AZOV battalion.

---

122 John Potash, "Do Americans Really Want to Support the Neo-Nazi Filled Western Ukrainian Government?" *CovertAction Magazine*, March 30, 2022.

"So, again," Van den Ende concluded,

> the Western media appear to be lying—blaming Russia for every atrocity in the war without proof, while failing to give any context for how the war started and who is responsible.[123]

Speaking of the fact that the far-right militias, such as the Azov Battalion, are supported by the United States, former high-ranking Swiss military analyst Jacques Baud observed:

> So, the West supported and continued to arm militias that have been guilty of numerous crimes against civilian populations since 2014: rape, torture and massacres.[124]

Adrien Boquet, a French journalist and former military officer, had a three-week humanitarian mission in Ukraine and was the subject of a story entitled "French Volunteer Outraged by Lies of Western Media, Revealed Truth about War Crimes in Ukraine." Describing facts that are hidden by the Western media, he focused especially on the Nazi forces and the resulting war crimes committed by the Ukrainian government. He said: "I was furious! Because what I see and hear on TV and what I saw there on the spot is a huge difference. It's disgusting.... I'm talking about the Azov fighters." He added:

> Azov fighters are everywhere. With neo-Nazi stripes. It shocks me that Europe supplies weapons to neo-Nazis. The symbols of the SS are embroidered everywhere on their uniforms. They do not hide their views. They advertise them. I worked with these people and treated them. They openly say that they are ready to destroy blacks and Jews ... I witnessed how the Ukrainian military shot through the knees of captured

---

123 Sonja Van den Ende, "U.S. Are Lying About Russian Atrocities in Mariupol, Says Embedded Reporter at Ground Zero," *CovertAction Magazine,* April 23, 2022.

124 Jacques Baud, "The Military Situation in The Ukraine." *The Postil Magazine,* April 1, 2022. https://www.thepostil.com/the-military-situation-in-the-ukraine/

Russian soldiers and shot at the head of employees with a rank higher than officer.[125]

Showing that the British and American publics are not very informed about even the best known of the Nazi groups, the London *Telegraph* published a puff-piece about the "Azov wives"—the wives of the fighters with the Azov battalion. The *Telegraph* story of May 15, 2022 failed to mention that the Azov fighters are neo-Nazis and that their wives support their activities. Sputnik News published a story showing a photo of three of the wives, including the wife of Lieutenant Colonel Denis Prokopenko, who was trapped in the bowels of the ruined Azov steel mill in Mariupol. In addition to the photo showing Prokopenko's wife wearing a Swastika t-shirt, another photo shows the three women lined up and giving the Nazi salute.[126]

Israel has even confirmed the CIA's role in supporting Ukraine's Nazism. A May 13, 2022, story in *Israel365 News* reported:

> [As to] Russian President Vladimir Putin's accusation that Ukraine advocated Nazism, the neo-Nazi Azov Battalion seemed proof of his claim. But further research seems to implicate the Central Intelligence Agency (CIA) in establishing and funding the white supremacist paramilitary. Sputnik News, a Russian state-owned news agency that is now inaccessible in the U.S., reported last week that Putin's claims of ties between the U.S. government and the Ukrainian neo-Nazi Azov Battalion were true.
>
> Formed in 2014, the Azov Special Operations Detachment is a right-wing extremist, neo-Nazi, formerly paramilitary, unit of the National Guard of Ukraine, based in Mariupol, in the Azov Sea coastal region.[127]

---

125 "Former French Officer Outraged By Lies of Western Media Revealed Truth about War Crimes In Ukraine." *State of the Nation,* May 19, 2022

126 James Tweedie, "Wife of Azov Commander Hailed in West is Pictured Giving Nazi Salute," *Sputnik News,* May 16, 2022.

127 "Israeli Media confirming CIA Trained Ukrainian Nazi Paramilitary," *Veterans Today,* citing "New Evidence Reveals CIA Trained, Armed Ukrainian Nazi Paramilitary Now Leading the Fight against Russia," *Israel365 News,* May 13, 2022.

Brazilian journalist Pepe Escobar, writing about Mariupol, the Sea of Azov port, noted:

> The NATO narrative is that Azovstal—one of Europe's biggest iron and steel works—was nearly destroyed by the Russian Army and its allied Donetsk forces who "lay siege" to Mariupol. The true story is that the neo-Nazi Azov battalion took scores of Mariupol civilians as human shields since the start of the Russian military operation in Ukraine, and retreated to Azovstal as a last stand.[128]

U.S. television claimed that the Russians were holding civilians at the Azovstal steel plant. But PressTV reported that on April 25, 2022, the Russian Defense Ministry announced that it would "unilaterally stop any hostilities" to allow civilian evacuation, adding that the civilians would be taken "in any direction they have chosen."[129]

In the third week of May, the last neo-Nazis hiding in the Azovstal plant surrendered. Russian military spokesman, Major-General Igor Konashenkov, said that 2,439 Azov Nazis and Ukrainian servicemen had laid down their arms since May 16, and that the entire Azovstal complex was now under control of Russian armed forces.[130]

Pepe Escobar put it this way: the group of "NATO-trained neo-Nazis . . . was either pulverized or forced to surrender like cornered rats."[131]

Remembering the Odessa Massacre

Recalling in 2022 the anniversary of the tragic event of eight years ago, Joe Lauria, the editor-in-chief of Consortium News, wrote:

---

128 Pepe Escobar, "How Mariupol Will Become a Key Hub of Eurasian Integration," *The Cradle,* March 29, 2022.

129 "Russia Announces Ceasefire around Steel Plant in Ukraine's Mariupol to Allow Civilian Evacuation," *Veterans Today,* April 25, 2022.

130 Fabio Giuseppe Carlo Carisio, "Mariupol Freed from the Zelensky's Satanist Nazis," *Gospa News,* May 22, 2022.

131 Pepe Escobar, "Russia Rewrites the Art of Hybrid War," *Unz Review,* May 20, 2022.

Authorities in the Ukrainian port city of Odessa have set a 24-hour curfew from May 1–3 to prevent protests commemorating the burning alive on May 2, 2014, of 48 people who had rejected the U.S.-backed coup in Kiev earlier that year....

On that day eight years ago hooligans and far-right groups deliberately set fire to a labor union building where protestors against the coup had taken refuge. Police did not intervene. Video footage shows at least one police officer and others firing their guns into the building. The crowd is cheering as many of the people trapped inside jumped to their deaths.... Pleas at the time from the United Nations and the European Union for Ukraine to investigate were ignored. This event became the trigger for the uprising in the Donbass. Eight days after the Odessa massacre, coup resisters in the far eastern provinces of Donetsk and Lugansk, bordering on Russia, voted in a referendum to become independent from Ukraine. The U.S.-backed coup government then launched a military attack against the breakaway provinces, which continued for nearly eight years.... It had been a tradition that on May 2, residents of Odessa come to the House of Trade Unions, where the tragedy occurred, to honor the memory of the victims. But this year the Ukrainian authorities decided to prevent any gathering on May 2nd. Everyone who left their home on May 2 would be detained under the terms of the curfew.[132]

Jeremy Kuzmarov wrote this about the Odessa massacre:

Eight years after the massacre, the International Action Center, a New York-based anti-war group founded by former U.S. Attorney General Ramsey Clark, hosted a public commemoration that included testimony from a survivor named Alexey who currently lives in Luhansk in eastern Ukraine.

---

132 Joe Lauria, "Curfew for Anniversary of Odessa Massacre That Sparked Rebellion," April 30, 2022.

Alexey spoke movingly about his friend and comrade, Andrey Brezevsky, who was beaten to death by neo-Nazi thugs with a metal bar after he jumped out of the Trade Unions Building to escape the fire. Brezevsky's mother, after her son's death, lost her teaching position at a local university after being denounced by right-wing groups.

Alexey emphasized that none of the perpetrators of the Odessa massacre was ever punished. In the aftermath of the atrocity, neo-Nazi groups mocked and persecuted the relatives of the victims, like Alexey's mother. The once bright city became "gloomy and sad," Alexey said. The massacre had not happened by accident, but was a "planned act of intimidation" by Ukraine's post-coup government. It was "designed to intimidate the opposition [and] was an act of political terrorism perpetrated by the Ukrainian state targeting unarmed civilians [the victims in the fire were all unarmed]."[133]

Is Funding for the Military-Industrial-Complex a Factor?

Diana Johnstone said in her second essay that, in World War II, "Military Keynesianism emerged as the key to prosperity. The Military-Industrial-Complex was born." Military Keynesianism is the doctrine that the economy needs to be boosted by military spending. Is this a factor in explaining the U.S.'s proxy war against Russia?

Glenn Greenwald, in a piece asking who benefits from U.S. military spending for the Ukraine war, suggests that this may be true.

While it is extremely difficult to isolate any benefit to ordinary American citizens from all of this, it requires no effort to see that there is a tiny group of Americans who do benefit greatly from this massive expenditure of funds. That is the industry of weapons manufacturers. So fortunate are they that the White

---

133 Jeremy Kuzmarov, "'The Once Bright City Became Gloomy and Sad:' Survivor of 2014 Odessa Massacre Reflects Back on Tragedy," *CovertAction Magazine,* May 10, 2022. https://covertactionmagazine.com/2022/05/10/the-once-bright-city-became-gloomy-and-sad-survivor-of-2014-odessa-massacre-reflects-back-on-tragedy/

House has met with them on several occasions to urge them to expand their capacity to produce sophisticated weapons so that the U.S. government can buy them in massive quantities.... [B]y transferring so much military equipment to Ukraine, the U.S. has depleted its own stockpiles, necessitating their replenishment with mass government purchases. One need not be a conspiracy theorist to marvel at the great fortune of this industry, having lost their primary weapons market just eight months ago when the U.S. war in Afghanistan finally ended, only to now be gifted with an even greater and more lucrative opportunity to sell their weapons by virtue of the protracted and always-escalating U.S. role in Ukraine. Raytheon, the primary manufacturer of Javelins along with Lockheed, has been particularly fortunate that its large stockpile, no longer needed for Afghanistan, is now being ordered in larger-than-ever quantities by its former Board member, now running the Pentagon, for shipment to Ukraine. Their stock prices have bulged nicely since the start of the war.[134]

The possible financial fruits of removing Putin from the Russian government are so great that the American government has been willing to spend astronomical amounts in this effort. In May 2022, "Congress passed and President Biden signed a $40 billion aid package for Ukraine much of which goes toward military assistance through September: that's more than $100 million a day."[135]

Has the U.S. Narrative About the Ukraine Been Sold by American Propaganda?

This book presents lots of reasons why people should be sympathetic to Russia's attempt to address the existential crisis created by NATO's move eastward, especially the 2014 coup engineered by the U.S.

---

134 Glenn Greenwald, "Biden Wanted $33B More for Ukraine. Congress Quickly Raised It to $40B. Who Benefits?" *Scheerpost,* May 11, 2022.

135 Ryan Swan, "U.S. Increases Aid to Over $100 Million per Day for Ukraine War: A Critique of the West's Militarized Approach," *CovertAction Magazine,* May 24, 2022.

government. And yet the American and European publics at large "stand with Ukraine" and accept the media's demonization of Russia and Putin. In response, Phillip Roddis wrote:

> I'm struggling for a way to penetrate the mass hypnosis my fellows have succumbed to over Ukraine. This war has been spun—by the most extensive, the most sophisticated and the most multi-dimensional propaganda system in history—as a gallant nation fighting for its freedom against a neighboring tyrant. . . . [The evidence to the contrary]—of U.S. crimes in this century alone . . . of NATO expansion . . . of Ukraine's post 2014 trajectory—scarcely register in the western mindset. . . . [Americans and Europeans have bought] the fact-defying fairy tale of a Washington-led west as a force for good in the world. . . . The emperor is naked but so what? Everyone has packed and gone to La La Land, a finger in each ear as they intone the mantra: Zelensky good, Putin baad.[136]

Caitlin Johnston similarly extolls, while hating, the effectiveness of U.S. propaganda. She admitted:

> Sometimes I can only stop and stare in awe at the power of the U.S. propaganda machine. Almost the entire global north has been paced [sic] into perfect alignment with cold war agendas geared toward securing U.S. unipolar dominance by an unprecedented propaganda and censorship campaign. . . . The human species is being led around like a dog on a leash by a collective mind control system of unparalleled and unprecedented sophistication that hardly anyone even notices. Imperial propaganda is the single most overlooked and underappreciated aspect of our society. . . . If you have a problem with someone highlighting the culpability of the most powerful government on earth in giving rise to this war, it's because imperial propaganda has turned you into a power-worshipping bootlicker. . . . Few people have trouble believing there's

---

136 Phillip Roddis, "Ukraine in La La Land," *Steel City Scribe,* April 23, 2022.

a uniquely evil tyrant in the world. They just have a hard time accepting that it's their own government.[137]

Economist Michael Hudson has a similar view. Writing that NATO and the U.S. have "done a wonderful job of controlling the public relations dimension of this war, making it appear as if somehow other countries are the aggressors, in not letting America exploit them, and making it appear as if Russia is the aggressor in Ukraine."[138]

Ukraine, Zelensky, and the Pandora Papers

President Zelensky's involvement with Neo-Nazis is something the American mainstream press does not like to mention. But another unmentionable is Zelensky's listing in the Pandora Papers. The Pandora Papers is the result of the "largest investigation in journalism history." It "exposes a shadow financial system that benefits the world's most rich and powerful."[139]

The document entitled "Frequently asked questions about the Pandora Papers and ICIJ" states:

> The Pandora Papers is an investigation into the shadowy offshore financial system that reveals the workings of a secret economy that benefits the wealthy and well-connected at the expense of everyone else. . . . The offshore financial system can drain trillions of dollars from treasuries, worsen wealth disparities and protect those who cheat and steal while depriving their victims of recourse. Studies have estimated that the world's ultra-wealthy own the bulk of the $11 trillion realm of offshore companies.[140]

137 Caitlin Johnstone, "The Awesome Power of US Propaganda: Notes from the Edge of the Narrative Matrix," *Daily Writings about the End of Illusions* (blog), March 18, 2022.

138 Benjamin Norton, "Economist Michael Hudson on Decline of Dollar, War Sanctions, Imperialism, Financial Parasitism," *Multipolarista,* May 11, 2022.

139 "Pandora Papers: An ICIJ Investigation," ICIJ [International Consortium of Investigative Journalists], 2021. https://www.icij.org/investigations/pandora-papers/

140 Dean Starkman, Fergus Shiel, Emilia Díaz-Struck, and Hamish Boland-Rudder, "Frequently asked questions about the Pandora Papers and ICIJ," International

The report about Ukraine and President Zelensky said:

> KIEV—Nowhere could the revelations from the Pandora Papers investigation hit harder than in Ukraine. The discovery of offshore accounts strike at the heart of the current government and power structure of a ruling class that rose to power on the promise of fighting corruption, including the television-star-turned-President Volodymyr Zelensky.
>
> The worldwide probe . . . included work by journalists from the Ukrainian media Slidstvo.Info, which connected the shady financial dealings of Zelensky's television production company Studio Kvartal 95 to the Ukrainian oligarch Igor Kolomoisky. Slidstvo found that the laundered money passed through the Cyprus branch of Kolomoisky-owned Privatbank, according to law enforcement officers....
>
> Among the . . . documents of offshore registrars are the names of some of the most powerful figures in Ukraine: Ivan Bakanov, the head of the Security Service of Ukraine, Serhii Shafir, the chief aide to the president, and President Zelensky himself are all there....
>
> For this is a story about the actor and head of Studio Kvartal 95, who played the president in the series and won in real life. Volodymyr Zelensky's successful show business career was created in Ukraine through a hidden financial network of offshore companies.
>
> Nine years ago, the popular Kvartal 95 goes to TV channel 1+1. Their shows and programs are hits on the channel owned by [billionaire] Igor Kolomoisky, who will later support Zelensky and the team not only as entertainers but also as politicians....
>
> According to the Pandora Papers, millions from Kolomoisky went not only to the accounts of Ukrainian companies close to Zelensky and his associates....

Consortium of Investigative Journalists, October 19, 2021. https://www.icij.org/investigations/pandora-papers/frequently-asked-questions-about-the-pandora-papers-and-icij/

Closely related, it was also reported by the *Wall Street Journal* in 2019 that Zelensky has a 3-story mansion, complete with 11 bedrooms and 14 bathrooms, in South Florida.[141]

The U.S. Claim that Russia's Attack on Ukraine Was Unprovoked

U.S. President Biden said Ukraine suffered "an unjustified attack by Russian military forces." Noam Chomsky reported that a Google search for the phrase "unprovoked invasion of Ukraine" returned "about 2,430,000 results" in less than half a second.[142]

But Don Hank and Jeremy Kuzmarov, writing in *CovertAction Magazine* in 2022, said: "Biden's assessment is wrong-headed if we consider that Russia has been repeatedly provoked—over the last eight years." In fact, they headlined their article: "Eyewitness Reports Indicate that Ukrainian Army Fired First Shots in War with Russia."[143]

After the Donbass region, with its two republics (Donetsk and Luhansk), voted for independence from Ukraine, the U.S.-installed Ukrainian government launched an "anti-terrorist" war against the provinces, with the assistance of the neo-Nazi Azov Battalion. In the eight-year war, "the Ukrainian Armed Forces and Azov have used artillery, snipers and assassination teams to systematically butcher more than 5,000 people (another 8,000 were wounded)—mostly civilians—in the Donetsk Peoples Republic," and "an additional 2,000 civilians were killed and 3,365 injured" in the Luhansk People's Republic.[144]

Sometimes the Donetsk and Luhansk provinces are called separatists or independentists. But as Jacques Baud has emphasized, the referendums they held were for "self-determination" or "autonomy."[145]

---

141 "A Three-Story Mansion with a Dock Suited for a Yacht in South Florida," *Wall Street Journal*, May 30, 2019.

142 C.J. Polychroniou, "Noam Chomsky: Propaganda Wars Are Raging as Russia's War on Ukraine Expands," *Truthout,* April 28, 2022, https://truthout.org/articles/noam-chomsky-propaganda-wars-are-raging-as-russias-war-on-ukraine-expands/

143 Don Hank and Jeremy Kuzmarov, "Eyewitness Reports Indicate Ukrainian Army Fired First Shots in War with Russia," *CovertAction Magazine*, February 24, 2022.

144 Steven Starr, "Ukraine & Nukes," *Consortium News,* March 3, 2022.

145 Baud, "The Military Situation in the Ukraine."

Speaking of a March 14 ballistic missile attack on a central main street in the city of Donetsk that killed 21 people and injured nearly 40 more people, Eva Bartlett said she was not surprised by the lack of media coverage: The Ukrainian war crimes do not "suit their narrative, a narrative that erases the eight years of Ukraine's war against the four million people of the Donbass republics, killing at least 14,000 people, to give a modest estimate."

Bartlett cited war crimes investigator Ivan Kopyl, who said the Ukrainian Tochka-U missile, which is used exclusively by the Ukrainian side, had cluster munitions, which are prohibited. Weeks later, another Tochka-U attack with prohibited cluster munitions hit a train station in the city of Kramatorsk killing 57 people, including 5 children, and wounded 109.[146]

Significantly, President Biden claimed that Tochka-U that hit this train station was fired by Russians. But as the website Veterans Today pointed out,

> Russians had stopped using this type of missile, in favor of the more effective and accurate Iskander in 2019. The Tochka-U came from Ukrainian-held territory ("Dobropolia. . . , where the 19th Ukrainian Missile Brigade is based") and, in any case, the serial number (Ш91579) (or in English Sh91579) shows that it was Ukrainian (this serial number "was record-ed in official documents as having been transferred from the USSR to Ukraine in 1991").[147]

Bartlett ended her essay by quoting journalist Roman Kosarev, who said: "Russia isn't starting a war, Russia is ending one."[148]

Again presenting the Russian side of the story was the Dutch woman, Sonja Van den Ende, who visited the republics of Donetsk and

---

146 Eva Bartlett, "They Saw and Heard the Truth—Then Lied About It: Media on Donbass Delegation Omitted Mention of Ukraine's 8Year War on the Autonomous Republics," *Nexus Newsfeed.com,* April 5, 2022.

147 "US/Biden Lied: Tochka that hit Train Station Has Serial Number Tied to Ukraine Only," *Veterans Today,* April 9, 2022; Russell Bentley, "Western Media Engages in a War on Truth," *CovertAction Magazine,* May 16, 2022.

148 Bartlett, "They Saw and Heard the Truth—Then Lied About It."

Luhansk as an embedded reporter with the Russian army. According to Van den Ende,

> Ministries have reported the high number of children killed [by the Ukrainian military] to various organizations, such as UNICEF, Human Rights Watch and Amnesty. But to this day, it hasn't been publicized. These human rights organizations only report if it is in their own interest, that is, if their Western donors instruct them to report on it.[149]

Jeremy Kuzmarov wrote a piece titled "Endowment for Democracy Deletes Records of Funding Projects in Ukraine," arguing that the deletion was necessary to preserve the big lie of an unprovoked Russian invasion. The National Endowment for Democracy (NED) is a CIA offshoot founded in the 1980s. As the late William Blum said, it "often does exactly the opposite of what its name implies." As a CIA offshoot, its assignment, as ProPublica said, "was established by Congress, in effect, to take over the CIA's covert propaganda efforts. But, unlike the CIA, the NED promotes U.S. policy and interests openly."[150]

The archived webpage for NED on February 25, 2022, showed that NED granted $22,294,281 from 2014 to 2022 for operations in Ukraine. But later that day, the webpage showed "No results found." With the Biden administration "intent on preserving the fiction that the Russian invasion/counter-offensive was unprovoked," said Kuzmarov, "censorship and the deletion of records [was] necessary."

Regarding the deleted evidence, *MintPress News* reported in April 2022 that the National Endowment for Democracy (NED) had spent over $22 million on propaganda efforts in Ukraine since 2014.[151]

149 Sonja Van den Ende, "Eye-Witness Report from Donbass: How the War Looks from the Russian Side," *CovertAction Magazine*, April 7, 2022.
150 ProPublica, "The National Endowment for Democracy Responds to Our Burma Nuclear Story—And Our Response," November 24, 2022.
151 "Documents Reveal US Gov't Spent $22M Promoting Anti-Russia Narrative in Ukraine and Abroad," *MintPress News*, April 3, 2022.

Does the Rest of the World Support the U.S. Efforts to Isolate Russia?

The Western media gives one the impression that most of the world agrees with the U.S.-NATO attempt to treat Putin-led Russia as a pariah, criminal state.

Laura Ruggeri, in her previously mentioned essay, argues that this is no surprise, because:

> The U.S. information warfare capability is unparalleled: when it comes to manipulating perceptions, producing an alternate reality and weaponizing minds, the U.S. has no rivals. The U.S. coercive deployment of non-military instruments of power to bolster its hegemony, and attack any state that challenges it, is also undeniable. And that's precisely why Russia was left with no other option than the military one to defend its interests and national security. . . . The U.S. information war arsenal is unmatched because it controls the Internet and its main gatekeepers of content such as Google, Facebook, YouTube, Twitter, Wikipedia. . . . It means the U.S. can exercise control over the noosphere, that "globe-spanning realm of the mind" that RAND in 1999 was already presenting as integral to the American information strategy. . . . Because neither Russia nor China can beat the U.S. in a game where it holds all the cards, the smart thing to do is to leave the gaming table, which is exactly what both powers are doing, each drawing on its specific strengths.[152]

Furthermore, international law professor Daniel Kovalik has written:

> [W]hile the U.S. is attempting to claim that the world is on its side in wanting to isolate Russia, the opposite is actually true. Thus, if one looks at the countries that either voted against, abstained from or simply did not vote at all on the UN General Assembly resolution condemning Russia's

---

152 Laura Ruggeri, "Is Russia Losing the Information War?" Strategic Culture Foundation, March 31, 2022.

actions—(against) Russia, North Korea, Eritrea, Belarus and Syria; (abstaining) China, India, Iran, Iraq, Algeria, Angola, Armenia, Bangladesh, Bolivia, Burundi, Central African Republic, Congo, Cuba, El Salvador, Equatorial Guinea, Kazakhstan, Kyrgyzstan, Laos, Madagascar, Mali, Mongolia, Mozambique, Namibia, Nicaragua, Pakistan, Senegal, South Africa, South Sudan, Sri Lanka, Sudan, Tajikistan, Tanzania, Uganda and Vietnam; (not voting) Azerbaijan, Burkina Faso, Cameroon, Eswatini, Ethiopia, Guinea, Guinea-Bissau, Morocco, Togo, Turkmenistan, Uzbekistan and Venezuela— one sees that countries representing the majority of the world's population and a huge portion of its land mass are not with the U.S. on this.[153]

Princeton Professor Emeritus and former UN Special Rapporteur Richard Falk agrees:

> Russia is more globally supported in the Geopolitical War than is the United States. The Global North controls the discourse prevailing on the most influential media platforms, creating the misleading impression that the whole world, except the outliers, are content with U.S. leadership.[154]

Antiwar.com's John Walsh makes the same point in an essay entitled "On Ukraine, the World Majority Sides With Russia Over U.S."[155] Pepe Escobar stated the point in percentages: "88% of the planet does not align with [Washington]."[156]

---

153 Daniel Kovalik, "Russia's Invasion of Ukraine Signifies the End of an Era of Unipolar American Power," *CovertAction Magazine,* March 24, 2022.

154 Richard Falk, "The Second Level Geopolitical War in Ukraine Takes Over," *CounterPunch,* April 29, 2022.

155 John V. Walsh, "On Ukraine, the World Majority Sides with Russia Over US," *Antiwar.com,* May 15, 2022.

156 Pepe Escobar, "Russia Rewrites the Art of Hybrid War," *Unz Review,* May 20, 2022.

Was the Alleged Massacre at Bucha a False Flag?

On the MSNBC show "Velshi," John Spencer of the Modern War Institute (a research center of the U.S. Military Academy) said he was ready to advocate war with Russia on the basis of Ukrainian claims that Russia had committed war crimes in the Ukrainian city of Bucha. The show's host, Ali Velshi, expressed agreement, saying:

> We are past the point of sanctions and strongly-worded con-demnations and the seizing of oligarchs' megayachts.... The world cannot sit by as Vladimir Putin continues this reign of terror.... Lines have been crossed and war crimes have been committed by Putin that make direct military intervention something NATO now must seriously consider.[157]

Spencer and Velshi both understood that direct military confronta-tion with Russia could lead to nuclear war, but they both thought the risk should be taken. This foolhardiness is amazing.

As for the event that gave rise to this atrocity, the possibility is ig-nored that the dead, and apparently dead, people of Bucha were put there as a false flag incitement to accuse the Russians of atrocities. But as we know about the faked incidents by the misnamed "White Helmets" in Syria,[158] indeed, NATO has a long history of staging false flag incidents. More immediately,

> The Russian Defence Ministry earlier slammed photos and video footage allegedly showing the bodies of civilians scattered around the streets of Bucha as staged by Ukrainian authorities to spread them in the Western media and accuse Russian troops of killing them. The Defence Ministry pointed

---

157 Trent Baker, "MSNBC's Velshi urges 'direct military involvement' from NATO to Stop Russia—'What is the point of these alliances if not to stop this?" *Breitbart,* April 4, 2022. https://www.breitbart.com/clips/2022/04/04/msnbcs-velshi-urges-direct-military-involvement-from-nato-to-stop-russia-what-is-the-point-of-these-alliances-if-not-to-stop-this/

158 "Bucha liberated from Russian invaders – Mayor," *Ukrinform,* April 1, 2022, https://www.ukrinform.net/rubric-ato/3445989-bucha-liberated-from-russian-invaders-mayor.html

out that Russian forces left the city on 30 March and that the town's mayor reported no bodies on the streets when he [smilingly] confirmed their departure the next day. . . . The footage and the photos only emerged four days later, when the Ukrainian Security Service and the media arrived in Bucha, the ministry's statement said.[159]

Scott Ritter reported:

[T]he Russian military said, "we had good relations with the local people. It was peaceful." The Russians said "we traded our dry rations for their dairy products." The citizens of Bucha would give them eggs, milk and cheese, and the Russians would give them dry rations—flour, salt, sugar, meat, etcetera. This was going on, then the Russians left. Anybody who engaged in that type of interaction with the Russians was now viewed as a collaborator.[160]

Interestingly, the Ukrainian police had reported that there was a "clearing Operation" in Bucha a day before the videos of dead bodies went viral.[161] According to Ritter, the Ukrainian national police announced they were going into Bucha "to carry out a cleansing operation to liquidate the collaborators." Ritter added that there was a videotape of

a senior political figure announcing on social media to the citizens of Bucha, "stay in your homes. The national police are carrying out a cleansing operation. Do not panic. Stay in your homes." She repeats it over and over again. Why? Because the police are in the streets, gunning people down, kicking in doors of people who were collaborating, and killing them.

---

159 "Russia Will Demand a UNSC Meeting Over Situation in Bucha After UK's Refusal," *Sputnik News,* April 4, 2022.

160 "Scott Ritter: A Conversation About Ukraine Part 1," *Ed Mays* Youtube video, 58:00, April 6, 2022. "https://www.youtube.com/watch?v=-fNrnWxXhP0

161 "Ukrainian Police Claimed 'Clearing Op' in Bucha a Day Before Videos of Dead Bodies Went Viral," *Sputnik International,* April 4, 2022.

The Ukrainian government said 412 civilians had been killed by the Russians, and the Western media claimed that proof was provided by satellite imagery. Jeremy Kuzmarov pointed out that "[t]he number of bodies in the satellite imagery is only six, however, which is well short of the total of 412 civilians that the Ukrainian government claimed Russian troops had massacred in Bucha."[162]

This was the event for which Biden said Putin should be tried by the World Court. Patrick Lawrence observed: "Joe Biden denounced the Bucha atrocities at 10:30 am Eastern time on April 4, at the very moment word came of them. At that moment he could not possibly have had any knowledge of what had transpired." Yet Biden said of Vladimir Putin:

> Well, the truth of the matter—you saw what happened in Bucha. This warrants him—he is a war criminal.... This guy is brutal. And what's happening in Bucha is outrageous, and everyone's seen it.

It is said that a picture is "worth a thousand words." But quite often one needs a few truthful words to know what the picture actually shows.[163] The *Hindustan Times* encouraged an independent investigation and added that there were "widespread hollow allegations against Moscow while there's evidence that it was in fact a cynical false flag operation, perpetrated by Kiev itself."[164]

Furthermore, researcher Evan Rief wrote a piece for *CovertAction Magazine* asking, "Was Alleged Russian Army Massacre of Civilians at Bucha Actually a False Flag Event Staged by Ukrainian Nazis?" Rief did not claim to have indisputable evidence. But he did have good reason for suspicion: A neo-Nazi Azov commander by the name of Sergey Korotkikh, who was a terrorist and murderer, "was not only among the first Ukrainian forces in the town along with his squad of terrorists, he

---

162 Jeremy Kuzmarov, "Remember the Maine: The Alleged Russian Atrocity at Bucha Looks Like Another in a Long Line of False Pretexts for War," *CovertAction Magazine,* May 13, 2022.

163 Patrick Lawrence, "The Great Acquiescence—Glory to Ukraine," *Consortium News,* April 16, 2022.

164 Rezaul H. Laskar, "'Cynical False Flag Operation by Kyiv': Russia on Bucha Killings, India Calls for a Probe," *Hindustan Times*, April 7, 2022.

was making jokes about shooting civilians as he entered. He would later happily post these videos on his official telegram channel."[165]

Turning to Russia, Moscow asked for the United Nations Security Council to discuss "the Provocation of the Kiev regime in Bucha." But "the British presidency of the UN Security Council did not agree."[166] Russia asked again, and the British refused again.

"We are shocked at the scale and brutality of the staging organized in Bucha in the best traditions of 'white helmet cinema,'" said Dmitry Polyansky, Russia's First Deputy Permanent Representative to the United Nations. "Today's Ukrainian neo-Nazis are completely faithful to Goebbels' old Nazi school of provocations and are trying to shift the blame to Russia."[167] Indeed, Polyansky said, "instructors of the notorious Syria-based White Helmets group have already been deployed to Ukraine."[168] He believed they were brought in to arrange for false flag attacks to accuse Russia of war crimes.[169]

Scott Ritter agreed. On April 5, 2022, Ritter tweeted:

> The Ukrainian National Police committed numerous crimes against humanity in Bucha. Biden, in seeking to shift blame for the Bucha murders, is guilty of aiding and abetting these crimes.

Twitter suspended Ritter for engaging in the prohibited behavior of questioning the claims of Ukrainian authorities that Russian soldiers had massacred civilians in Bucha. When Ritter was asked about this on the Rachel Blevins Show ("Twitter Jail for Questioning the Narrative + the U.S. 'Info War' Against Russia with Scott Ritter"), he pointed out

---

165 Evan Rief, "Was Alleged Russian Army Massacre of Civilians at Bucha Actually a False Flag Event Staged by Ukrainian Nazis?" *CovertAction Magazine,* April 6, 2022.

166 Tim Korso, "Russia Will Demand a UNSC Meeting Over Situation in Bucha After UK's Refusal," *Sputnik News,* April 4, 2022.

167 "Moscow will insist on holding a UN Security Council meeting on Monday over the provocation in Bucha, despite Britain's attempts to refuse to organize the meeting," *Tass,* April 4, 2022.

168 *RT,* April 25, 2022.

169 "White Helmets Instructors Deployed to Ukraine, Moscow claims," *RT,* April 25, 2022.

that while Biden claimed that the Russians were responsible, on April 4, 2022 the Pentagon said that it "can't independently confirm atrocities in Ukraine's Bucha."[170]

Ritter pointed out, furthermore, that if the dead bodies had been left to rot on the street for nearly two weeks, they would be badly bloated and decomposed with black faces and putrid liquid coming out of them— which was not shown in the satellite imagery. Ritter also said evidence that could be extracted from the images showed that the bodies appeared to have been killed within 24–36 hours of their discovery—meaning that they were killed after the Russians withdrew from Bucha.[171]

In any case, the alleged atrocity served the U.S.: On April 28, the House of Representatives approved by a vote of 417–10[172] the Lend-Lease bill allowing the Biden administration to lend or lease defense materials to Ukraine in a manner similar to the program adopted for Britain during World War II. President Biden said the "atrocities that the Russians are engaging in are just beyond the pale."[173]

Jeremy Kuzmarov of *CovertAction Magazine* wrote an article about this episode, the title of which reads "The Alleged Russian Atrocity at Bucha Looks Like Another in a Long Line of False Pretexts for War."[174]

That Bucha was a false flag was confirmed by Adrien Boquet, a journalist and retired military officer in France who was spending three weeks in Ukraine on a humanitarian mission. One lie that he spoke of involved the incident at Bucha which he himself witnessed. Outraged by the lies, he reported that "Bucha was staged. The bodies of the victims were moved from other places and deliberately placed in such a way as to produce a shocking shooting," and added that "a lot of reporters from the U.S. are working in Ukraine, filming the staged scenes."[175]

---

170 "Pentagon can't independently confirm atrocities in Ukraine's Bucha, official says," *Reuters*, April 4, 2009.

171 Kuzmarov, "Remember the Maine."

172 Patricia Zengerle, "U.S. Congress Revives World War Two-era "Lend-Lease" Program for Ukraine," Reuters, April 28, 2022.

173 "Remarks By President Biden at Signing of S. 3522," *The Whitehouse,* May 9, 2022.

174 Jeremy Kuzmarov, "Remember the Maine: The Alleged Russian Atrocity at Bucha Looks Like Another in a Long Line of False Pretexts for War," *CovertAction Magazine,* May 13, 2022.

175 "French Volunteer Outraged by Lies of Western Media, Revealed Truth about War Crimes in Ukraine," *Southfront,* May 12, 2022.

In early August 2022, the world became alarmed by reports of shelling of the Zaporizhzhia nuclear power plant in Ukraine. Each side blamed the other, with the Ukrainians accusing the Russians of "nuclear terror" and of threatening a Chernobyl-like catastrophe tantamount to dropping a nuclear bomb on the country.[176] However, the Russian claim of Ukrainian responsibility was far more credible insofar as Russia had taken over the plant militarily early in the conflict (though Ukrainians continued to operate it). Also, if the Russians wanted to create a nuclear catastrophe, why not attack one of the plants deeper into Ukrainian territory and farther from Russia? While information is sketchy, given the evidence of the willingness of Ukrainian forces to carry out murderous false-flag attacks, possibly including a missile that landed in Poland (see below), it is plausible that this was one such operation. In any case, because the Ukrainians were consistently portrayed as the good guys and the Russians as the bad, many people doubtless retained the idea that the Russians, in addition to their other sins, had heedlessly risked causing another Chernobyl.

Is America Supporting Democracy in Ukraine?

In an essay titled "Risking Nuclear War for a Corrupt, Increasingly Repressive Ukraine," the Cato Institute's Ted Galen Carpenter wrote:

> In addition to lavishing arms on Ukraine, Washington is sharing key military intelligence with Kyiv. The United States is skirting very close to becoming an outright belligerent in an extremely dangerous war. It would be imprudent for U.S. leaders to put America at such risk even if Ukraine were the most splendid, pristine democracy in history. It is utterly irresponsible to do so for an appalling corrupt and increasingly authoritarian country. Yet that is an accurate characterization of today's Ukraine.

Concerning President Zelensky in particular, Carpenter wrote:

---

176 Tim Lister, Yulia Kesaieva, and Tara John, "UN chief condemns 'suicidal' shelling around Ukrainian nuclear plant," *CNN,* August 8, 2022.

Matters have become decidedly worse in a wartime setting. Zelensky promptly used the war as a justification for outlawing 11 opposition parties and combining all national television stations into one platform to ensure a unified message.[177]

In addition, Jeremy Kuzmarov reported in *CovertAction Magazine* that:

Vasily Prozorov, a former officer with the Security Services of Ukraine (SBU), stated soon after his defection to Russia in 2018 that the SBU had been advised by the CIA since 2014. . . . Prozorov's revelations take on extremely ominous implications in light of a report by The Grayzone Project that detailed the SBU's participation in a campaign of assassination, kidnapping and torture overseen by Ukrainian President and Western media darling Volodymyr Zelensky.[178]

In April 2020 Max Blumenthal and Esha Krishnaswamy posted an article called "Zelensky's Hardline Internal Purge," pointing out that Western media have covered up the anti-democratic nature of President Zelensky's administration:

Zelensky and top officials in his administration have sanctioned a campaign of kidnapping, torture, and assassination of local Ukrainian lawmakers accused of collaborating with Russia. . . . With training from the C.I.A. and close coordination with Ukraine's state-backed neo-Nazi paramilitaries, Ukraine's SBU security service has [been] filling its vast archipelago of torture dungeons with political dissidents. . . . While Zelensky spouts bromides about the defense of democracy before worshipful Western audiences, he is using the war

---

177 Ted Galen Carpenter, "Risking Nuclear War for a Corrupt, Increasingly Repressive Ukraine," *Antiwar.com*, April 26, 2022.
178 Jeremy Kuzmarov, "CIA Behind Secret Plots to Kidnap, Torture and Assassinate Ukrainian Dissidents for President Zelensky, says Ukraine Defector," *CovertAction Magazine*, April 25, 2022.

as a theater for enacting a blood-drenched purge of political rivals, dissidents and critics.[179]

After discussing the Zelensky regime's banning of opposition parties, Caitlin Johnstone observed:

> This is the Free World that we are risking nuclear annihilation in order to protect, folks. Are we sure we want to do this? Is this fight really worth risking the life of every terrestrial organism for? It's a question we should all be contemplating very seriously.[180]

What Are the Chances of a Nuclear War?

Ted Galen Carpenter also addressed the danger of nuclear weapons. Concerned that U.S. and European officials were not taking the issue with sufficient seriousness, he wrote that what these officials

> do not seem to comprehend is that Ukraine is a vital Russian security interest, and the Kremlin likely will do whatever is necessary—probably even the use of tactical nuclear weapons—to prevent a defeat. The failure to understand just how important Ukraine is to Russia caused Western leaders to disregard Moscow's warnings over more than a decade against making Kyiv a NATO member or an informal military ally. For the same reason, they seem to be making an even more dangerous blunder by ignoring the Kremlin's latest warnings about dire consequences if NATO uses Ukraine as a pawn in a proxy war against Russia.[181]

As it concerns Russia's use of tactical nuclear weapons in Ukraine, in the decree signed by Putin in 2020, Basic Principles of the Russian

---

179 Max Blumenthal and Esha Krishnaswamy, "Zelensky's Hardline Internal Purge," *Consortium News,* April 20, 2020.

180 Caitlin Johnstone (blog), May 5, 2022.

181 Ted Galen Carpenter, "Ukraine Is a Russian Vital Interest, and Moscow Will Behave Accordingly," *The National Interest,* May 4, 2022.

Federation's State Policy in the Domain of Nuclear Deterrence, the Russian Federation declares its right to use nuclear weapons in either one of two situations: (1) "in response to the use of nuclear weapons and other types of weapons of mass destruction against it and/or its allies"; (2) "in the case of aggression against the Russian Federation with the use of conventional weapons, when the very existence of the state is put under threat."[182]

Focusing not broadly on U.S. and European leaders, as Carpenter did, but on Joe Biden in particular, Caitlin Johnstone affirmed that "Ukraine Alone Makes Biden the Worst U.S. President in a Long Time." The reason is that the war in Ukraine "is a proxy war being waged by one of the world's two top nuclear forces against the world's other top nuclear force," and yet:

> [T]he Biden administration is actually hindering diplomatic efforts to negotiate an end to this war, and it has refused to provide Ukraine with any kind of diplomatic negotiating power regarding the possible rollback of sanctions and other U.S. measures to help secure peace.... This is therefore a war that could very easily result in the death of everyone on earth.... Even if humanity survives this standoff ..., Biden will still have been an unforgivably depraved president for allowing it to get this close.[183]

Edward Curtin has also written about this issue, saying:

> The nuclear weapons are primed and ready to fly. The U.S. insists on its first-strike right to launch them. It openly declares it is seeking the overthrow of the Russian government. Russia says it will use nuclear weapons only if its existence is

---

182 Stated in Fabio Giuseppe Carlo Carisio, "Putin Celebrates the Victory. 'War in Ukraine against Nazis and NATO Plans.' Nuclear Nightmare for NWO," *Gospa News,* May 9, 2022.

183 Caitlin Johnstone, "Ukraine Alone Makes Biden the Worst US President in a Long Time," Daily Writings about the End of Illusions, May 8, 2022. (Johnstone was inspired to write this essay by a tweet from Scott Horton, "Biden's refusal to attempt to negotiate an end to the war in Ukraine is the greatest scandal in American political history.")

threatened, which has become increasingly so because of U.S. provocations over a long time period and its current expanding arming of Ukraine's government and its neo-Nazi forces.[184]

Ray McGovern, commenting on Senate testimony by Director of National Intelligence Avril Haines on the likelihood of nuclear war with Russia, said that her "logic" when analyzed, amounted to this syllogism:

Major Premise: We don't want to end up in WWIII, using nuclear weapons.
Minor Premise: Putin may use them if he perceives that he is losing the war in Ukraine.
Conclusion: Thus the U.S. will do what it takes to make Putin "perceive" he is losing in Ukraine.

McGovern ended his essay with this suggestion: "Reasonable policy-makers would be well advised to change the Conclusion resting beneath those premises in the fateful syllogism depicted above."[185]

Furthermore, the organization to which McGovern belongs, Veteran Intelligence Professionals for Sanity, put out a memorandum for the U.S. president titled "Nuclear Weapons Cannot Be Un-invented." The first five points were:

1. The growing possibility that nuclear weapons might be used, as hostilities in Ukraine continue to escalate, merits your full attention.

2. For almost 77 years, a common awareness of the awesome destructiveness of atomic/nuclear weapons created an (ironically stabilizing) balance of terror called deterrence. Nuclear-armed countries have generally avoided threatening to use nukes against other nuclear-armed countries.

184　Edward Curtin, "It's About Time," *OffGuardian,* May 1, 2022.
185　Ray McGovern, "US Counting on Putin to Signal before Using Nukes," *Antiwar. com,* May 12, 2022.

3. Putin's recent reminders of Russia's nuclear weapons capability can easily fit into the category of deterrence. It
   can also be read as a warning that he is prepared to use
   them in extremis.

4. Extremis? Yes; Putin regards Western interference in
   Ukraine, particularly since the coup d'état in Feb. 2014,
   as an existential threat. In our view, he is determined to rid
   Russia of this threat, and Ukraine is now a must-win for
   Putin. We cannot rule out the possibility that, backed into
   a corner, he might authorize a limited nuclear strike with
   modern missiles that fly many times the speed of sound.

5. Existential threat? Moscow sees U.S. military involvement in Ukraine as precisely the same kind of strategic
   threat President Kennedy saw in Khrushchev's attempt to
   put nuclear missiles in Cuba in violation of the Monroe
   Doctrine. Putin complains that U.S. "ABM" missile sites
   in Romania and Poland can be modified, by simply insert-
   ing an alternate compact disk, to launch missiles against
   Russia's ICBM force.[186]

McGovern and his VIPS fellow members assume that a hot war
between the U.S. and Russia, which would likely become nuclear, is one
that the U.S. thinks should be avoided. But Kevin Barrett, who calls the
neoconservatives "[t]he real rulers of the U.S. empire," wrote that they
are "bent on world conquest."

> A decision has apparently been made behind the scenes to
> fight World War III sooner rather than later, in service to the
> Wolfowitz Doctrine that the U.S. will tolerate no challenges
> to its global hegemony. The neocons have made their position
> clear: They will either rule the planet unilaterally or destroy it.
> That is why the Empire and its vassals are inflicting economic
> devastation on their own people, and the people of the world,

---

186 Veteran Intelligence Professionals for Sanity, "Nuclear Weapons Cannot Be Un-
Invented," *Antiwar.com,* May 1, 2022.

as they frantically mobilize for the biggest and most destructive war in human history.[187]

This, of course, would be madness. But who is to say that the neocons are not mad?

How Easily Could the War Have Been Avoided?

An opinion piece by Zeeshan Aleen for MSNBC cites top analysts who say that it was a careless if not "negligent" gamble not to accede to Putin's demand that Ukraine remain neutral and not join NATO, which would likely have prevented the war. Aleen writes,

> Analysts say it's widely known that Ukraine had no prospect of entering NATO for many years, possibly decades. . . . But by dangling the possibility of Ukraine's NATO membership for years but never fulfilling it, NATO created a scenario that emboldened Ukraine to act tough and buck Russia—without any intention of directly defending Ukraine with its firepower if Moscow decided Ukraine had gone too far. But for the West to offer to compromise on Ukraine's future entry into NATO would have required admitting the limitations of Western power.

Anatol Lieven, senior research fellow on Russia and Europe at the Quincy Institute for Responsible Statecraft, told Aleen, "It was the desire of Western governments not to lose face by compromising with Russia. . . . But it was also the moral cowardice of so many Western commentators and officials and ex-officials who would not come out in public and admit that this [Ukraine joining NATO] was no longer a viable project."

George Beebe, a former director of Russia analysis at the CIA and special adviser on Russia to former Vice President Dick Cheney, offered Aleen this analysis: "The choice that we faced in Ukraine . . . was whether Russia exercised a veto over NATO involvement in Ukraine on the

---

187 Kevin Barrett, "It's the War Mobilization, Stupid!" *Veterans Today,* May 16, 2022.

negotiating table or on the battlefield. And we elected to make sure that the veto was exercised on the battlefield, hoping that either Putin would stay his hand or that the military operation would fail."

The author summarizes: "The West didn't want to set limits on NATO's enlargement and influence or lose face. So what it did was gamble."[188] Gamble, that is, with the lives of countless Ukrainians and with the existence of the nation itself in its then-present form.

Another proposal about how easy it would have been for the war not to happen was provided by Michael Morrissey in an essay called "War Madness." He wrote:

> Germany is especially to blame for ignoring the history that made it possible for Germany even to exist as a state in its current form. It was the primary beneficiary of the 1990 treaty that allowed reunification, on the condition that no foreign troops or nuclear weapons would be deployed in the former East German territory.... Germany should have been the first country to object to this expansion and violation of the spirit, if not the letter, of the agreement that made it possible for it to exist as a whole country again, and even join NATO in a military alliance against the very country, Russia, that had sacrificed so much (27 million lives!) in order to defeat it in its former incarnation as the "Third Reich".... If [Olav] Scholz had [declared] formally that Germany, for one, would never allow Ukraine into NATO, that in itself might well have been enough for Russia to call off the invasion, [as] the NATO charter clearly requires any decision on enlargement to be unanimous.... It could and should have also refused to scuttle its multi-billion-euro Nordstream 2 deal with Russia.[189]

---

188 Zeeshan Aleen, "Russia's Ukraine Invasion May Have Been Preventable," *MSNBC.com,* March 4, 2022.

189 Michael David Morrissey, "War Madness," *Fire Dog* (blog), May 5, 2022, https://morrissey.substack.com/

Why Can't We Debate the Wisdom of Official Policy Toward Ukraine?

We are not allowed to read or listen to programs provided by websites that present the views of Russia, such as Sputnik News and RT.

We are not even allowed to read or hear discussions about this very issue—for example, a podcast by Michael J. Brenner, Professor Emeritus of International Affairs at the University of Pittsburgh and a Fellow of the Center for Transatlantic Relations at SAIS/Johns Hopkins. The podcast was called "American Dissent on Ukraine is Dying in Darkness."[190] In an email, he said he had given up expressing his opinions on the subject. With the subject line "Quittin' Time," Brenner declared one of the main reasons:

> [I]t is manifestly obvious that our society is not capable of conducting an honest, logical, reasonably informed discourse on matters of consequence. Instead, we experience fantasy, fabrication, fatuousness and fulmination.[191]

In a similar vein, Marco Carnelos, a former Italian diplomat, published in *Middle East Eye* an essay titled, "Russia-Ukraine War: In the West's Response, Emotion Has Overcome Reason." Carnelos complained:

> It has all become a dangerous zero-sum game: where Russia appears in its own words to be confronted with a binary choice—win this war or be destroyed, while the West is prepared to settle for nothing less than regime change in Moscow. . . . Every topic is viewed through a prism of black or white; any nuance has been erased. Either you support Ukrainians' heroic struggle against ruthless Russians no matter the costs and the consequences, or you are a Putin stooge.

---

190 Michael J. Brenner, "American Dissent on Ukraine is Dying in Darkness," with Robert Scheer (host), *Scheer Intelligence* [talk show], April 15, 2022.
191 Brenner, *Scheer Intelligence.*

Any questioning of Ukraine's real democratic credentials is considered political blasphemy.[192]

Another example: Alan Macleod of *Mint Press News* posted a piece titled "An Intellectual No-Fly Zone: Online Censorship of Ukraine Dissent Is becoming the New Norm." This article was considered so dangerous that Macleod and *Mint Press News* were told by the the popular online payment company PayPal: "You can no longer use PayPal."

Then PayPal did the same thing with regard to Consortium News. Joe Lauria of Consortium News wrote a major essay about the growing censorship in the West for the PEN International Writers for Peace Committee, which he began by mentioning the PayPal decision: "PayPal does not agree with our news coverage, and very likely especially on Ukraine, and are trying to hurt us financially." Lauria's main point is that "[t]he press must remain free to tell a more complete story" about the causes of the Ukraine war. In discussing these causes, he wrote:

> The first was NATO expansion eastward, despite promises to [then-Soviet president Mikhail] Gorbachev. The other causes were the U.S.-backed coup in 2014, the 8-year civil war against the coup resisters in Donbass, the non-implementation of the Minsk accords, the failure of the West to take seriously Russia's treaty proposals in December for a new security architecture in Europe, and the last cause is the very influential role of neo-Nazis, including the Azov Regiment, which is part of the Ukraine state military. Corporate media reported on the massing of Russian troops at the border in the winter, but not on the 60,000 Ukrainian troops on the Donbass contact line. It was like describing a chess board with only black pieces. All these causes of the war are left out of Western media reporting on Ukraine.

As was stated above, "The problem is to create a suitably offensive incident and depict Russia as the aggressor." Depicting Russia as the

---

192 Marco Carnelos, "Russia-Ukraine War: In the West's Response, Emotion Has Overcome Reason," *Middle East Eye,* April 25, 2022.

aggressor was accomplished by the Western media, primarily by acts of omission. Lauria continues:

> Omitting key causes of the Russian invasion paints a totally different picture of what's happening. It's what Western leaders and media want you to believe. And if a media organization tries to report what's omitted, to give a fuller picture, we now know that Western governments will go after you in violation of every tenet of free speech and press freedom.[193]

Freedom of speech is a matter of concern with regard to social media as well. The resignation of the former CEO of Twitter, Jack Dorsey, led to the publication of a new "crisis misinformation policy" under the new CEO. The new policy statement gave these examples of the kind of content that will violate the policy:

- False coverage or event reporting, or information that mischaracterizes conditions on the ground as a conflict evolves;
- False allegations regarding use of force, incursions on territorial sovereignty, or around the use of weapons;
- Demonstrably false or misleading allegations of war crimes or mass atrocities against specific populations;
- False information regarding international community response, sanctions, defensive actions, or humanitarian operations.

The immediate implications of this were addressed by the website 21st Century Wire:

> Censorship giant Twitter has announced that it will increase its policing of any posts about the war in Ukraine, as it releases a new round of thought speech policies designed to "reduce amplification" of any opinions from persons or independent media outlets which the Big Tech firm considers "untrustworthy" sources.

---

193 Joe Lauria, "West's Free Speech Threatened by Ukraine War," *Consortium News,* May 18, 2022.

In addition, Twitter will be actively shielding its global users from any news sources which it considers to be affiliated with a "Russian state media source," in its attempt to shape public opinion by controlling the conversation on its platform to reflect NATO and western mainstream media's preferred narrative of the conflict.

Critics of Twitter have accused it of systematically suppressing any reporting which depicts Ukrainian war crimes, and promoting any reports which accuse Russia of wrongdoing—a decidedly partisan approach which effectively transforms the platform into an extension of the U.S. and NATO's information warfare military operations.[194]

The fact that PayPal, Twitter, U.S. television and some websites are working with the U.S. Government to support its policies means that business and government are working together—one of the definitions of fascism. President Biden has said that America is defending democracy against non-democratic systems of government. But in his commitment to use Ukraine against Russia, he has resorted to these fascistic measures to keep the press from revealing the full truth about his plan.

What went wrong? In trying to use Ukraine to weaken and even remove Putin, the Biden administration had to distort the truth. It had to pretend that the Maidan coup did not happen, that the post-coup Ukrainian government was not selected by the United States, that this government had not been persecuting and killing Russian-speaking Ukrainians, that many Ukrainians did not in World War II fight for the Germans and that today Ukraine is not heavily influenced by Nazis, that the CIA did not work closely with Nazis, that Zelensky did not outlaw other political parties and imprison rivals, and so on. The true story about Ukraine is so terrible that every effort has been made to try to block every avenue of truth which would enable most Americans to

---

194 News Wire, "Twitter Announces Increased Censorship Over Ukraine," *21st Century Wire,* May 20, 2022. https://21stcenturywire.com/2022/05/20/twitter-announces-increased-censorship-over-ukraine/ [Editor's note: David Ray Griffin concluded his writing on this work before Elon Musk's exposure of massive FBI interference with Twitter.]

see the falsity of Biden's claims. In short, the American government is resorting to fascism to defend democracy.

Caitlin Johnstone discusses another implication of the "fact that both Silicon Valley and the mainstream news media have accepted it as a given that it is their job to manipulate public thought about this war." As a result,

> The Ukrainian government is quickly learning that it can say anything, literally anything about Russia, without any evidence at all, and the western mainstream press will report it as an actual news story.

As the title of a Johnstone article says, "Western Media Run Blatant Atrocity Propaganda for the Ukrainian Government." She continues:

> The latest story making the rounds is a completely unevidenced claim made by a Ukrainian government official that Russians are going around raping Ukrainian babies to death.

This extraordinary story was run by U.S. websites, although the story said that the website "could find no independent evidence for the claim." Caitlin Johnstone complained:

> This is what passes for journalism in the western world today. Reporting completely unfounded allegations against U.S. enemies based solely on assertions by a government official demanding more weapons and sanctions against those enemies.[195]

Within a little over a week *Newsweek* reported that the Ukrainian official responsible for these atrocity stories was fired by the Ukrainian parliament "because of the unevidenced nature of those claims." Johnstone then observed:

---

195 Caitlin Johnstone, "Western Media Run Blatant Atrocity Propaganda for the Ukrainian Government," caitlinjohnstone.com, May 21, 2022.

This latest development shows that even the Ukrainian government is more skeptical of Ukrainian government claims than the western mainstream press.[196]

Did the U.S. Media Whitewash Ukraine?

Canadian photojournalist Eva Bartlett, who has written about Gaza and Syria, has weighed in on the eight-year war on the two autonomous republics of the Donbass region, the Donetsk People's Republic and the Lugansk People's Republic. Writing now from the Donbass where she is similarly bearing witness, Bartlett points out that "whitewashing Ukrainian forces' crimes, unfortunately does achieve its intended effect: duping Western viewers into believing the opposite of reality—that the liberators are the war criminals."[197]

Ted Galen Carpenter brought direct attention to whitewashing in the title of his essay of May 17, 2022: "The News Media's Ukraine Whitewash Grows Worse." His article begins:

> The U.S. news media's treatment of the Ukraine issue has long been characterized by flagrant favoritism. Reports from organizations such as Human Rights Watch, Transparency International, and Freedom House showing that Ukraine's actual conduct differed markedly from its carefully crafted image as a dedicated young democracy received little coverage in the mainstream press.

Carpenter continued:

> That willingness to conceal Ukraine's corruption and authoritarianism has grown even worse since the outbreak of war with Russia. Media coverage moved quickly from ignoring or minimizing inconvenient information about Kyiv's political

---

196 Johnstone, "Ukrainian Official Behind Western Media Reports Of Russian Atrocities Fired By Ukrainian Parliament," *Daily Writings about the End of Illusions* (blog), June 1, 2022.

197 Eva K. Bartlett, "They Saw and Heard the Truth—Then Lied About It: Media on Donbass Delegation Omitted Mention of Ukraine's 8 Year War on the Autonomous Republics."

and economic system to channeling outright Ukrainian propaganda. . . . Contents in the *Washington Post* and the *New York Times*, which set the agenda and tone throughout much of the U.S. news media on any issue, similarly have conveyed a solidly pro-Ukraine perspective. Moreover, there are very few competing accounts in those outlets from Russian news sources or even from American analyses that challenge the dominant narrative.

Giving an example, Carpenter spoke of the Azov battalion:

An especially egregious performance has occurred with respect to the role of the Azov battalion (now the Azov regiment) in Ukraine's defense effort. The Azov battalion was notorious for years before the Russian invasion as a bastion of extreme nationalists and outright Nazis. [Carpenter cites a 2017 article in The Hill by Lev Golinken, "The Reality of Neo-Nazis in Ukraine Is Far from Kremlin Propaganda."] That aspect proved to be more than just a source of embarrassment for Ukraine's supporters when the unit became a crucial player in the battle for the city of Mariupol. The Western (especially U.S.) press sought to portray Ukraine's resistance to the Russian siege as a heroic effort similar to the battle of Stalingrad in World War II. The prominence of the Azov regiment among the defenders certainly should have complicated that media portrayal. Yet most accounts simply focused on the suffering of Mariupol's population, the heartless villainy of the Russian aggressors, and the tenacity of the city's brave defenders. Such accounts typically ignored the presence of Azov fighters among the defenders or failed to disclose their ideological pedigree. A *Washington Post* story, for example, merely described the Azov regiment as "a nationalist outfit."[198]

---

198 Ted Galen Carpenter, "The News Media's Ukraine Whitewash Grows Worse," *Antwar.com,* May 7, 2022.

Sixteen Lies Told by the U.S. Government

In May of 2022, Richard Ochs published an article in *CovertAction Magazine* titled "The 16 Biggest Lies the U.S. Government Tells America about the Ukraine War." Here is the list:

1. "Ukraine is a democracy"
2. "National sovereignty is sacred"
3. "Putin is a war criminal"
4. "The world condemns Russia's invasion"
5. "Putin has threatened to use nuclear weapons"
6. "With his back against the wall, Putin will resort to chemical warfare, just like in Syria"
7. "Putin may resort to biological warfare"
8. "Russia is targeting civilians in Ukraine"
9. "Russia will make false-flag attacks"
10. "If Putin prevails in Ukraine, he will attack NATO countries next"
11. "Russia is threatening nuclear power plants"
12. "Russia's invasion threatens the whole world"
13. "The U.S. has a 'free press' while Russia's news is controlled"
14. "Russia is planning cyber-attacks on the U.S."
15. "Russia is killing children."
16. "Russia may use tactical nuclear weapons."

The article explains why each lie is in fact a lie (although it is true that Russia may resort to nuclear weapons, but only, as explained earlier, in case of nuclear attack or other existential threat).[199]

---

199 Richard Ochs, "The 16 Biggest Lies the U.S. Government Tells America about the Ukraine War," *CovertAction Magazine,* May 18, 2022.

The New York Times *Signaled a Change of Plans*

On May 19, 2022, the editorial board of the *New York Times*, through which "the powers that rule us" can signal a change of plans, did so on May 19. The phrase, "the powers that rule us," was used by Paul Craig Roberts in a piece titled "NY Times Has Abandoned Hope for Victory over Russia." Roberts says that "the powers that rule us have changed the narrative" when the *Times* "abandoned the neoconservative demand for victory over Russia: A decisive military victory for Ukraine over Russia, in which Ukraine regains all the territory Russia has seized since 2014, is not a realistic goal.... Russia remains too strong."[200] Also, "In the eyes of the [*Times*] editorial writers, the war has become a U.S. proxy war against Russia using Ukrainians as cannon fodder—and it is careening out of control."

John Walsh commens on this statement: "This has not become a proxy war; it has always been a proxy war." For the neocons, who follow what Todd Pierce calls Cheneyism (see p. 135), "the goal has always been a proxy war to bring down Russia."[201]

Roberts writes:

> The powers that rule us have used the *New York Times* to open a front against the neoconservatives who control U.S. foreign policy. We will see if the neoconservative warmongers can be brought to heel before they unleash Armageddon.... The powers that rule us have recognized that Washington is unprepared and unfit for a wider war and have ordered the NYT to bring the situation under control.[202]

But it appears the Biden administration ignored the suggestion from the *NYT* editorial board, as two days later Biden signed a $40 billion military aid package to Ukraine. Scott Ritter then pointed out that this was a game-changer—but in the opposite direction:

---

200 Paul Craig Roberts, "The NY Times Has Abandoned the Neocon Demand for Victory over Russia," *Paul Craig Roberts* (blog), May 26, 2022. https://paulcraigroberts. org

201 John V. Walsh, "New York Times Repudiates Drive for 'Decisive Military Victory' in Ukraine, Calls for Peace Negotiations," *Counterpunch,* May 23, 2022.

202 Roberts, "NY Times Has Abandoned."

Russia started the special military operation with a limited number of troops and with clearly stated objectives that were designed to be achieved with this limited number of troops. Today, Russia still has the same number of troops and the same objectives. But instead of going up against the Ukrainian military as it existed at the start of the conflict, it's now going up against a Ukrainian military that is supported by a weapons package that by itself nearly matches the defense budget for Russia in all of one year. I think the defense budget for Russia in 2021 was around $43 billion.. . . [Russia is] still going to be confronted with a hostile Ukraine that is more closely linked to NATO's today than they were when the conflict started.[203]

Ryan Swan wrote that this new amount meant that the U.S. was giving more than $100 million a day for the Ukraine war.[204]

Chris Hedges wrote a concise account of what the U.S. commitment to unchecked militarism means for Americans:

No high speed trains. No universal health care. No viable Covid relief program. No respite from 8.3 percent inflation. No infrastructure programs to repair decaying roads and bridges, which require $41.8 billion to fix the 43,586 structurally deficient bridges, on average 68 years old. No forgiveness of $1.7 trillion in student debt. No addressing income inequality. No program to feed the 17 million children who go to bed each night hungry. No rational gun control or curbing of the epidemic of nihilistic violence and mass shootings. No help for the 100,000 Americans who die each year of drug overdoses. No minimum wage of $15 an hour to counter 44

203 "Russia to Score Major Victories in Donbass, Must Adapt to New NATO Game," *Sputnik News,* May 25, 2022.

204 Ryan Swan, "U.S. Increases Aid to Over $100 Million per Day for Ukraine War: A Critique of the West's Militarized Approach," *CovertAction Magazine,* May 24, 2022.

years of wage stagnation. No respite from gas prices that are projected to hit $6 a gallon.[205]

Hedges added:

> The proposed budget for the Environmental Protection Agency (EPA) is $11.881 billion. Ukraine alone gets more than double that amount. Pandemics and the climate emergency are afterthoughts. War is all that matters. This is a recipe for collective suicide.

Hedges quotes Marjorie Taylor Greene, a conservative Republican congresswoman, who said: "$40 billion dollars but there's no baby formula for American mothers and babies. . . . Stop funding regime change and money laundering scams." Hedges concluded by saying: "Greene is demented, but Raskin and the Democrats peddle their own brand of lunacy. We are going to pay a very steep price for this burlesque."[206]

U.S. Bioweapon Labs in Ukraine

Testifying to the U.S. Senate, Under Secretary of State for Political Affairs Victoria Nuland said on March 8, 2022: "There are biological research laboratories in Ukraine. We are currently concerned that the Russian militants may take control of them. We are working with the Ukrainian side to ensure that the materials of biological research do not fall into the hands of Russian forces."

Prior to Nuland's testimony, said MintPress News, the existence of U.S. bioweapon labs in Ukraine had been labelled "fake news" and a "conspiracy theory." But there were reports validating these stories. One was from journalist Dilyana Gaytandzhieva, who "has spent years investigating U.S.-funded biological laboratories in Eastern Europe." Her reports, said MintPress News, "have proven that Pentagon-funded laboratories have conducted potentially lethal experiments on thousands of soldiers in Ukraine and Georgia." In 2018, she reported "that the U.S. embassy in Tbilisi, Georgia, was complicit in secretive military programs

---

205 Chris Hedges, "The USA: 'No Way Out but War.'"
206 Hedges.

and that Pentagon scientists had transported "frozen human blood and pathogens as diplomatic cargo for a secret U.S. military program."[207]

Some individuals even tried to claim that the story that Nuland admitted that the U.S. has biolabs in Ukraine was a fake. For example, VoxUkraine said that its VoxCheck Team showed that the story is not true because the quotation from Nuland was taken out of context.[208] And "[d]espite Nuland's confirmation, Biden Administration officials continue[d] to insist the claims are false."

But then a second validation came from former soldier, Congresswoman, and presidential candidate Tulsi Gabbard, who said: "there are 25+ U.S.-funded biolabs in Ukraine which if breached would release and spread deadly pathogens to U.S./world" and therefore must be secured in order to prevent new pandemics.[209] Republican Senator Romney accused Gabbard of "parroting false Russian propaganda," suggesting that her "treasonous lies may well cost lives."[210]

On March 8, 2022, the website National Pulse published an article from June 18, 2010 entitled "Biolab Opens in Ukraine." It said that "former President Barack Obama spearheaded an agreement leading to the construction of biolabs handling 'especially dangerous pathogens' in Ukraine." The story appeared the same day that Victoria Nuland told the Senate about the need to keep the Russians from taking control of the U.S. biological laboratories.

With that background, Pepe Escobar said the U.S. government was in a state of panic, citing a phone call by Secretary of Defense Lloyd Austin to Russian Defense Minister Sergei Shoigu. He said:

> It's now confirmed by one of my top intel sources. The call was a direct consequence of panic. The United States Government (USG) by all means wants to scotch the detailed Russian investigation—and accumulation of evidence—on

---

207 Dan Cohen, "US Admits to Funding Biological Laboratories in Ukraine, with Dilyana Gaytandzhieva," *MintPress News,* March 12, 2022.

208 "FAKE: Victoria Nuland Admitted that US has Biolabs in Ukraine," *VoxUkraine,* March 17, 2022.

209 Ewan Palmer, "Tulsi Gabbard Clarifies Ukraine Bio Labs Remarks after Widespread Outrage," *Newsweek,* March 15, 2022.

210 Ibid.

the U.S. bioweapon labs in Ukraine, as I outlined in my previous column.[211]

In that previous column, Escobar had discussed the results of Chief of Russian Radiation, Chemical, and Biological Protection Force Igor Kirillov's investigation. Describing the results as "astonishing," Escobar summarized the results thus:

> U.S. bioweapon ideologues comprise the leadership of the Democratic Party. By linking with non-governmental biotechnology organizations, using the investment funds of the Clintons, Rockefellers, Soros and Biden, they profited from additional campaign financing—all duly concealed. In parallel, they assembled the legislative basis for financing the bioweapons program directly from the federal budget. COVID-19 vaccine manufacturers Pfizer and Moderna, as well as Merck and [Donald Rumsfeld's] Gilead, were directly involved.
>
> U.S. specialists tested new drugs in the Ukraine biolabs in circumvention of international safety standards. . . . These findings, amply documented, suggest a vast "legitimized" bioweapon racket reaching the highest levels of the American body politic.[212]

Escobar then points out why the Pentagon is in a panic about the U.S./Ukrainian biolabs program: "There's no doubt the Russians plan to thoroughly unmask it for the benefit of world public opinion, starting with a War Crimes Tribunal."[213]

---

211 Pepe Escobar, "Russia Rewrites the Art of Hybrid War," *Unz Review,* May 20, 2022.
212 Escobar, "Russia Rewrites the Art of Hybrid War."
213 Escobar, "Russia Rewrites the Art of Hybrid War."

Indicators of Ukraine's True Situation on the Battlefield

1. The May 19 piece by the editorial board of the *New York Times*, which was titled "NY Times Has Abandoned Hope for Victory over Russia," said that the hope for a "decisive victory" is not realistic, because Russia "remains too strong." Reinforcing that point, the *Washington Post* said that "Moscow has continued to earn about the same amount of money from fossil fuel sales as it did before the invasion."[214]

2. By May the mainstream media had begun to report truthfully about how poorly the Ukrainian forces are doing. The *Washington Post* led the way with an article titled "Ukrainian Volunteer Fighters in the East Feel Abandoned." It stated that "many troops in eastern Ukraine have been surviving on one potato per day and deserting their posts because they feel their leaders have turned their backs on them and they're being sent to certain death." Regarding a particular military company, the *Post* reported that this company by March of 2022 had been reduced from 120 men to 54, and that the experience of this company offered "a rare and more realistic portrait of the conflict and Ukraine's struggle to halt the Russian advance in parts of Donbass."[215]

The *Washington Post* story broke the dam, leading to several other stories explaining how poorly the Ukrainian military was doing. On June 11, the Moon of Alabama website listed several stories that had appeared the previous day. One of these was a *Newsweek* story, "Ukraine's at Risk of Losing War with Russia: Military Official."[216] Another was a *NYT* story, "Shortage of Artillery Ammunition Saps Ukrainian Frontline Morale."[217]

As predicted on the Moon of Alabama website on June 9, the blame game began. On June 10, Biden threw Zelensky under the bus. Biden said that he had warned, in the weeks before the war began on February

---

214 "European Union Agrees to Phase Out Most Russian Oil," *Washington Post*, May 16, 2022.

215 "Ukrainian Volunteer Fighters in the East Feel Abandoned," *Washington Post*, May 27, 2022.

216 Zoe Strozewski, "Ukraine's at Risk of Losing War with Russia: Military Official," *Newsweek*, June 10, 2022.

217 Thomas Gibbons-Neff, Andrew E. Kramer & Natalie Yermak, "Shortage of Artillery Ammunition Saps Ukrainian Frontline Morale," *The New York Times*, June 10, 2022.

24, that Putin was going to attack. "There was no doubt," Biden said. "And Zelensky didn't want to hear it."[218]

3. Complementary to how poorly Ukraine was doing is how well Russia has been doing. An assessment was provided by Scott Ritter on May 30, 2022:

> After more than ninety days of incessant Ukrainian propaganda, echoed mindlessly by a complicit western mainstream media that extolls the battlefield successes of the Ukrainian armed forces and the alleged incompetence of the Russian military, the Russians are on the cusp of achieving the stated goal of its operation, namely the liberation of the newly independent Donbass Republics of Lugansk and Donetsk, which Russia recognized two days before its invasion.[219]

Ritter added that Putin had said that the purpose of the Russian operation was to restore "the DPR and the LPR within the administrative borders of the Donetsk and Lugansk regions, which is enshrined in the constitutions of the republics." Ritter also quoted the head of the Russian armed forces, General Sergei Rudskoy, who said: "The combat capabilities of Ukraine's Armed Forces have been significantly reduced, which allows us, once again, to concentrate our main efforts on achieving the main goal—the liberation of Donbass."[220]

Also good news for Russia was a story by Anatol Lieven, reporting that Russia's centrist elite were becoming more supportive of the war because they sensed that the U.S. was using the conflict to destroy their country.[221]

4. Secretary of Defense Lloyd Austin contacted the Russian Minister of Defense, for the first time since February 18, urging an "immedi-

---

218 Associated Press, "Biden: Zelensky Didn't Want to Hear US Info," June 11, 2022.
219 Scott Ritter, "Phase Three in Ukraine," May 30, 2022.
220 Scott Ritter, "Phase Three in Ukraine," May 30, 2022.
221 Anatol Lieven, "Why Russian Intellectuals Are Hardening Support for War in Ukraine," Responsible Statecraft, June 6, 2022.

ate ceasefire in Ukraine." Austin also "emphasized the importance of maintaining lines of communication." Why would he ask for a ceasefire, asked Moon of Alabama on May 14, if Ukraine was winning the war?— and goes on to cite considerable evidence that the opposite is the case.[222]

5. Kissinger called for negotiations in a speech at Davos in May 2022. As Mike Whitney has explained, the war was hurting America and its allies, and it strengthened its main rival, China, so Kissinger had decided the war should end: "Negotiations need to begin in the next two months before it creates upheavals and tensions that will not be easily overcome.[223] Ukraine had said it would only resume peace talks with Russia if Moscow surrendered the territory it had gained since the invasion started on February 24, which by summer's end would include the entire eastern region contiguous with Crimea. It appears that, just as Biden rejected the attempt by the *New York Times* editorial board to convince him to give up the war, he also rejected Kissinger's more modest attempt proposing giving up some territory. First Biden said he would "not pressure the Ukrainian governmentin in private or public—to make any territorial concessions."[224] But on June 3, Biden acknowledged for the first time "that Ukraine may eventually have to cede land to Russia if it wants to reach a 'negotiated settlement' and end the death and destruction." Biden said he would not tell Kyiv how to proceed, but that it appeared to him "that at some point along the line, there's going to have to be a negotiated settlement here."[225]

6. Biden then published a *NYT* op-ed on May 31 in which he focused on possible negotiations. Dee Knight said that this reflected a new reality:

---

222 "If Ukraine Is Winning Why Is The U.S. Requesting A Ceasefire?" *Moon of Alabama,* May 14, 2022. https://www.moonofalabama.org/2022/05/if-ukraine-is-winning-why-is-the-us-requesting-a-ceasefire.html

223 Mike Whitney, "Kissinger Nails It. For Once," *Global Research,* June 3, 2022.

224 Joseph R. Biden Jr., "What America Will and Will Not Do in Ukraine," *The New York Times*, May 31, 2022.

225 Gerald Celente, "Ukraine May Have to Give Up Some Land in 'Negotiated Settlement,' Biden Says," *Global Research,* June 6, 2022.

As the *Guardian*'s economics editor Larry Elliott wrote on June 2, things are not "going according to plan. On the contrary, things are going very badly indeed." His conclusion is that "sooner or later, a deal will be struck."[226]

Moon of Alabama took a stronger position:

> The professional military and intelligence people know exactly what is up. The Ukraine is already in a very bad situation and from here on it can only get worse. . . . I am sure they are urging . . . for immediate negotiations. . . . It is the White House for which such an outcome is not what it had hoped to achieve.[227]

Dave DeCamp reported on June 11 that according to the Associated Press:

> While there is some sentiment among European leaders for Ukraine to make concessions to Russia to achieve peace, top U.S. and NATO officials are encouraging Ukraine to keep fighting.[228]

Bernard noted on the Moon of Alabama website that White House could not allow a negotiated settlement. He explained:

> It is currently blocking any negotiations because admitting to a loss in Ukraine would give the Republicans more ammunition to damage Biden.[229]

---

226 Dee Knight, "Joe Biden's Saber-Rattling Threatens World War III—with China and Russia," *CovertAction Magazine,* June 8, 2022.

227 "Washington Starts Blame Game Over Defeat In Ukraine," *Moon of Alabama,* June 9, 2022. https://www.moonofalabama.org/2022/06/washington-starts-blame-game-over-defeat-in-ukraine.html

228 Dave DeCamp, "Ukraine Fears It Might Lose Western Support Over 'War Fatigue,'" *Antiwar.com,* June 11, 2022.

229 "Washington Starts Blame Game Over Defeat In Ukraine," op. cit.

It was not clear, at the end of the summer (2022), how Biden could wait until 2024 to engage in negotiations. But that did seem to be the plan.

Despite these indications that the war was not going in Ukraine's favor, the Western media spin continued to be that a Ukraine victory was in sight, or at least was possible, presumably to justify continued billions in aid in the form of military equipment. Thus the mainstream media portrayed the Ukrainian re-taking of the city of Kherson in November 2022 as a turning point, making the headlines for days, with Zelensky proclaiming that it was the beginning of the end of the war, now with a victorious Ukraine. Scott Ritter, however, gave a more sober assessment, calling it a Pyrrhic victory, i.e., one not worth the cost:

> . . . headline grabbing does not translate into battlefield success. At the same time Russia is preserving its most precious resource—its manpower—Ukraine will be squandering thousands more lives to obtain propaganda value from photographs showing the Ukrainian flag raised in Kherson.[230]

It is noteworthy that when public officials—for example, the Chairman of the Joint Chiefs of Staff, General Mark Milley, and a group of progressives in the House—talked or wrote about a negotiated or diplomatic settlement, they were quickly criticized and pressured to walk it back. "The Ukrainians are taking the lead" was official policy. But the stated objective of the Ukrainian government was to recover all territory including Crimea—a completely unrealistic goal. Secretary of Defense Lloyd Austin offered a realistic assessment: "I don't see this war ending anytime soon."[231] Such pessimistic appraisals by military leaders, contrasting with the official pep-talking propaganda, should have been taken seriously considering the Russian intent to deploy some hundreds of thousands of additional troops in the near future.

The policy of leaving fateful decisions up to the Ukrainian leadership was placed in an unsettling light with an incident November 16, when a missile hit a farm in Poland near the border with Ukraine, killing two people. Russia was immediately blamed, and a flurry of high-level

---

230 Scott Ritter Extra, "On Kherson," November 10, 2022. https://www.scottritterextra. com/p/on-kherson

231 PBS News Hour, November 16, 2022.

discussion ensued about whether, since Poland is a NATO member, this should draw NATO directly into the conflict in accordance with the provisions of its collective defense treaty, and more specifically, whether a no-fly zone should be established over Ukraine, despite the fact that this could have led to a nuclear exchange. But the missile was quickly determined to have been of Ukrainian origin, and the official spin was then that it was an anti-aircraft missile fired from Ukraine that went off track.

Zelensky refused to admit that it was not of Russian provenance. Either this was collective delusion on the part of the Ukrainian command structure, or they were persevering in a propaganda line irrespective of the truth. Scott Ritter made the point that a missile intended to shoot down a Russian aircraft would not have been pointed towards Poland in any event, suggesting a false-flag attack intended to bring NATO into the conflict.[232]

Top Ukrainian military leader General Valery Zaluzhny made a noteworthy admission in an interview with the *Economist*:

> I know I can defeat this enemy. But I need resources. I need 300 tanks, 600–700 infantry fighting vehicles, 500 howitzers. Then, I think, it is quite realistic to reach the frontiers on February 23. But I can't do it with two brigades. I get what I get, but less than I need.[233]

A straightforward reading of these remarks is that he believed the war would be lost unless they received a large amount of equipment that was quite unlikely to be forthcoming. Even if he was engaging in hyperbole, it is in strong contrast to contemporaneous reports in the West that "they now have the Russians on the back foot" and the like.

The fact that the U.S. has consistently backed the course of action of the zealously anti-Russian, ultra-nationalist government, even while all indications were that it was a waste of human lives, bolsters the claim that its aim all along was to use Ukraine to weaken Russia as a player on the grand chessboard.

---

232 Scott Ritter, "A False Flag Over Poland?" *Scott Ritter Extra* (blog), Nov. 18, 2022. https://www.scottritterextra.com/p/deab6162-d4d2-4e1c-ade0-68471cc9ec4d

233 "An Interview with General Valery Zaluzhny, Head of Ukraine's Armed Forces," *The Economist*, December 15, 2022.

At the time of this writing, it is impossible to predict with certainty what an end to this war, with its horrible human cost, will look like. But one thing is clear: it was brought about and kept going by America's quest for global hegemony.

To Summarize

Expansion of NATO was, from Russia's perspective, an existential threat, but the West condemned its response as gratuitous aggression.

The encirclement of Russia took a qualitative leap with the 2014 coup in Ukraine, which replaced a Russia-friendly government with a Russia-hating government. The coup was quickly followed by a law stating that Russian was no longer an official language of Ukraine. Also, the Russian-speaking citizens were forbidden to express their values, norms, and culture.

After the coup, Crimea was returned to Russia. The West likes to say that it was Russian aggression, that it "invaded" Crimea. But Russia's navy was already in the naval base at Sebastopol in Crimea. And Crimea as a whole was returned by means of a democratic vote (only roughly 10 per cent of Crimeans wanted to remain with Ukraine).

The war was primarily, as John Mearsheimer said in 2014, the responsibility of the United States. But Kiev was also partly responsible. In 2015, it signed the Minsk II agreement, which said that the Kiev government would grant autonomy (self-government) to the eastern, Russian-speaking regions, Donetsk and Lugansk. But Kiev did not implement the agreement.

In 2014, the anti-Russian regime in Kiev started an eight-year war on the Russian-speaking provinces, killing thousands of civilians—over 14,000. Neo-Nazis spearheaded the killing.

One of the most futile attempts by the American media to hide the truth about Ukraine was to claim that there was no significant presence of neo-Nazis. But their influence was deep and well-documented.

President Zelensky has been treated as a man of the people by American television, indeed, even as a saint who spoke only the gospel truth, such as when he spoke of Russian atrocities. But people might have been less inclined to accept his honesty if they knew more about him—that he is a multi-millionaire, with enough money stashed offshore to be covered by the Pandora Papers, to say nothing of his increasingly dictatorial rule in Ukraine.

Various developments—an op-ed by the *New York Times* editorial board, stories appearing in the mainstream media reporting how poorly the Ukrainian military was doing and how well Russia was doing, indications by Colonel Douglas Macgregor and Henry Kissinger that the war was essentially over, Defense Secretary Austin's call for a ceasefire, the U.S. concern that its bioweapons would be exposed—indicated that further resistance by Ukraine was widely perceived to be of no avail and to be courting disaster. But with both sides determined to fight on and Ukraine being under no pressure from its benefactors to seek a settlement, the killing and destruction nevertheless continued with, to paraphrase Secretary Austin, no end in sight.

16

Conclusion: Facing Up to the True Nature of the American Empire

The desire for an American Empire has existed for long time, virtually from the beginning of the United States of America.[1] But it only achieved hegemonial status as a result of World War II, through which the American Empire replaced the British Empire as the ruling power on the planet, both militarily and economically. This replacement did not just happen spontaneously, but as the result of planning (see Shoup and Minter, *Imperial Brain Trust* 2004).

With the 1988–89 demise of the Soviet Union, The American Empire became the unipower, no longer having to worry about a competing empire having approximately equal power. The 2001 attacks of 9/11 gave the U.S. the perceived right to go after those presumably responsible. People and governments were in general supportive of the U.S.'s "War on terror." But not everyone was convinced.

In Harold Pinter's 2005 Nobel Prize acceptance speech, "Art, Truth & Politics," he said:

> The crimes of the USA have been systematic, constant, vicious, remorseless, but very few have talked about them. You have to hand it to America. It has exercised a quite clinical manipulation of power worldwide while masquerading as a force for universal good. It's a brilliant, even witty, highly successful act of hypnosis.[2]

---

1   David Ray Griffin, *The American Trajectory: Divine or Demonic?* (Clarity Press, 2018).

2   Harold Printer, "Art, Truth & Politics," 2005 Nobel Prize Acceptance Speech.

Since that time, many others have seen through the propaganda and recognized that the United States, far from being the rightful leader of the "international community," is the most dangerous country in the world—the main source of terrorism, the primary threat of impending environmental disaster, which could result in the extinction of human civilization.

Seeing Through the U.S. Unipolar Aspiration

British blogger Phillip Roddis, who like Pinter spoke of hypnosis, wrote:

> I'm struggling for a way to penetrate the mass hypnosis my fellows have succumbed to over Ukraine. This war has been spun—by the most extensive, the most sophisticated and the most multi-dimensional propaganda system in history—as a gallant nation fighting for its freedom against a neighboring tyrant. . . . [Americans and Europeans have bought] the fact-defying fairy tale of a Washington-led west as a force for good in the world.[3]

Australian blogger Caitlin Johnstone has certainly not been convinced that the United States, in spite of its awesome power to propagandize people, is good. She declared:

> The power structure loosely centralized around the United States is without question the single most depraved and destructive on earth. No one else has spent the 21st century waging wars that have killed millions and displaced tens of millions. No one else is circling the planet with military bases and working to destroy any nation on earth which disobeys it. Not Russia. Not China. Nobody.
>   This would after all be the same empire that is currently circling the planet with hundreds of military bases and waging wars which have killed millions and displaced tens of millions

---

3   Phillip Roddis, "Ukraine in La La Land," *Steel City Scribe,* April 23, 2022.

just since the turn of this century. Its sanctions and blockades are starving people to death *en masse* every single day.

It works to destroy any nation which disobeys its dictates by toppling their governments via CIA coups, proxy armies, partial and full-scale invasions, and the most egregious number of election interferences in the entire world, while threatening the entire species with nuclear brinkmanship on multiple fronts.[4]

To promote the American unipolar aspiration is to risk nuclear holocaust. As Noam Chomsky puts it, the issue is *Hegemony or Survival: America's Quest for Global Dominance.*[5] The Ukraine war has made it only too clear that a small but dangerous group of Americans, who are unfortunately now running the country, are willing to risk nuclear war in order to achieve and maintain this global hegemony. These people seem to believe that unless the U.S. controls the whole world, including China and Russia, life is not worth living.

Jeffrey Sachs, Director of the Center for Sustainable Development of Columbia University, sees the war in Ukraine as

the culmination of a 30-year project of the American neoconservative movement. The Biden Administration is packed with the same neocons who championed the U.S. wars of choice. . . . The neocon track record is one of unmitigated disaster, yet Biden has staffed his team with neocons. As a result, Biden is steering Ukraine, the U.S., and the European Union towards yet another geopolitical debacle.[6]

Caitlin Johnstone puts it more bluntly:

---

4 Caitlin Johnstone, "Perhaps the US Should Shut the Fuck Up about Respecting Other Countries' Sovereignty," *Daily Writings about the End of Illusions,* February 22, 2022.

5 Noam Chomsky, *Hegemony or Survival: America's Quest for Global Dominance,* Holt, 2004.

6 Jeffrey Sachs, "Ukraine Is the Latest Neocon Disaster," *JDS* (blog), June 27, 2022. https://www.jeffsachs.org

There's a lot in the news right now but none of it is as important as the fact that we're being shoved toward nuclear war for no good reason by a few idiots who want to rule the world. Again, the real risk of nuclear war is not that any side will deliberately start one but that the explicit agreement in "Mutually Assured Destruction" will be set into motion by a nuke being deployed by accident, miscommunication, miscalculation or malfunction as things escalate. . . . [and just] so we're clear, the U.S. empire is rapidly restructuring the systems people look to for information about the world in order to ensure iron-fisted control over our dominant narratives while it scrambles to subvert its rivals in cold war maneuverings and secure unipolar planetary hegemony.[7]

"The main message of the neocons," said Jeffrey Sachs, "is that the U.S. must predominate in military power in every region of the world and must confront rising regional powers that could someday challenge U.S. global or regional dominance, most importantly Russia and China." But that is precisely the view that led, said Sachs, the Biden administration to such disaster in Ukraine.[8]

Continuing to Aim for a Unipolar World is Unrealistic.

Dani Rodrik, a professor of international economy at Harvard, said:

In truth, other countries would rather live in a world without domination, where smaller states retain a fair degree of autonomy, have good relations with all others, are not forced to choose sides, and do not become collateral damage when major powers fight it out. The sooner U.S. leaders recognise that others do not view America's global ambitions through the same rose-tinted glasses, the better it will be for everyone.[9]

---

7   Caitlin Johnstone, "The Most Joe Biden Thing Ever: Notes from the Edge of the Narrative Matrix," May 4, 2022.

8   Jeffrey Sachs, "Ukraine Is the Latest Neocon Disaster," op. cit.

9   Dani Rodrik, "The Other Side of US Exceptionalism," *Project Syndicate,* June 8, 2022.

In the words of Pepe Escobar, "The era of the unipolar world is over."[10] Arte Moeini elaborates, arguing that the U.S.-led Western bloc, the world's last ideological empire, will ensure its own demise:

> The world looks altogether different than it did in 1991 or even 2001. A United States that has carried out two decades of costly wars and failed nation-building projects in the Middle East, all while China ascended, isn't the self-assured hegemon it was when the Twin Towers came down. It is wishful thinking to believe that the shift to multipolarity—with the rise of China and multiple regional centers of power ending America's global dominance as the sole hegemon—could be stopped militarily. . . . The demise of the Soviet Union eliminated one of the faces of the modern Janus that was the postwar ideological international order. . . . As one form of universalism—liberalism—eliminated its competition for world domination, it paradoxically lifted the mental fog of ideology, permitting the return of particularity—rootedness, locality, community, and civilization. . . . Only in America and within its liberal imperial domain, the ruling class has continued to resist these shifts, using its vast resources to insist on old utopian ideals and demanding still more globalism and homogeneity. . . . [T]he world's last ideological empire has united the non-Western civilizations in resistance. . . . [T]he systemic international trends that have accelerated multipolarity and weakened ideological hegemony show no signs of subsiding. Together they point to the dawn of a new world: a global realignment, away from universalist aspirations and marking the beginning of a post-ideological age. . . . Once the dust of tragedy settles, the Ukraine crisis will be remembered as ideology's last stand, a herald for this coming new world order. America's leaders would be wise to adapt to this new reality, instead of insisting on conducting foreign policy through tired shibboleths and expired ideological constructs.[11]

---

10 Pepe Escobar, "Exile on Main Street: The Sound of the Unipolar World Fading Away," *Information Clearing House,* June 26, 2022.

11 Arte Moeini, Ron Paul Institute, July 8, 2022.

According to Caitlin Johnstone,

> The strongest argument for a multipolar world is that main-
> taining a unipolar one necessarily requires endless violence
> and continually escalating nuclear brinkmanship. It is literally
> unsustainable. There's no valid reason nations can't just get
> along and collaborate toward the greater good of humanity
> without one of them trying to dominate all the others. The
> unipolarist impulse to rule the earth stops this peaceful
> and collaborative world from emerging. There is no "Pax
> Americana." Unipolarism is the opposite of peace.[12]

In another essay, Johnstone added: "It doesn't need to be like this. There's
no reason our planet needs to be dominated by any one single power
structure, especially if doing so means risking complete annihilation."[13]

According to economist Michael Hudson, the new cold war started
by the United States "is a fight to impose rentier-based finance capitalism on the entire world."[14] However, Hudson wrote,

> Empires often follow the course of a Greek tragedy, bringing
> about precisely the fate that they sought to avoid. That cer-
> tainly is the case with the American Empire as it dismantles
> itself in not-so-slow motion. . . . For more than a generation
> the most prominent U.S. diplomats have warned about what
> they thought would represent the ultimate external threat: an
> alliance of Russia and China dominating Eurasia. America's
> economic sanctions and military confrontation has driven
> them together, and is driving other countries into their emerg-
> ing Eurasian orbit. . . . So I am somewhat chagrined as I watch
> the speed at which this U.S.-centred financialised system
> has de-dollarized over the span of just a year or two. . . . I

12 Caitlin Johnstone, "US Interventionism Always Makes Things Worse," *Notes from the Edge of the Narrative Matrix* (blog), April 5, 2022.
13 Caitlin Johnstone, "The Huge Gap between How Serious Nuclear War Is and How Seriously It's Being Taken," March 16, 2022.
14 Benjamin Norton, "Economist Michael Hudson on decline of dollar, sanctions war, imperialism, financial parasitism," *Multipolarista,* May 9, 2022.

thought that de-dollarization would be led by China and Russia moving to take control of their economies to avoid the kind of financial polarization that is imposing austerity on the United States. But U.S. officials are forcing them to overcome whatever hesitancy they had to de-dollarize. . . . A truly new international economic order is emerging. . . . Trump's mode of expression and mannerisms may have been uncouth, but America's neocon gang has much more globally threatening confrontation obsessions.[15]

Concerning the war in Ukraine, Hudson noted,

[Y]ou think the war is all about Ukrainians and NATO fighting Russians, and it's really a war by the United States to use the NATO-Russia conflict as a means of locking in control over its allies and the whole Western world, and in Janet Yellen's words, re-establishing American unipolar power. . . . Because Biden has said again and again, "We've got to destroy Russia because if we destroy Russia, we will cut it off in China, and then we can go against China as our real enemy." So, we've got to cut up the world potentially opposing us, first Russia and then China, maybe India, too. And he's been very explicit in this, so you can imagine where this leaves China and India. India has already said, "Well, look, we're economically linked to Russia. We're going to continue to link."

In contrast to the brave talk about "go[ing] against China as our real enemy," Patrick Lawrence, wrote:

It has been clear since the Biden regime's earliest months that it has no idea how to address China or what a sound China policy would look like. Secretary of State Antony Blinken's calamitous encounter with Chinese counterparts in Alaska in

---

15 Michael Hudson, "The American Empire Self-Destructs," *Michael Hudson* (blog), March 6, 2022. https://michael-hudson.com

March 2021 was the first indication of this, though hardly the last.[16]

Biden's confusion was apparent when he said in Tokyo that the U.S. would intervene militarily if China attempted to take over Taiwan. Biden warned that a Chinese attack on Taiwan would be "similar to what happened in Ukraine." Biden seemed doubly confused. First, America has a one-China policy, so it has no commitment to defend Taiwan. Second, there is no parallel between Ukraine and Taiwan: Ukraine is losing, not winning, the war with Russia, and China can readily take control of Taiwan.

More generally, Alfred McCoy pointed out in June, 2022, that Zbigniew Brzezinski, a devotee of Halford Mackinder's view that "Who rules the World-Island [Eurasia plus Africa] commands the World," had warned that the United States must, in McCoy's words,

> preserve its strategic "perch on the Western periphery" of Eurasia through NATO; it must prevent "the expulsion of America from its offshore bases" along the Pacific littoral; and it must block the rise of "an assertive single entity" in the "middle space" of that vast landmass.[17]

McCoy concludes with Oxford scholar John Darwin that after World War II, Washington achieved its "colossal imperium . . . on an unprecedented scale" by becoming the first power ever to control the strategic axial points "at both ends of Eurasia." But, McCoy continues, the situation has changed. Whereas Brzezinski had said that the United States had to maintain three conditions to keep its empire, two of those conditions have not been maintained, one potentially and the other definitely. "China has, . . . been moving in that region, militarily, politically, and diplomatically, potentially winning over islands that were once an American preserve." In any case, the U.S. has "clearly failed to meet Brzezinski's critical third criteria for the preservation of its global power," because "the rise

16   Patrick Lawrence, "Biden's Taiwan Talk," *Consortium News,* May 31, 2022.
17   Alfred McCoy, "What Difference Does a War Make?: The Geopolitics of the New Cold War." https://www.researchgate.net/publication/361482519_What_Difference_Does_a_War_Make_The_Geopolitics_of_the_New_Cold_War"

of China as 'an assertive single entity' in the pivotal 'middle space' of Eurasia could potentially prove a fatal geopolitical blow to Washington's global ambitions." McCoy concludes by saying:

> In this century as in the last one, the geopolitical struggle over Eurasia has proven to be a relentless affair, one that, in the years to come, will likely contribute both to Beijing's rise and to the ongoing erosion of Washington's once formidable global hegemony.[18]

Concerning the Chinese, Michael Hudson points out that

> ... for them banking and credit is still a public utility. That's the most important sector to be [saved] in China, and that's what makes China so different from the United States. . . . [B]ankers are in charge of China through the Treasury, which is run by party officials that are not seeking to make capital gains for wealthy families but are using finance to build up their industry and infrastructure and make themselves independent of the West, so that America can never do to China what it did [in the Yeltsin era] to Russia.[19]

In an essay titled "Last Tango in Washington?" Michael Brenner writes about the American "blunder of trying to use a Ukraine crisis as the lever to bring down Putin, and Russia with him." Urging us to "[d]im the lights, the party's almost over," Brenner says that "Washington's radical weaponizing of the mechanisms for managing international finance has accelerated the move away from dollar supremacy." He thinks that American leaders have not fully understood the implications of the fact that the "already deeply entrenched Sino-Russian partnership is the key geo-strategic development of the 21st century." Stating the root problem, Brenner says:

---

18 McCoy, "What Difference Does a War Make?"
19 Michael Hudson, "Ukraine 4 Steps On," *Michael Hudson* (blog), May 3, 2022. https://michael-hudson.com/

Collective American self-esteem, belief in being Destiny's child, the ordained No. 1 in the world, has been our society's foundation stone. We have not matured beyond that magical dependence on myth and legend—to our, and the world's, misfortune.[20]

Reflecting on the U.S. blunders, George Galloway demanded: "Are We Ruled by Idiots?" That was answered by Joe Lauria of Consortium News. In a response similar to that of Michael Hudson, Lauria said, in paraphrase, that the U.S. and NATO are still living in a world in which they determine things; they have not yet adjusted to the new realities.[21]

NATO's declaration at the late-June NATO summit in Madrid indicated it had not adjusted to the new realities either. While a *NYT* report on the final document of the summit said NATO regards Russia as "the most significant and direct threat to our security," the document, for the first time, "also describes China as a direct challenge to the defensive alliance, which was first created after World War II as a bulwark against Soviet aggression."[22]

In response, the Chinese mission accused NATO of "provoking confrontation." It added that, whereas NATO said that "other countries pose challenges," in reality it is NATO that is creating problems around the world.

In an opinion piece in the journal *Foreign Policy*, Angela Stent points out that Russia has in no way made itself into a pariah in the world through its actions in Ukraine, since both China and India have refused to participate in the West's sanctions war, and Russia has strengthened ties in the Middle East, including Israel, and in Africa, which has largely refrained from criticizing Russia.[23] Adding to this China's massive "Belt and Road" initiative, an infrastructure project intended to link with some 150 countries, the idea of a unipolar world centered in Washington looks increasingly divorced from reality.

---

20   Michael Brenner, "Last Tango in Washington?" *Consortium News,* June 16, 2022.

21   George Galloway, "Are We Ruled by Idiots?" *Consortium News,* June 17, 2022.

22   Steven Erlanger and Michael D. Shear, "A More Muscular NATO Emerges as West Confronts Russia and China," *The New York Times*, June 29, 2022.

23   Angela Stent, "The West Versus the Rest: Welcome to the 21st Century's Cold War," *Foreign Policy,* May 2, 2022. https://foreignpolicy.com/2022/05/02/ukraine-russia-war-un-vote-condemn-global-response/

In an article titled "By Making China the Enemy, NATO Is Threatening World Peace," Jonathan Cook writes:

> Washington's greatest fear is that, as its economic muscle atrophies, Europe's vital trading links with China and Russia will see its economic interests—and eventually its ideological loyalties—shift eastwards, rather than stay firmly in the western camp.

For a vision contrasting with the unipolar world-vision of American neocons, one might consult President Putin's speech to the Valdai Discussion Club in Moscow on October 27, 2022, where he criticized the arrogance of Western elites and urged recognition of the new reality of a multipolar world. He appealed to the authentic liberal and pluralistic tradition of the West, in contrast to "the neoliberal model," which imposes a single universal value system upon all. He called for cultural and religious diversity, and concluded by talking about a "symphony of human civilization." If one might further elaborate on Putin's analogy, the French horn section cannot be allowed to turn their bells outward and play louder than everyone else because they think their sound is the best.

Advocacy for a Christian Approach to Foreign Policy

The United States has always claimed to be a Christian nation, though its foreign policy has been anything but Christian, as this book has demonstrated. By adopting what one might term a Christian foreign policy, could the United States begin to address the problems discussed above? The U.S. is rightfully hated and feared, and its present plan to expand its empire is unrealistic. Russia and China are both too powerful to be defeated, especially now that they have formed an alliance. They together constitute the bulk of Mackinder's World-Island.

It must be acknowledged that institutional Christianity throughout its history has generally not been notable for its opposition to despotic regimes; indeed, it has been notorious for working hand in glove with imperialism and colonialism. On the other hand, that Jesus preached an anti-imperialist message has been well established by scholarship.[24]

But what would a genuinely Christian foreign policy be? Obviously, it would be based on Christian principles. At the same time, it must be acknowledged that we live in a pluralistic world where other religions and philosophies are at play. For Christians in America to evaluate their country's foreign and domestic policies in a way that can be received as relevant by peoples of other traditions, both inside and outside the United States, we need to uphold a moral position that, while being Christian, is also shared by peoples of other traditions.

Could the Golden Rule fill the bill? Catholic theologian Hans Küng, who led the way toward the articulation of a global ethic, pointed out that at least most religious and philosophic traditions affirm some version of what Christians have called the Golden Rule:[25]

- Jesus of Nazareth: "So in everything, do to others what you would have them do to you, for this sums up the Law and the Prophets" (Matthew 7:12).

- Islam: "None of you is a believer as long as he does not wish for his brother what he wishes for himself."

- Jainism: "Human beings should ... treat all creatures in the world as they would want to be treated themselves."

The Golden Rule, however, has often been criticized, usually on the grounds that what we like is not necessarily what others would like. For example, George Bernard Shaw famously quipped: "Do not do unto others as you would that they should do unto you. Their tastes may be different."[26] But as Walter Stace countered:

---

24 See Richard A. Horsley, *Jesus and Empire: The Kingdom of God and the New World Disorder* (Minneapolis: Fortress, 2003); David Ray Griffin, John B. Cobb, Richard A. Falk, and Catherine Keller, *The American Empire and the Commonwealth of God*, 140–47.

25 Hans Küng, *A Global Ethic for Global Politics and Economics* (Oxford University Press, 1998).

26 George Bernard Shaw, *Man and Superman* (Archibald Constable & Co., 1903), 227.

Mr. Bernard Shaw's remark "Do not do unto others as you would that they should do unto you. Their tastes may be different" is no doubt a smart saying. But it seems to overlook the fact that "doing as you would be done by" includes taking into account your neighbor's tastes as you would that he should take yours into account. Thus the "golden rule" might still express the essence of a universal morality.[27]

Stace's answer is well taken. However, there is still a problem with using the Golden Rule as a universal ethical principle. It works well within a family and between good friends, and perhaps even within a tiny village. But the Golden Rule cannot provide a moral principle that could be followed in relation to an endless train of strangers and indeed, most of the world. There is also the problem of so doing, *ad infinitum*: There may be no end to the things that some people would like us to do for them.

But these problems may be avoided if the negative formulation of the principle were to be pursued. Sometimes called the Silver Rule, which is widely accepted, it can be seen as implicit in the Golden Rule:

- Judaism: Rabbi Hillel, who probably influenced Jesus, gave this formulation: "That which is hateful to you, do not unto another. This is the whole Torah. The rest is commentary."[28]

- Confucianism: "What you yourself do not want, do not do to another person."[29]

- Buddhism: "Hurt not others in ways that you yourself would find hurtful."[30]

- Hinduism: "One should not behave towards others in a way which is unpleasant for oneself: that is the essence of morality."[31]

- Zoroastrianism: "Whatever is disagreeable to yourself do not do unto others."[32]

---

27   Walter T. Stace, *The Concept of Morals* (MacMillan Company, 1937), 136.
28   Babylonian Talmud , Shabbat folio 31a.
29   Analects of Confucius 15:23.
30   Udana-Varga 5:18.
31   Mahabharata XIII, 114, 8.
32   Shayast-na-Shayast 13:29.

- The Incas: "Do not to another what you would not yourself experience."[33]

This principle is also, as philosopher Simon Blackburn pointed out, contained in virtually every ethical tradition.[34] Here are three examples in Greek philosophy:

- Thales: "Avoid doing what you would blame others for doing."

- Isocrates: "Do not do to others that which angers you when they do it to you."

- Sextus the Pythagorean: "What you do not want to happen to you, do not do it yourself either."[35]

Although an ethical position based on the Golden or Silver Rule might seem at first glance too narrow, all ethical issues can be stated in terms of it. The main point for Christians is that the Golden Rule, understood as containing the Silver Rule, enables the pursuit of a moral principle that is Christian and also universal.

A rights-based approach to morality is especially natural for Americans, since it is rooted in the American Declaration of Independence, which speaks of entitlements founded on "the laws of nature and of nature's God" and says that all people "are endowed by their Creator with certain unalienable rights."

Former UN independent expert Alfred de Zayas formulated 25 principles of international order in his groundbreaking book, *Building a Just World Order*, in which he wrote: "The paramount principle of international order is Peace." He elaborated:

> Peace is not the peace of cemeteries. The United Nations Charter commits all States to promoting *Peace with Justice*. The Preamble and articles 1 and 2 of the Charter stipulate that the principal goal of the Organization is the promotion and maintenance of peace. This entails the prevention of

---

33   Manco Capoc (founder of the Peruvian empire).
34   Simon Blackburn, *Ethics: A Very Short Introduction* Oxford: Oxford University Press), 101.
35   "The Sentences of Sextus -- The Nag Hammadi Library". *www.gnosis.org*.

local, regional and international conflict, and in case of armed conflict, the deployment of effective measures aimed at peace-making, reconstruction and reconciliation. The production and stockpiling of weapons of mass destruction constitutes a continuing threat against peace.2 Hence, it is necessary that States negotiate in good faith for the early conclusion of a universal treaty on general and complete disarmament under effective international control3. Peace is much more than the absence of war, and necessitates an equitable world order, characterized by the gradual elimination of the root causes of conflict, including extreme poverty, endemic injustice, privilege and structural violence. [36]

American philosopher Henry Shue of Oxford University developed a rights-based position in great detail, and specifically in relation to U.S. foreign policy. In his book *Basic Rights*, Shue focused on those rights that are most basic in the sense that they are common to all human beings. Rights are basic, said Shue, if the "enjoyment of them is essential to the enjoyment of all other rights."[37] Such rights, Shue says, constitute "the morality of the depths," because they specify "the line beneath which no one is to be allowed to sink."[38]

The basic rights approach is reflected in the United Nations' Universal Declaration of Human Rights, which says in Article 3 that "everyone has the right to life" and in Article 25 that "every man, woman and child has the inalienable right to be free from hunger and malnutrition."[39] As United Nations scholar James Nickel wrote, the unifying idea behind the Universal Declaration is "the idea of a decent or minimally good life for all people."[40]

Besides the right to life and adequate food, Shue pointed out that a minimally good life also requires "minimal economic security, or

---

36   Alfred de Zayas, *Building a Just World Order* (Clarity Press, 2001), 47.
37   Henry Shue, *Basic Rights: Subsistence, Affluence, and U.S. Foreign Policy*, 2nd ed. (Princeton University Press, 1996), 19.
38   Shue, *Basic Rights*, 18.
39   James Nickel, *Making Sense of Human Rights: Philosophical Reflections on the Universal Declaration of Human Rights* (University of California Press, 1987), 51.
40   Nickel, *Making Sense of Human Rights*, 23.

subsistence, meaning unpolluted air, unpolluted water . . . , adequate clothes, adequate shelter, and minimal preventive public health care."[41]

Thanks in large part to the UN's Declaration of Rights, the human-rights approach to morality has become increasingly universal. This approach can easily be phrased in terms of the Silver Rule: I would not want to be deprived of any of these things to which all people have a right, so I should not deprive any other people of any of these things.

Moreover, the Silver Rule should not be regarded as simply applicable to individuals. To say that we should not deprive other people of adequate food entails that we do not want our government to deprive any of the peoples of the world of any of these rights—so our political efforts and preferences should be guided by the Silver Rule.

The distinction between basic and non-basic rights has vast implications. Basic rights, by virtue of being basic, should trump all non-basic rights. Rights that are essential to life are people's vital interests in the most literal sense of the term. The vital interests of people should always take precedence over the non-vital interests of others. Even if these non-vital interests could be considered rights, they are not basic rights and hence can be trumped.

A society can be just, therefore, only if its laws and institutions are such as to guarantee that the non-vital rights and preferences of some are not protected at the expense of the vital interests of others. Some people hold that an interest in having an unlimited amount of money gives one a right to make it, along with a right to have all the luxury items one desires. But insofar as a right to such riches and luxuries exists—it is really a desire, not a right—it would be immoral to allow this "right" to trump the vital necessities, and hence basic rights, of others.

Shue noted that John Locke, whose writings inspired much in early American thought, "had taken for granted that the right to accumulate private property was limited by a universal right to subsistence."[42]

In light of these moral principles, the "right" of Jeff Bezos and Elon Musk to accumulate more and more money would, in a moral system of national and global governance, be trumped by the basic rights of Americans and people around the world to have nontoxic air,

---

41   Shue, *Basic Rights*, 19.
42   Shue, *Basic Rights*, 153, referring to John Locke, *Two Treatises of Government*, Book II, Ch. V.

non-polluted water to drink, adequate water for agriculture, thriving marine life, and a sea-level that will not force them to move.

Another major implication: Rights entail demands. Basic rights are, in Shue's words, "everyone's minimum reasonable demands upon the rest of humanity."[43] The truth of this point can be easily seen: If everyone has a right to adequate food, then everyone else has the duty not to prevent the exercise of this right. In addition, the basic rights of human beings implies duties beyond a merely negative duty not to violate them. It also implies positive duties to protect the rights of people to have, for example, adequate food and then, if this protection fails, to provide aid to those who fall victim to social failures or natural disasters. This means that we in America have a duty not only to prevent our government from violating the rights of people in other countries to have adequate food but also, because we are a wealthy country, to provide genuine aid peoples in poor countries, without strings attached.

Aiding all the poor people in the world to have adequate food is obviously not something that we as individuals or even America as a whole could do. But a global government could organize the world and its economy so that no one would starve. Also, the requirement to protect people's rights can be phrased in terms of the Silver Rule: We want our basic rights to be protected, so we should work toward a global community in which the basic rights of all people are protected.

The USA likes to see itself as a basically Christian country. There is still a sense in which this is true, in terms of nominal identification with Christianity. But to be substantively Christian, America's policies would need to reflect Christianity's most basic moral principle, the Golden Rule (understood as containing the Silver Rule). In other words, we should judge U.S. foreign policy in terms of the Silver Rule.

For Christians to regard America as reflecting their values, its foreign policies should not, at least not flagrantly, violate the Silver Rule. But they do.

- The United States has sought to create a universal empire that could dictate the political and economic policies, and perhaps even cultural policies, of other countries. But on the other hand, Americans

---

43 Shue, *Basic Rights*, 153, referring to John Locke, *Two Treatises of Government*, Book II, Ch. V

would dislike having our country's political and economic policies determined by any another country, such as Russia or China.

- The United States has overthrown 30 governments during the Cold War alone and continued this practice afterwards. But Americans would not want its government to be overthrown by outside powers. Indeed, Americans became very upset by the idea (albeit subsequently disproved) that Russia had influenced the U.S. presidential election in 2016.

- Policies dictated by the United States have caused the standard of living in many countries to be lowered, leaving many of their citizens with inadequate food, water, and health care. But Americans would be very upset if China, after becoming stronger than the U.S., adopted policies that decreased Americans' food, drinking water, and available medical care.

- America used nuclear weapons on Japan, even though there was no military necessity for this use.[44] Needless to say, Americans would be outraged if Russia or angry terrorists used nuclear weapons on us or anywhere else.

More generally, U.S. foreign policy could be judged in terms of an updated list of "ten commandments," such as:

1. Don't slaughter people.

2. Don't deprive people of food and water.

3. Don't steal people's oil and other natural resources.

4. Don't steal people's personal property.

5. Don't deprive people of their freedom.

6. Don't cause people needless pain.

7. Don't terrorize people.

8. Don't rape people.

9. Don't humiliate people.

10. Don't treat people as mere means to your ends.

---

44   See David Ray Griffin, *The American Trajectory: Divine or Demonic?*, 153–166.

These commandments can be reworded in terms of the Silver Rule. For example: "I would not like my family members to be murdered, so neither I nor my government should murder other people." Likewise, I would not like to be terrorized, so I should try to prevent my government from terrorizing other people.

Normalizing America's Status in the World

The United States could and should become just a normal country, one among many, rather than insisting on being #1. Just as Ukraine must remove its Nazis from positions of influence, the U.S. must keep the warmongering neocons from having positions of influence. This would mean that U.S. foreign policy would no longer be directed by those adhering to the doctrine that the U.S. should control the world.

As the first two points of this section indicate, the previous policies of the U.S. are increasingly unsuccessful. Besides being hated, the United States is increasingly neither feared nor respected. An indicator is provided by the failing U.S. attempt to bully other countries into supporting its sanctions on Russia. As John Walsh noted,

> Out of 195 countries, only 30 have honored the U.S. sanctions on Russia. That means about 165 countries in the world have refused to join the sanctions. Those countries represent by far the majority of the world's population.

Walsh concluded:

> For those who look forward to a multipolar world, this is a welcome turn of events emerging out of the cruel tragedy of the U.S. proxy war in Ukraine. The possibility of a saner, more prosperous multipolar world lies ahead—if we can get there.[45]

---

45   John V. Walsh, "On Ukraine, the World Majority Sides with Russia," *Antiwar.com*, May 5, 2022.

The people currently running the U.S. State Department do not look forward to a multipolar world. They and President Biden have had the habit of dominance so long that they will probably be unable to switch to a more realistic view. But this does not change the fact that the United States needs to make this transition.

It would be helpful if the U.S. foreign policy would become more moral, adopting the Silver Rule. But if that is too much to ask, it would be good for the United States to at least become realistic.

This fits with the ideas of Philip Giraldi of the Council for the National Interest. In line with the name of his organization, Giraldi says:

> [T]here is absolutely no standard of genuine national security that motivates the U.S.'s completely illegal aggression in many parts of the world. What occurs may be linked to a desire to dominate or a madness sometimes described as "exceptionalism" and/or "leadership of the free world," neither of which has anything to do with actual security.

Giraldi also said: "[L]et us shrink the U.S. military until it is responsive to actual identifiable threats. Let's elect a president who will follow the sage advice of President John Quincy Adams who declared that 'Americans should not go abroad to slay dragons they do not understand in the name of spreading democracy.'"

Finally, Giraldi mused, "one can only imagine an America that is at peace with itself and with what it represents while also being considered a friend to the rest of the world."[46]

What the United States should do can also be stated negatively. This was done by John Kiriakou on July 4, 2022, when he gave several reasons why he could not celebrate the United States. One of these was:

> I can't celebrate a country this year that sends unaccountable billions of dollars to a government in Ukraine known widely for its corruption, while the United States has underfunded

---

46   Philip Giraldi, "If You Want a War with Iran, Russia, China and Venezuela Tell Me Why and How It Would Benefit Americans," *Unz Review,* June 21, 2022.

schools, an embarrassment of a healthcare system and a national infrastructure in shambles.[47]

Notably, the latter two commentators were formerly employed by the CIA.

In summary

The unipolar aspiration of the United States has led it to be despised. It is no longer realistic, and the United States would actually improve the prospects of Americans as well as the rest of the world if its foreign policy would align with the Silver Rule.

---

47   John Kiriakou, "Hold the Fireworks," *Consortium News,* July 5, 2022.

Index